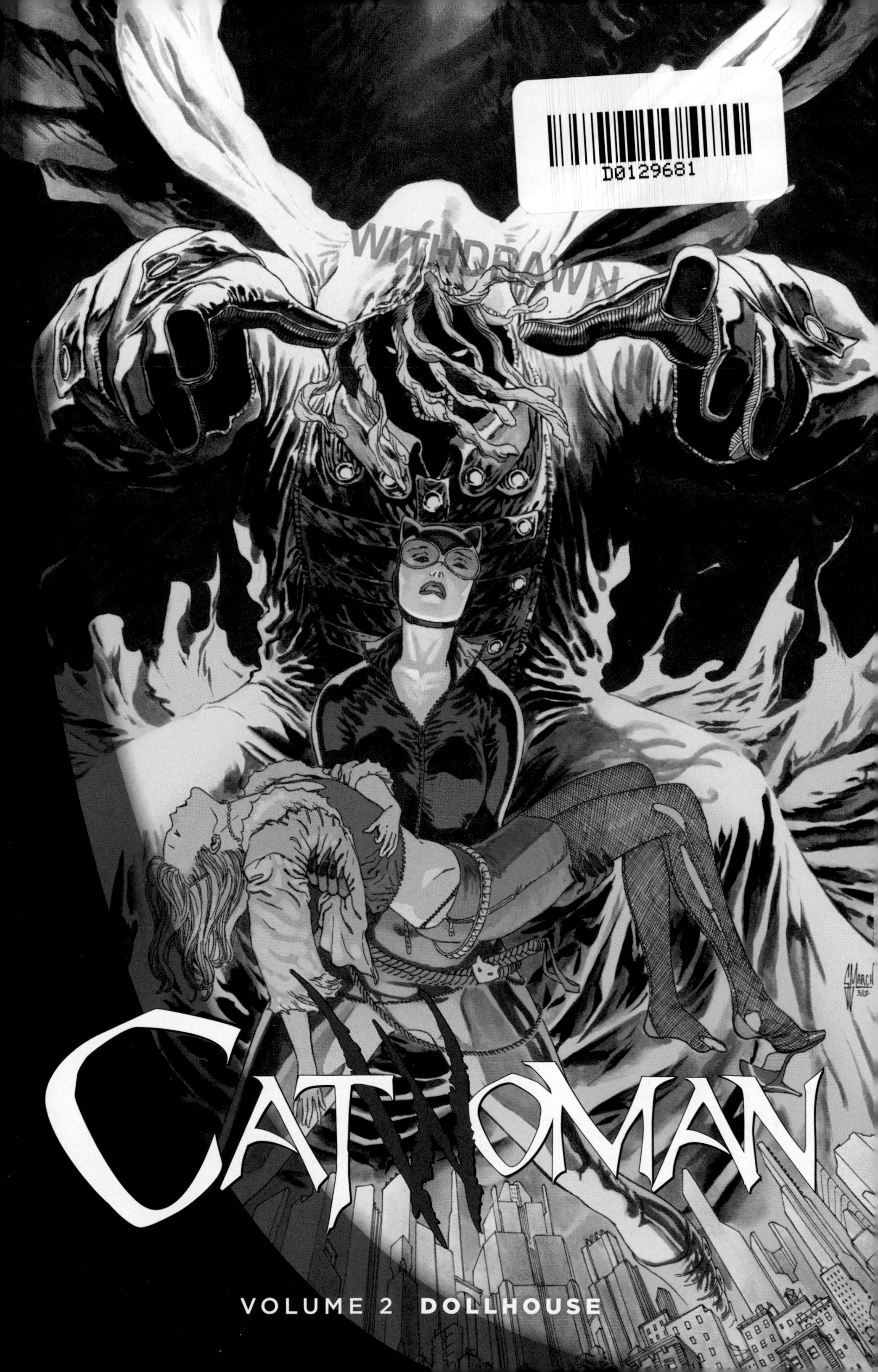
CATWOMAN
VOLUME 2 DOLLHOUSE

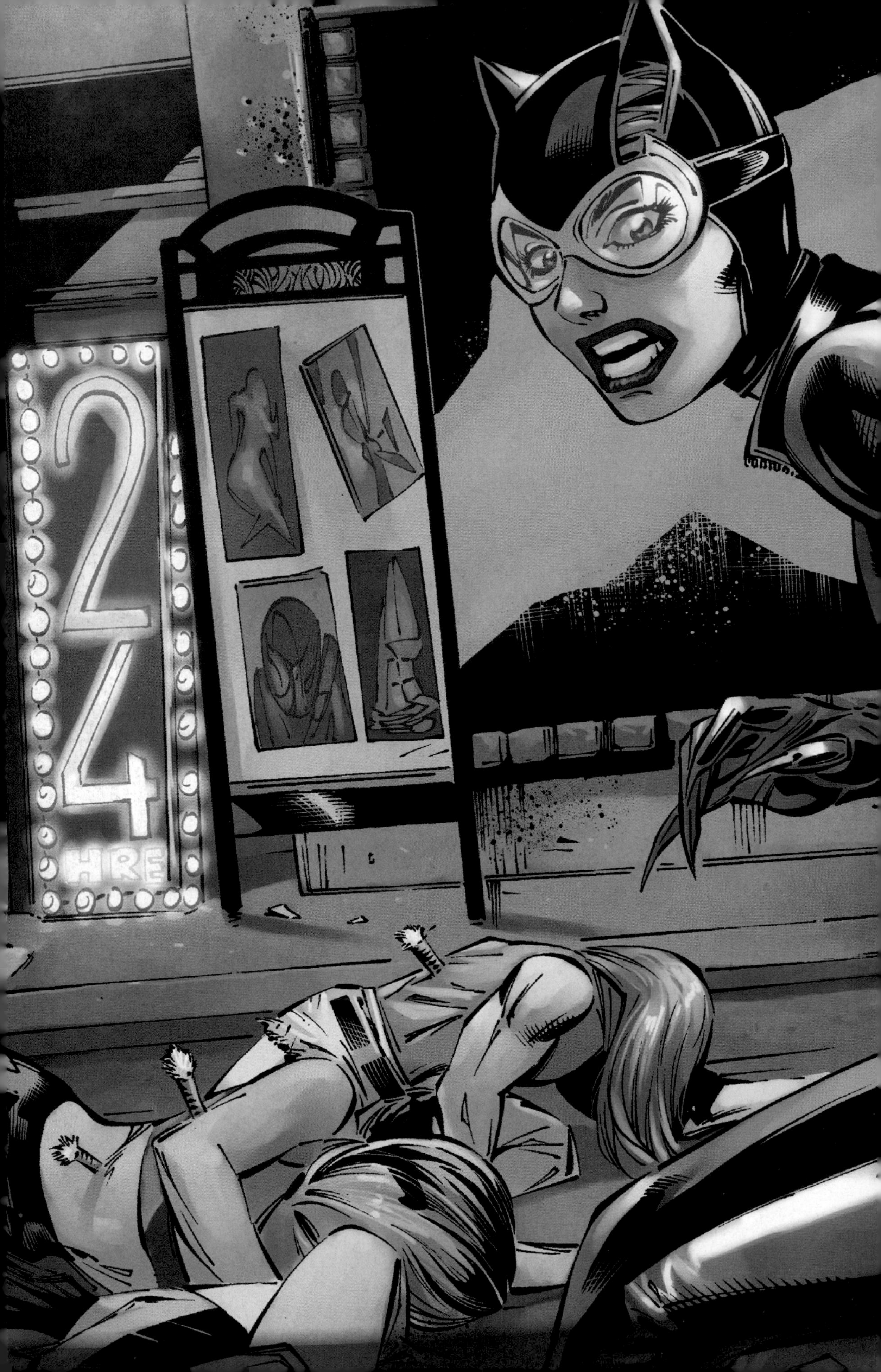
24
HRS

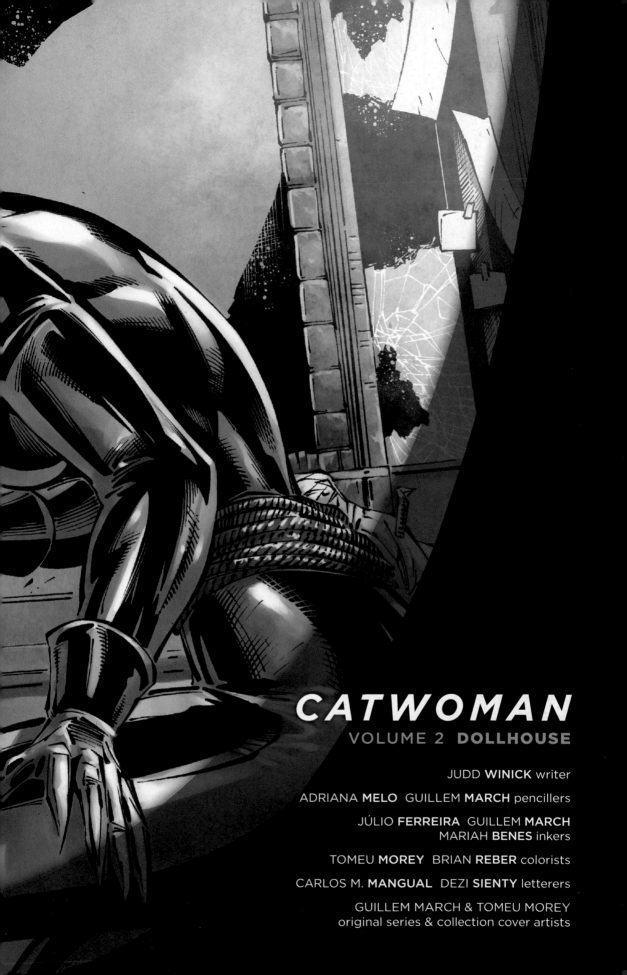

CATWOMAN
VOLUME 2 DOLLHOUSE

JUDD **WINICK** writer

ADRIANA **MELO** GUILLEM **MARCH** pencillers

JÚLIO **FERREIRA** GUILLEM **MARCH**
MARIAH **BENES** inkers

TOMEU **MOREY** BRIAN **REBER** colorists

CARLOS M. **MANGUAL** DEZI **SIENTY** letterers

GUILLEM MARCH & TOMEU MOREY
original series & collection cover artists

RACHEL GLUCKSTERN Editor – Original Series RICKEY PURDIN Assistant Editor – Original Series
JEB WOODARD Group Editor – Collected Editions ROBIN WILDMAN Editor – Collected Edition ROBBIE BIEDERMAN Publication Design

BOB HARRAS Senior VP – Editor-in-Chief, DC Comics

DIANE NELSON President DAN DIDIO and JIM LEE Co-Publishers
GEOFF JOHNS Chief Creative Officer
AMIT DESAI Senior VP – Marketing & Global Franchise Management
NAIRI GARDINER Senior VP – Finance SAM ADES VP – Digital Marketing BOBBIE CHASE VP – Talent Development
MARK CHIARELLO Senior VP – Art, Design & Collected Editions JOHN CUNNINGHAM VP – Content Strategy
ANNE DEPIES VP – Strategy Planning & Reporting DON FALLETTI VP – Manufacturing Operations
LAWRENCE GANEM VP – Editorial Administration & Talent Relations
ALISON GILL Senior VP – Manufacturing & Operations HANK KANALZ Senior VP – Editorial Strategy & Administration
JAY KOGAN VP – Legal Affairs DEREK MADDALENA Senior VP – Sales & Business Development
DAN MIRON VP – Sales Planning & Trade Development NICK NAPOLITANO VP – Manufacturing Administration
CAROL ROEDER VP – Marketing EDDIE SCANNELL VP – Mass Account & Digital Sales
SUSAN SHEPPARD VP – Business Affairs COURTNEY SIMMONS Senior VP – Publicity & Communications
JIM (SKI) SOKOLOWSKI VP – Comic Book Specialty & Newsstand Sales

CATWOMAN VOLUME 2: DOLLHOUSE

DC Comics, 4000 Warner Blvd., Burbank, CA 91522
A Warner Bros. Entertainment Company.
Printed by RR Donnelley, Salem, VA, USA. 8/28/15. Third Printing.

ISBN: 978-1-4012-3839-1

PEFC Certified
Printed on paper from sustainably managed forests and controlled sources
PEFC
PEFC/29-31-75
www.pefc.org

Library of Congress Cataloging-in-Publication Data

Winick, Judd.
Catwoman. Volume 2, Dollhouse / Judd Winick, Adriana Melo, Guillem March.
p. cm.
"Originally published in single magazine form in Catwoman 7-12."
ISBN 978-1-4012-3839-1
1. Graphic novels. I. Melo, Adriana. II. March, Guillem, 1979- III. Title. IV. Title: Dollhouse.
PN6728.C39W57 2012
741.5'973—dc23

2012040573

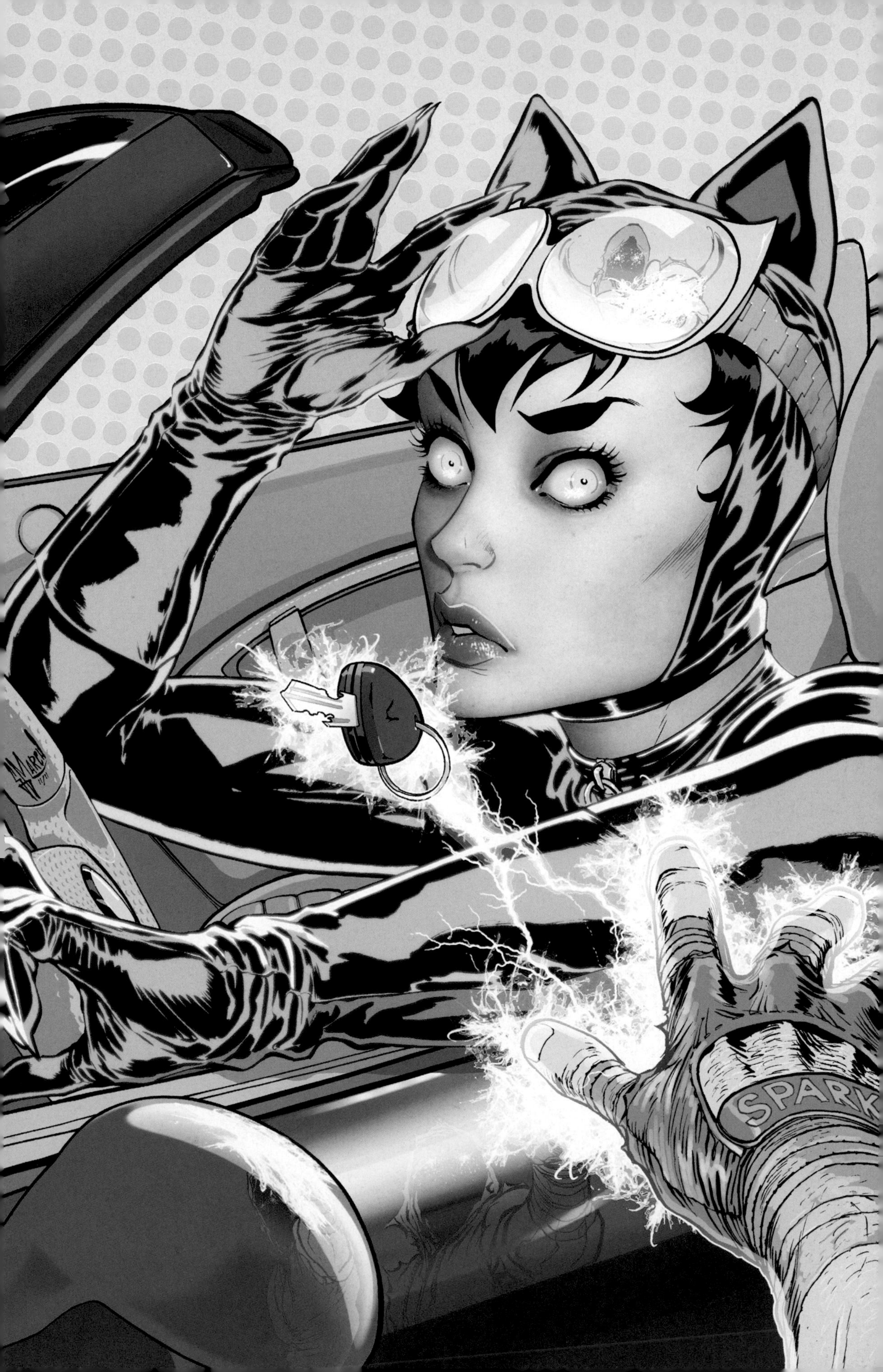
SPARK

JUDD WINICK writer **ADRIANA MELO** penciller **MARIAH BENES** inker

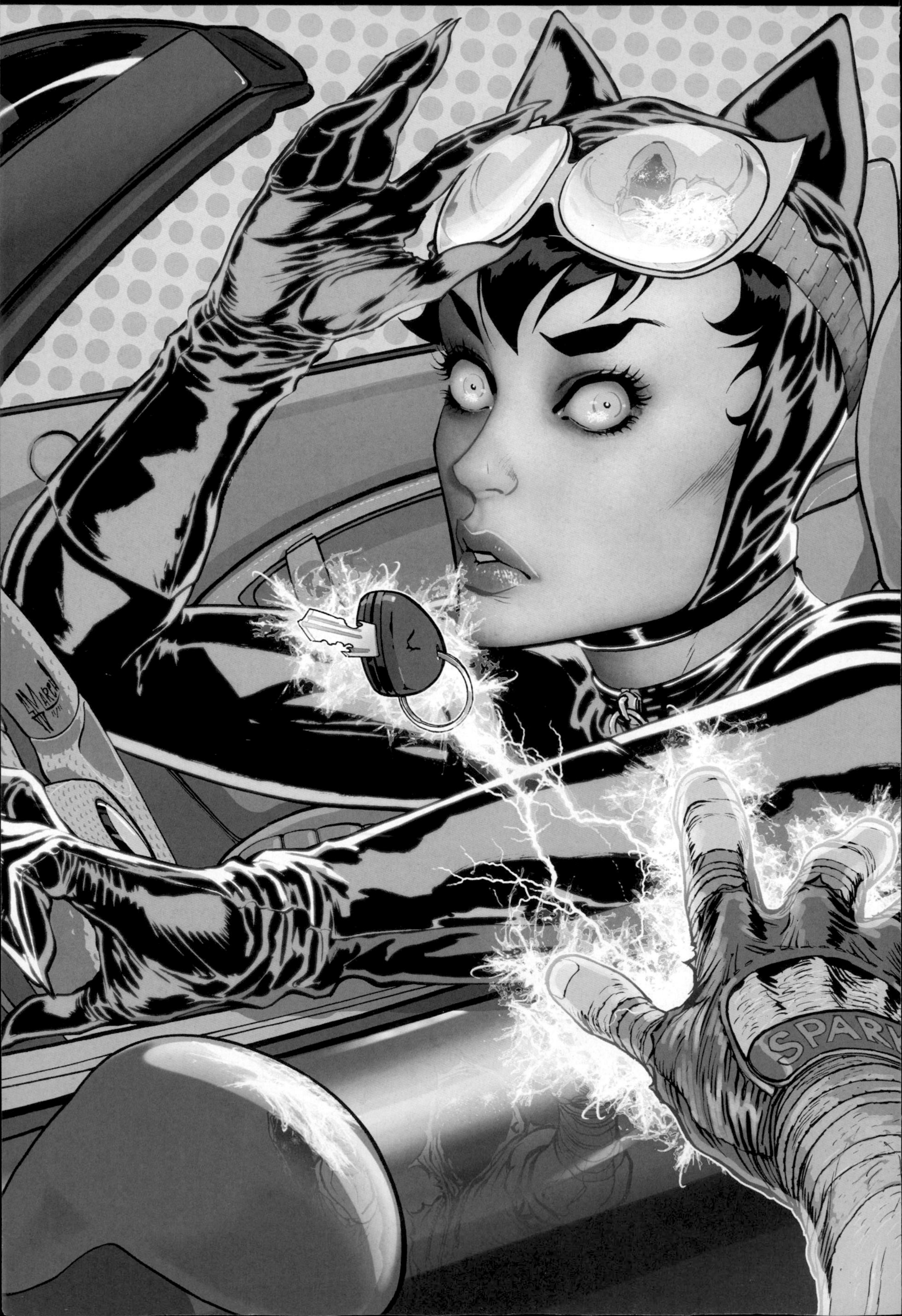

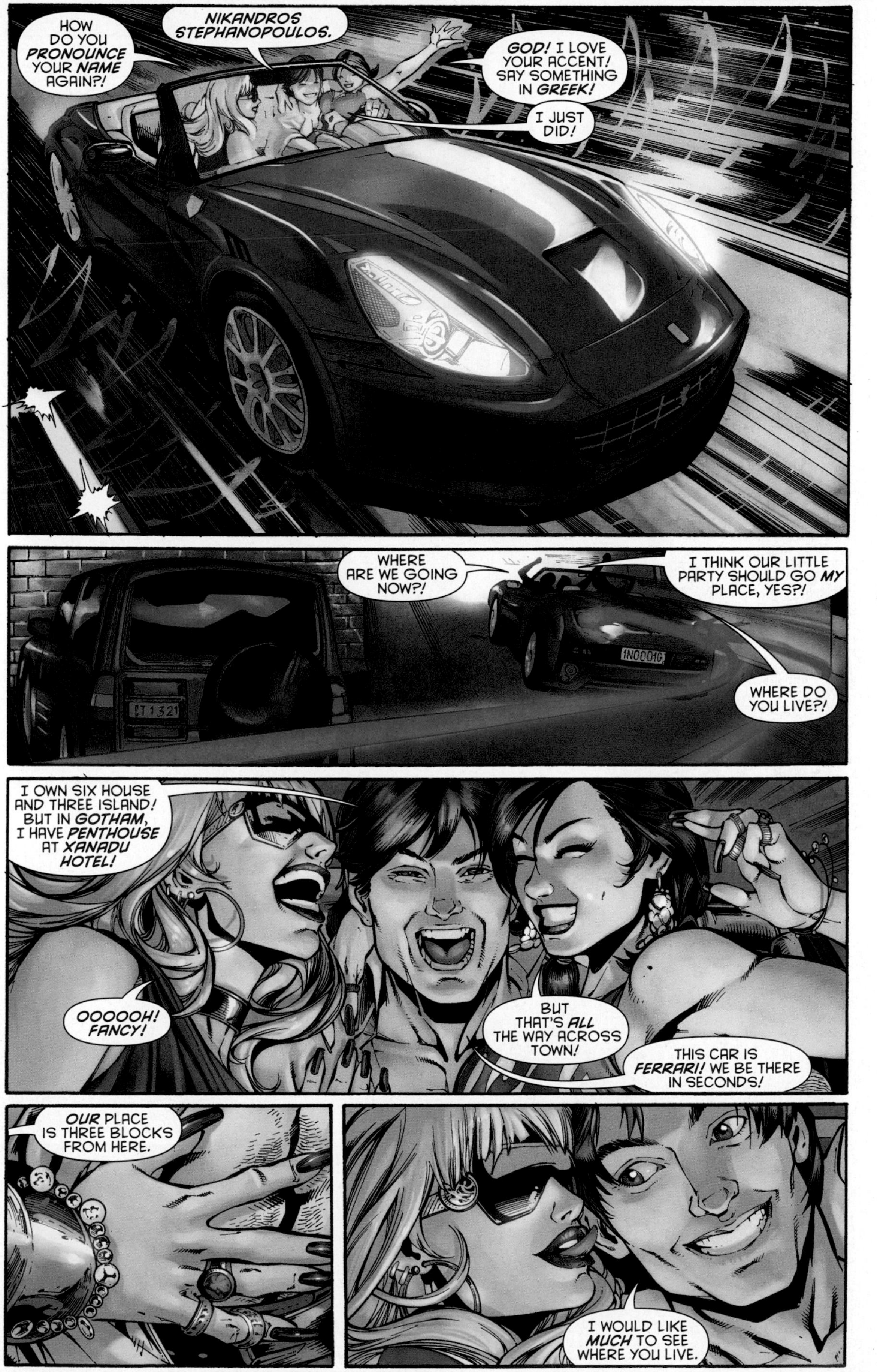
HOW DO YOU PRONOUNCE YOUR NAME AGAIN?!
NIKANDROS STEPHANOPOULOS.
GOD! I LOVE YOUR ACCENT! SAY SOMETHING IN GREEK!
I JUST DID!
WHERE ARE WE GOING NOW?!
I THINK OUR LITTLE PARTY SHOULD GO MY PLACE, YES?!
WHERE DO YOU LIVE?!
I OWN SIX HOUSE AND THREE ISLAND! BUT IN GOTHAM, I HAVE PENTHOUSE AT XANADU HOTEL!
OOOOOH! FANCY!
BUT THAT'S ALL THE WAY ACROSS TOWN!
THIS CAR IS FERRARI! WE BE THERE IN SECONDS!
OUR PLACE IS THREE BLOCKS FROM HERE.
I WOULD LIKE MUCH TO SEE WHERE YOU LIVE.

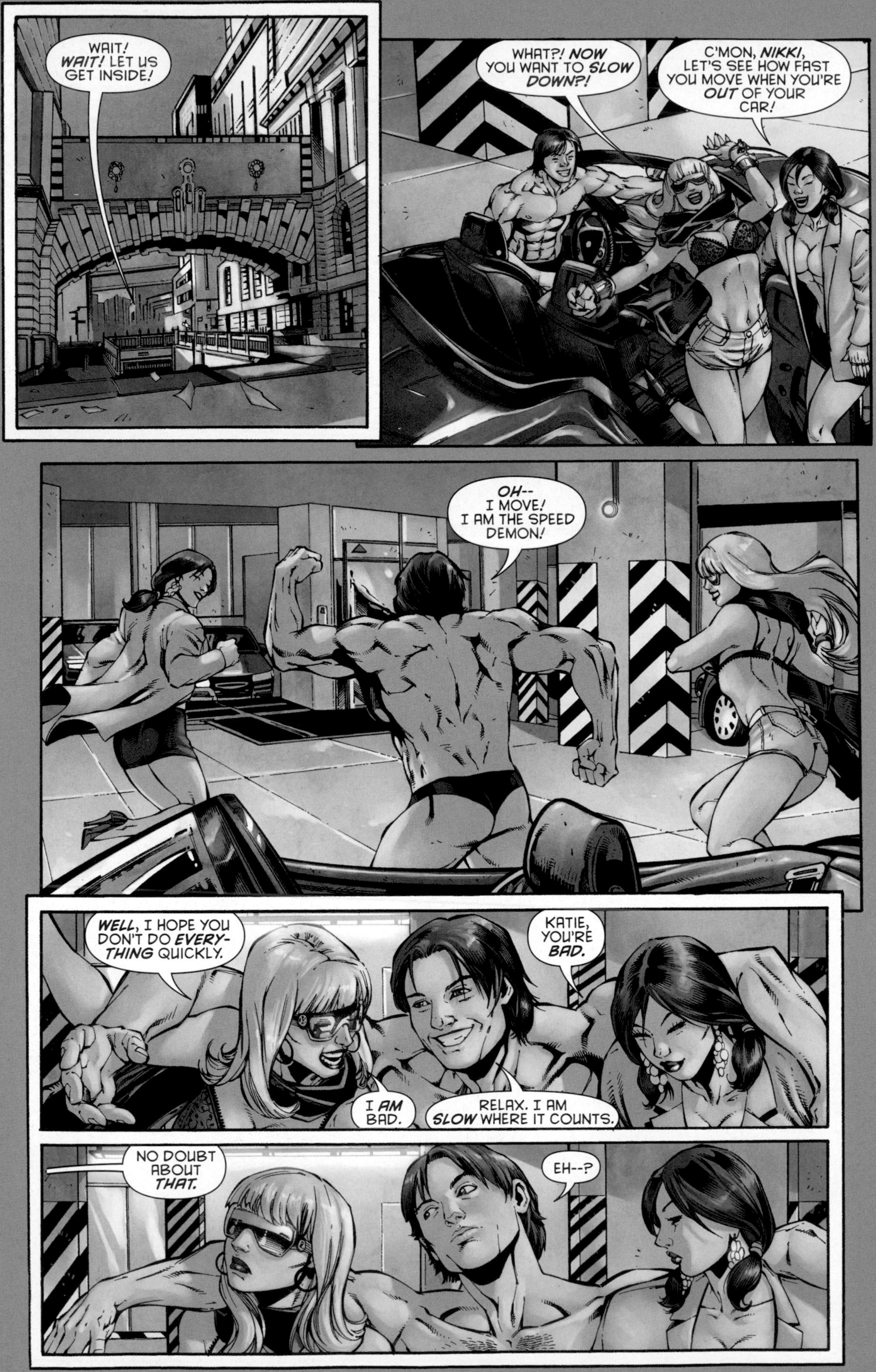
WAIT! WAIT! LET US GET INSIDE!
WHAT?! NOW YOU WANT TO SLOW DOWN?!
C'MON, NIKKI, LET'S SEE HOW FAST YOU MOVE WHEN YOU'RE OUT OF YOUR CAR!
OH-- I MOVE! I AM THE SPEED DEMON!
WELL, I HOPE YOU DON'T DO EVERYTHING QUICKLY.
KATIE, YOU'RE BAD.
I AM BAD.
RELAX. I AM SLOW WHERE IT COUNTS.
NO DOUBT ABOUT THAT.
EH--?

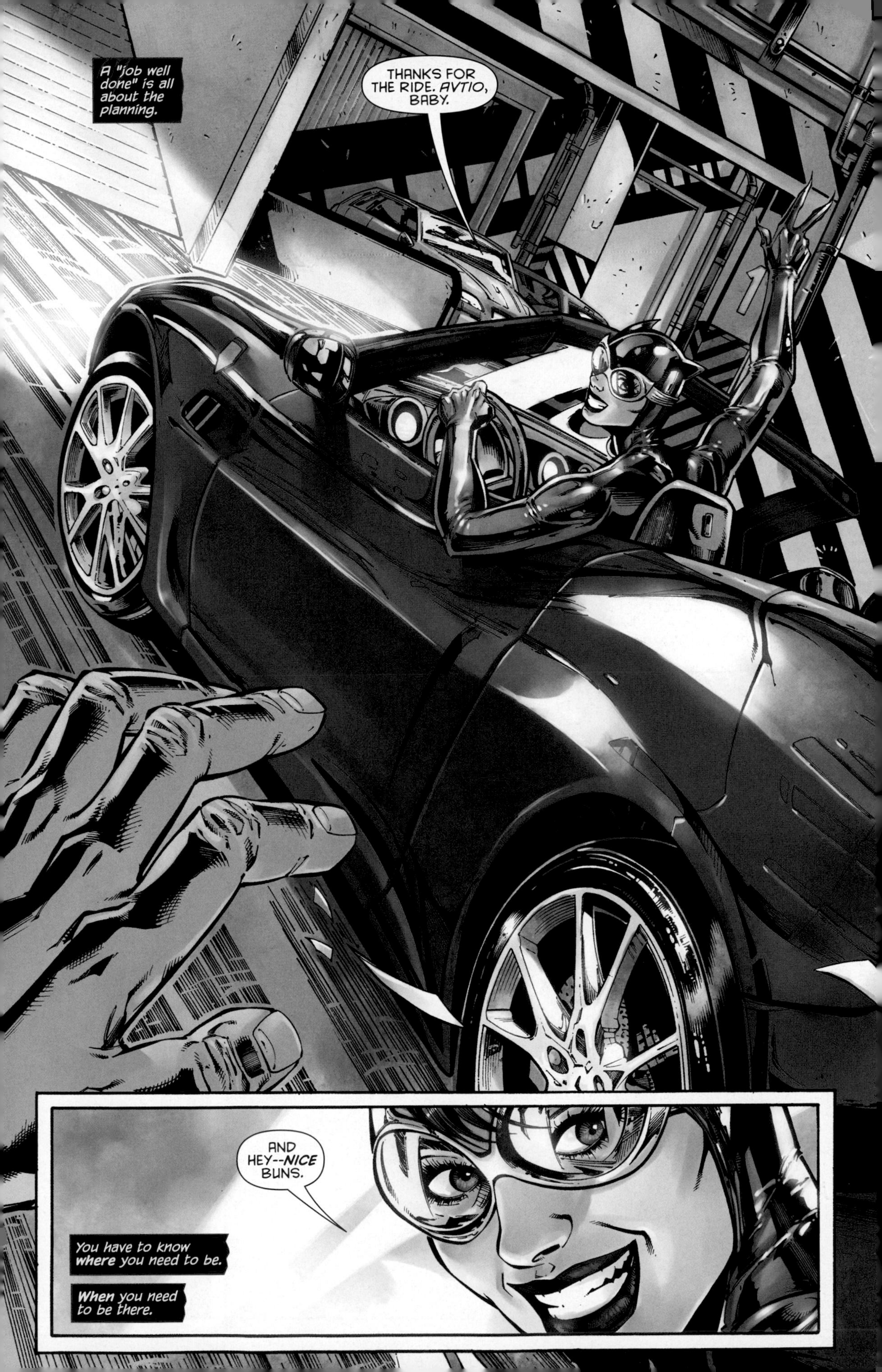
A "job well done" is all about the planning.
THANKS FOR THE RIDE. AVTIO, BABY.
AND HEY--NICE BUNS.
You have to know where you need to be.
When you need to be there.

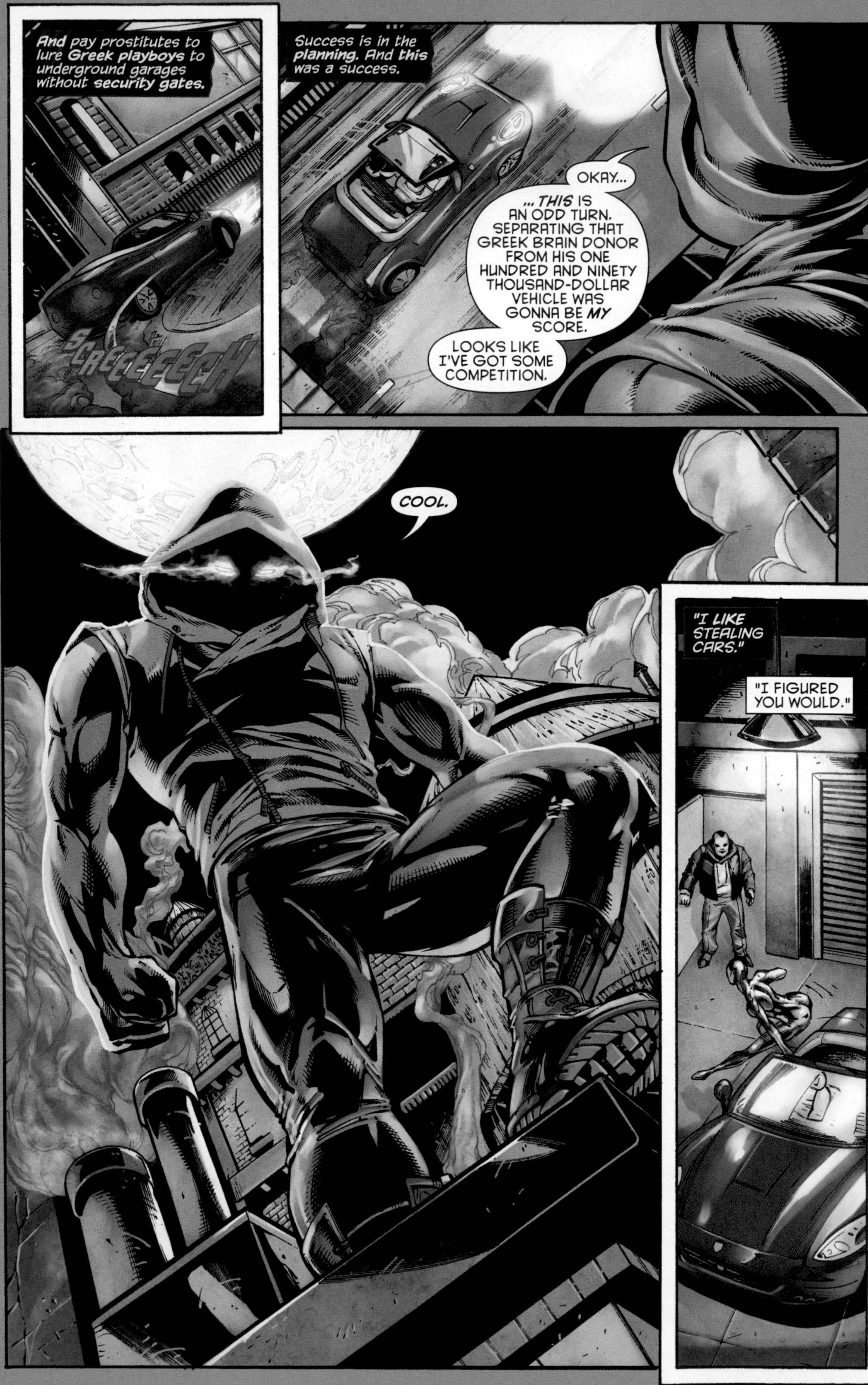
And pay prostitutes to lure Greek playboys to underground garages without security gates.
SCREEEEEECH
Success is in the planning. And this was a success.
OKAY...
...THIS IS AN ODD TURN. SEPARATING THAT GREEK BRAIN DONOR FROM HIS ONE HUNDRED AND NINETY THOUSAND-DOLLAR VEHICLE WAS GONNA BE MY SCORE.
LOOKS LIKE I'VE GOT SOME COMPETITION.
COOL.
"I LIKE STEALING CARS."
"I FIGURED YOU WOULD."

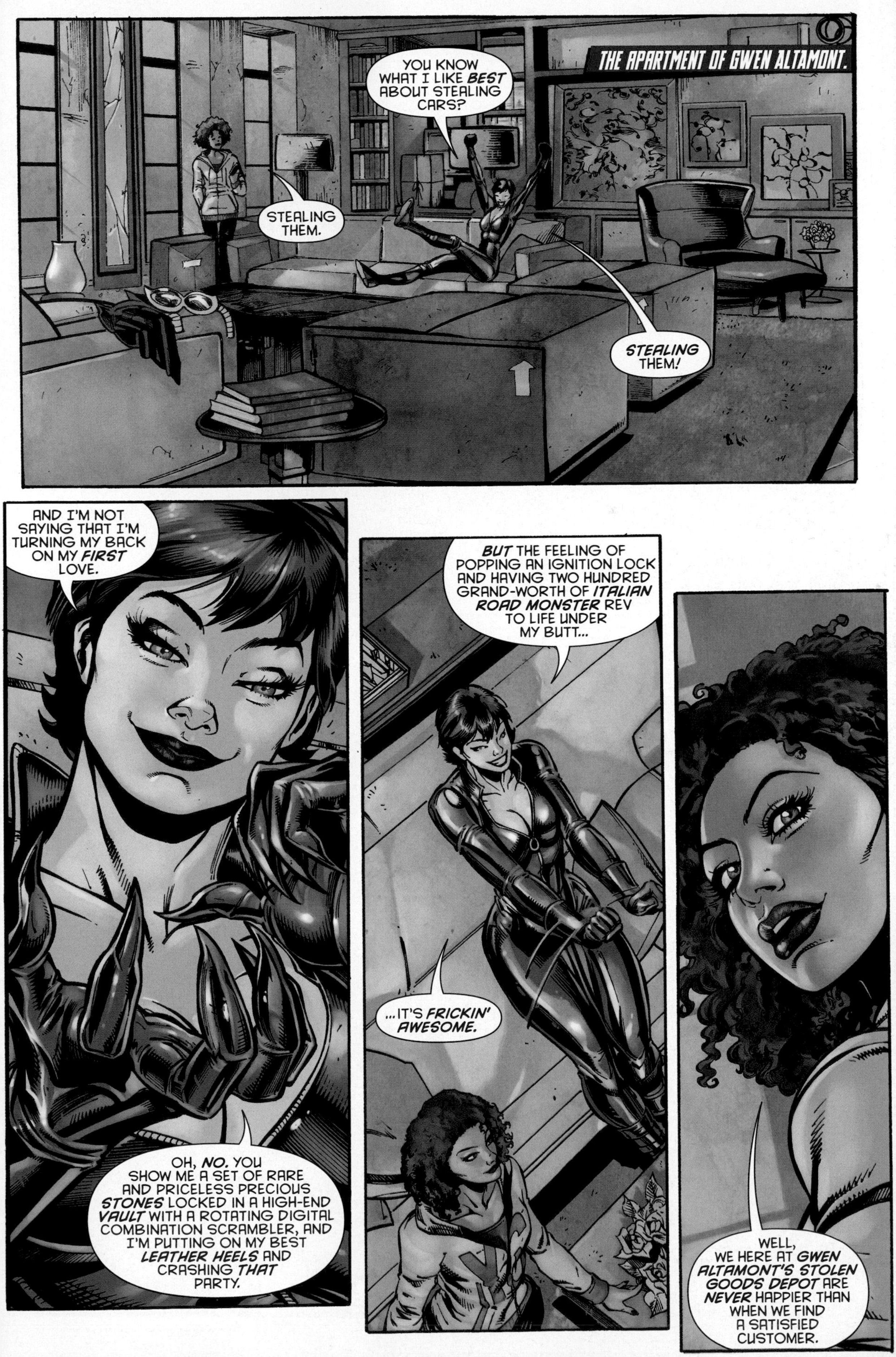
THE APARTMENT OF GWEN ALTAMONT.
YOU KNOW WHAT I LIKE BEST ABOUT STEALING CARS?
STEALING THEM.
STEALING THEM!
AND I'M NOT SAYING THAT I'M TURNING MY BACK ON MY FIRST LOVE.
OH, NO. YOU SHOW ME A SET OF RARE AND PRICELESS PRECIOUS STONES LOCKED IN A HIGH-END VAULT WITH A ROTATING DIGITAL COMBINATION SCRAMBLER, AND I'M PUTTING ON MY BEST LEATHER HEELS AND CRASHING THAT PARTY.
BUT THE FEELING OF POPPING AN IGNITION LOCK AND HAVING TWO HUNDRED GRAND-WORTH OF ITALIAN ROAD MONSTER REV TO LIFE UNDER MY BUTT...
...IT'S FRICKIN' AWESOME.
WELL, WE HERE AT GWEN ALTAMONT'S STOLEN GOODS DEPOT ARE NEVER HAPPIER THAN WHEN WE FIND A SATISFIED CUSTOMER.

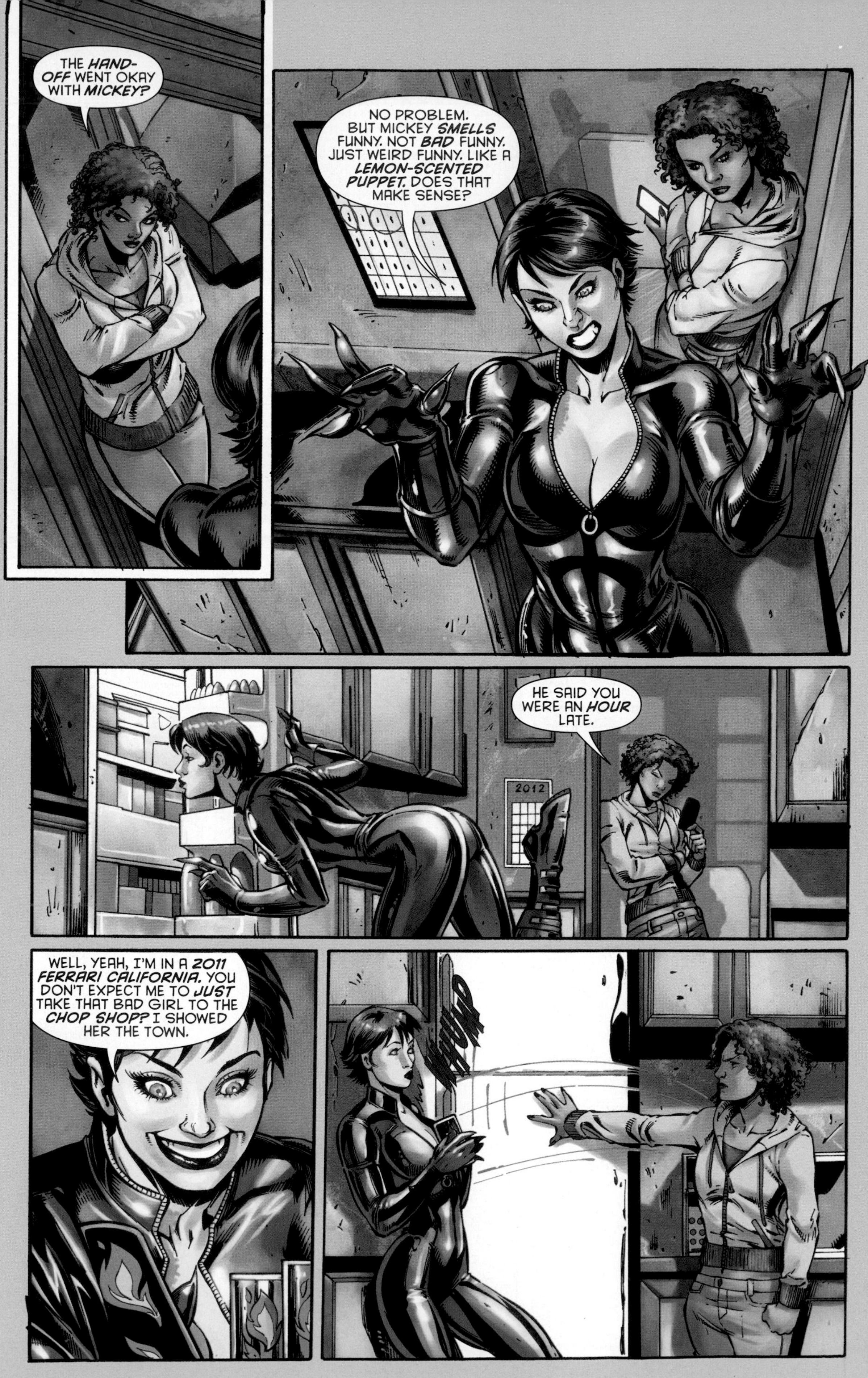
THE HAND-OFF WENT OKAY WITH MICKEY?
NO PROBLEM. BUT MICKEY SMELLS FUNNY. NOT BAD FUNNY. JUST WEIRD FUNNY. LIKE A LEMON-SCENTED PUPPET. DOES THAT MAKE SENSE?
HE SAID YOU WERE AN HOUR LATE.
2012
WELL, YEAH, I'M IN A 2011 FERRARI CALIFORNIA. YOU DON'T EXPECT ME TO JUST TAKE THAT BAD GIRL TO THE CHOP SHOP? I SHOWED HER THE TOWN.
WHUMP

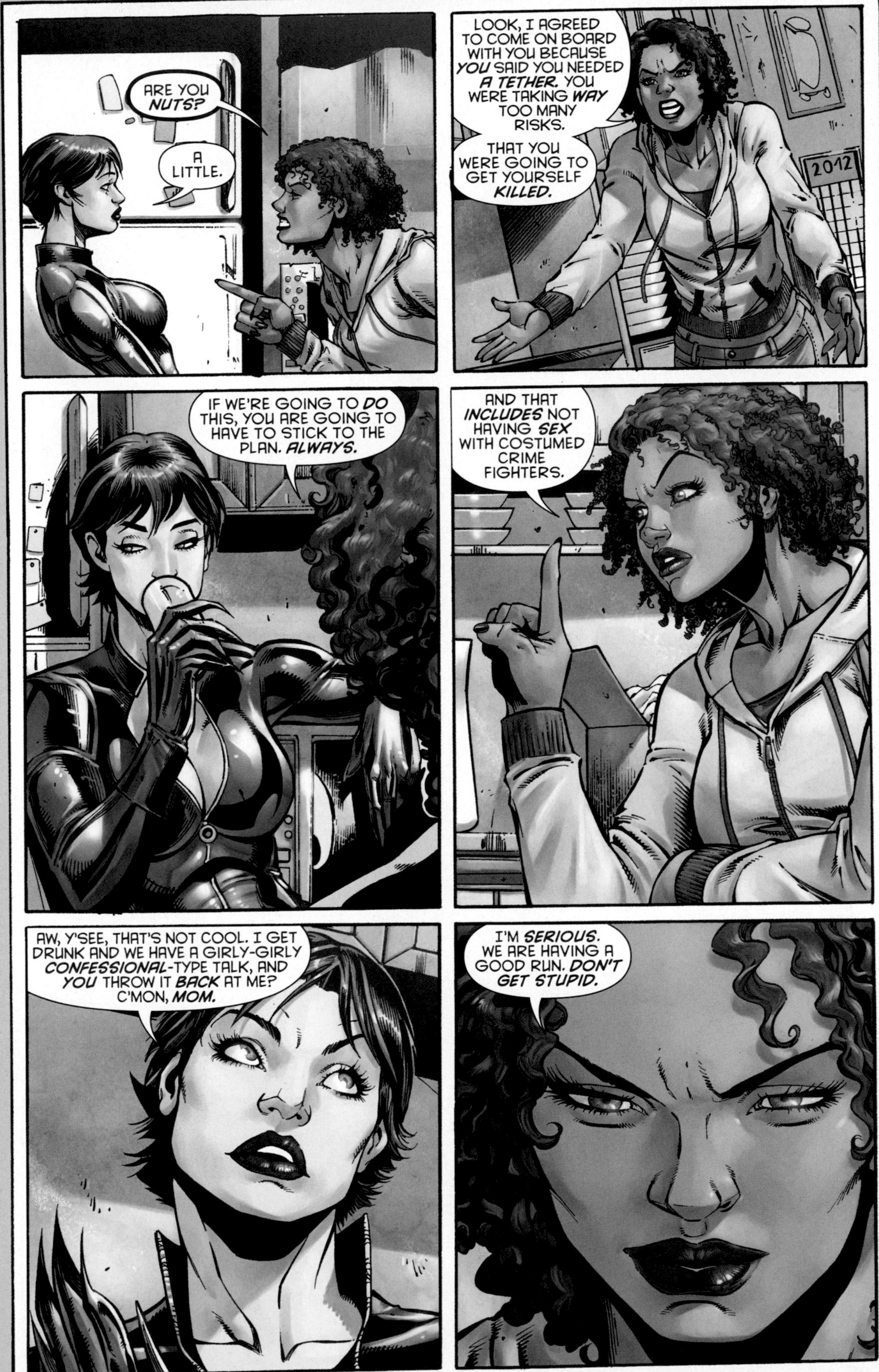
ARE YOU NUTS?
A LITTLE.
LOOK, I AGREED TO COME ON BOARD WITH YOU BECAUSE YOU SAID YOU NEEDED A TETHER. YOU WERE TAKING WAY TOO MANY RISKS.
THAT YOU WERE GOING TO GET YOURSELF KILLED.
2012
IF WE'RE GOING TO DO THIS, YOU ARE GOING TO HAVE TO STICK TO THE PLAN. ALWAYS.
AND THAT INCLUDES NOT HAVING SEX WITH COSTUMED CRIME FIGHTERS.
AW, Y'SEE, THAT'S NOT COOL. I GET DRUNK AND WE HAVE A GIRLY-GIRLY CONFESSIONAL-TYPE TALK, AND YOU THROW IT BACK AT ME? C'MON, MOM.
I'M SERIOUS. WE ARE HAVING A GOOD RUN. DON'T GET STUPID.

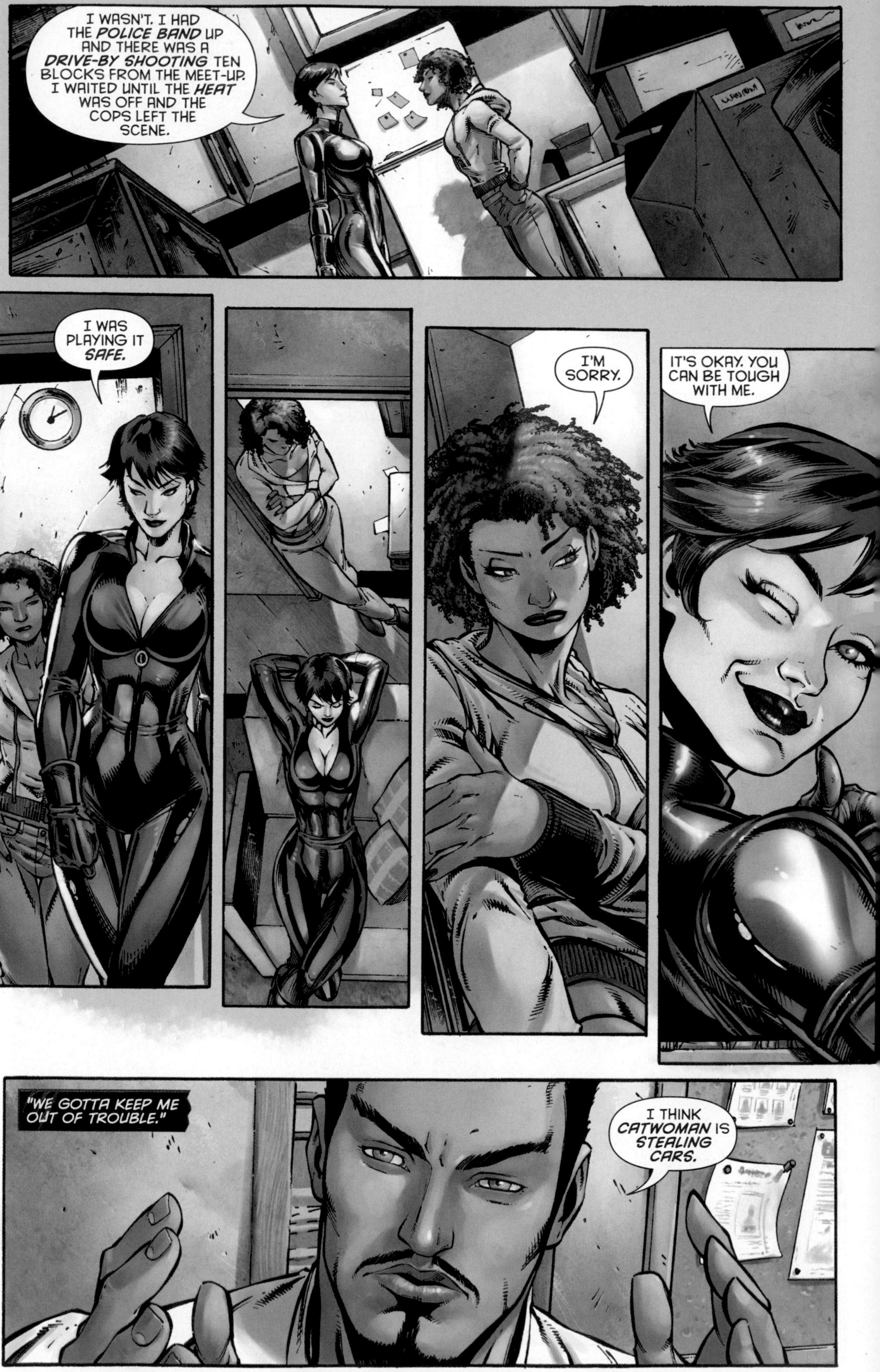
I WASN'T. I HAD THE POLICE BAND UP AND THERE WAS A DRIVE-BY SHOOTING TEN BLOCKS FROM THE MEET-UP. I WAITED UNTIL THE HEAT WAS OFF AND THE COPS LEFT THE SCENE.
I WAS PLAYING IT SAFE.
I'M SORRY.
IT'S OKAY. YOU CAN BE TOUGH WITH ME.
"WE GOTTA KEEP ME OUT OF TROUBLE."
I THINK CATWOMAN IS STEALING CARS.

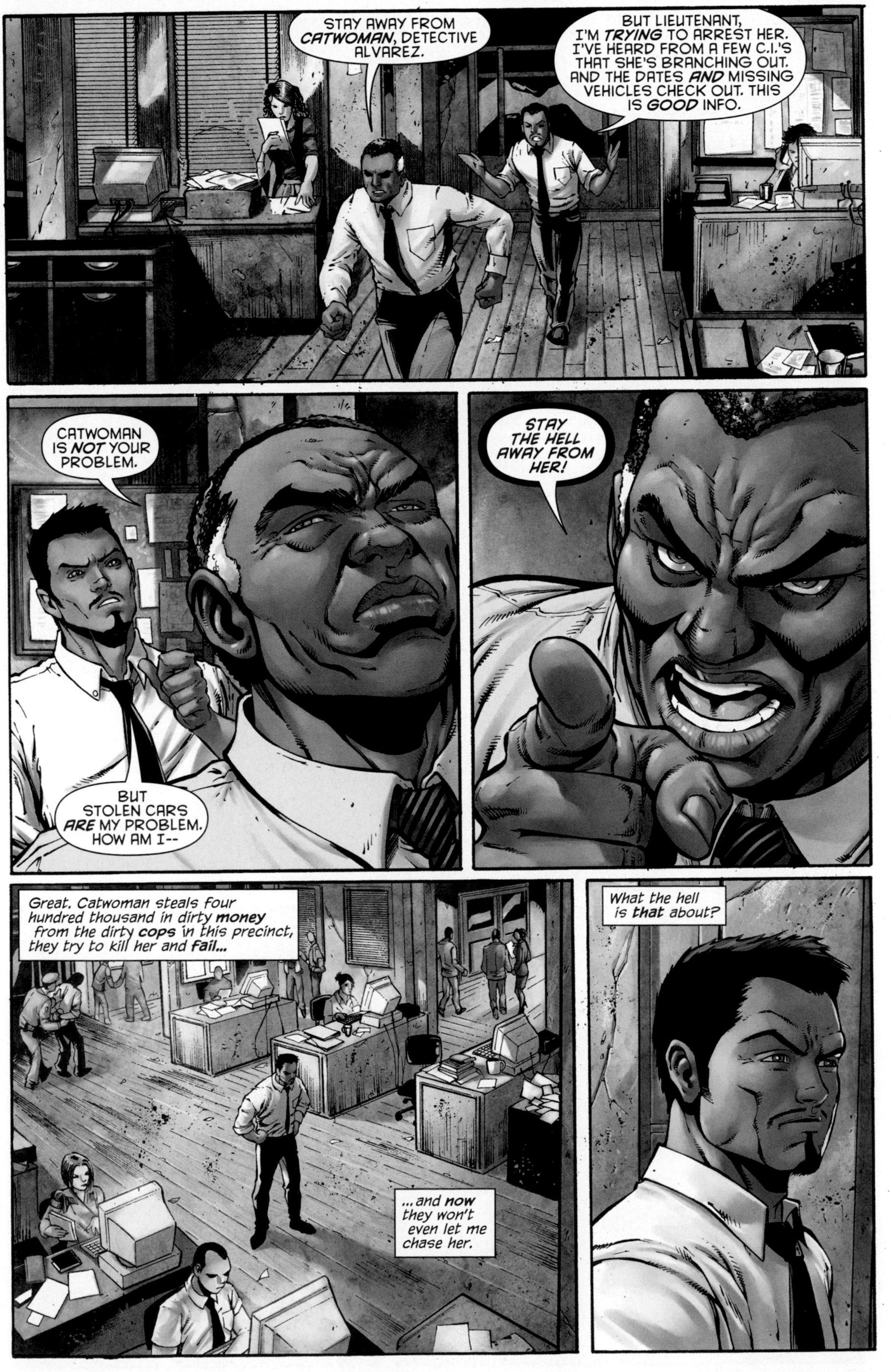
STAY AWAY FROM CATWOMAN, DETECTIVE ALVAREZ.
BUT LIEUTENANT, I'M TRYING TO ARREST HER. I'VE HEARD FROM A FEW C.I.'S THAT SHE'S BRANCHING OUT. AND THE DATES AND MISSING VEHICLES CHECK OUT. THIS IS GOOD INFO.
CATWOMAN IS NOT YOUR PROBLEM.
BUT STOLEN CARS ARE MY PROBLEM. HOW AM I--
STAY THE HELL AWAY FROM HER!
Great. Catwoman steals four hundred thousand in dirty money from the dirty cops in this precinct, they try to kill her and fail...
...and now they won't even let me chase her.
What the hell is that about?

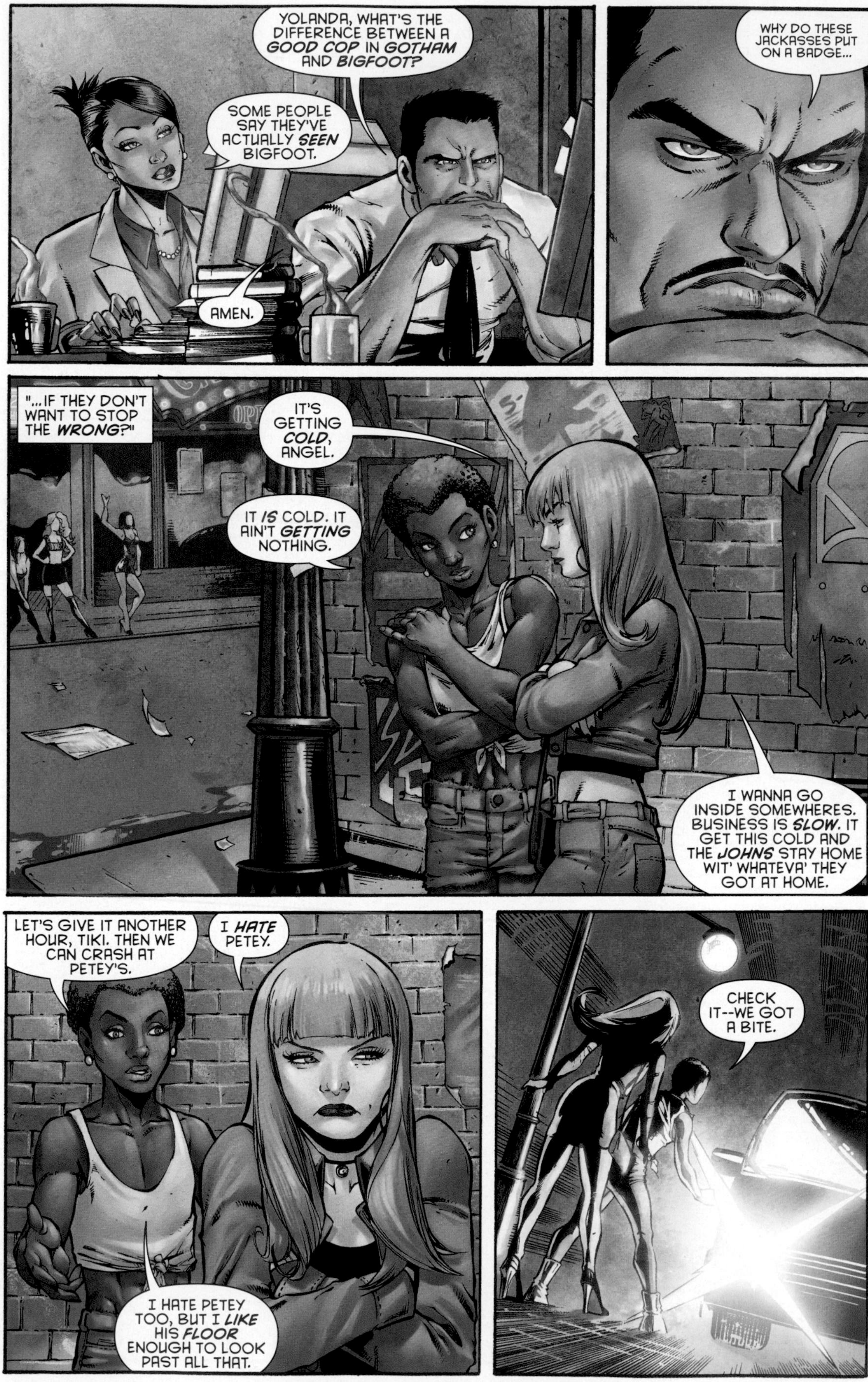
YOLANDA, WHAT'S THE DIFFERENCE BETWEEN A *GOOD COP* IN *GOTHAM* AND *BIGFOOT?*
SOME PEOPLE SAY THEY'VE ACTUALLY *SEEN* BIGFOOT.
AMEN.
WHY DO THESE JACKASSES PUT ON A BADGE...
"...IF THEY DON'T WANT TO STOP THE *WRONG?*"
IT'S GETTING *COLD*, ANGEL.
IT *IS* COLD. IT AIN'T *GETTING* NOTHING.
I WANNA GO INSIDE SOMEWHERES. BUSINESS IS *SLOW*. IT GET THIS COLD AND THE *JOHNS* STAY HOME WIT' WHATEVA' THEY GOT AT HOME.
LET'S GIVE IT ANOTHER HOUR, TIKI. THEN WE CAN CRASH AT PETEY'S.
I *HATE* PETEY.
I HATE PETEY TOO, BUT I *LIKE* HIS *FLOOR* ENOUGH TO LOOK PAST ALL THAT.
CHECK IT--WE GOT A BITE.

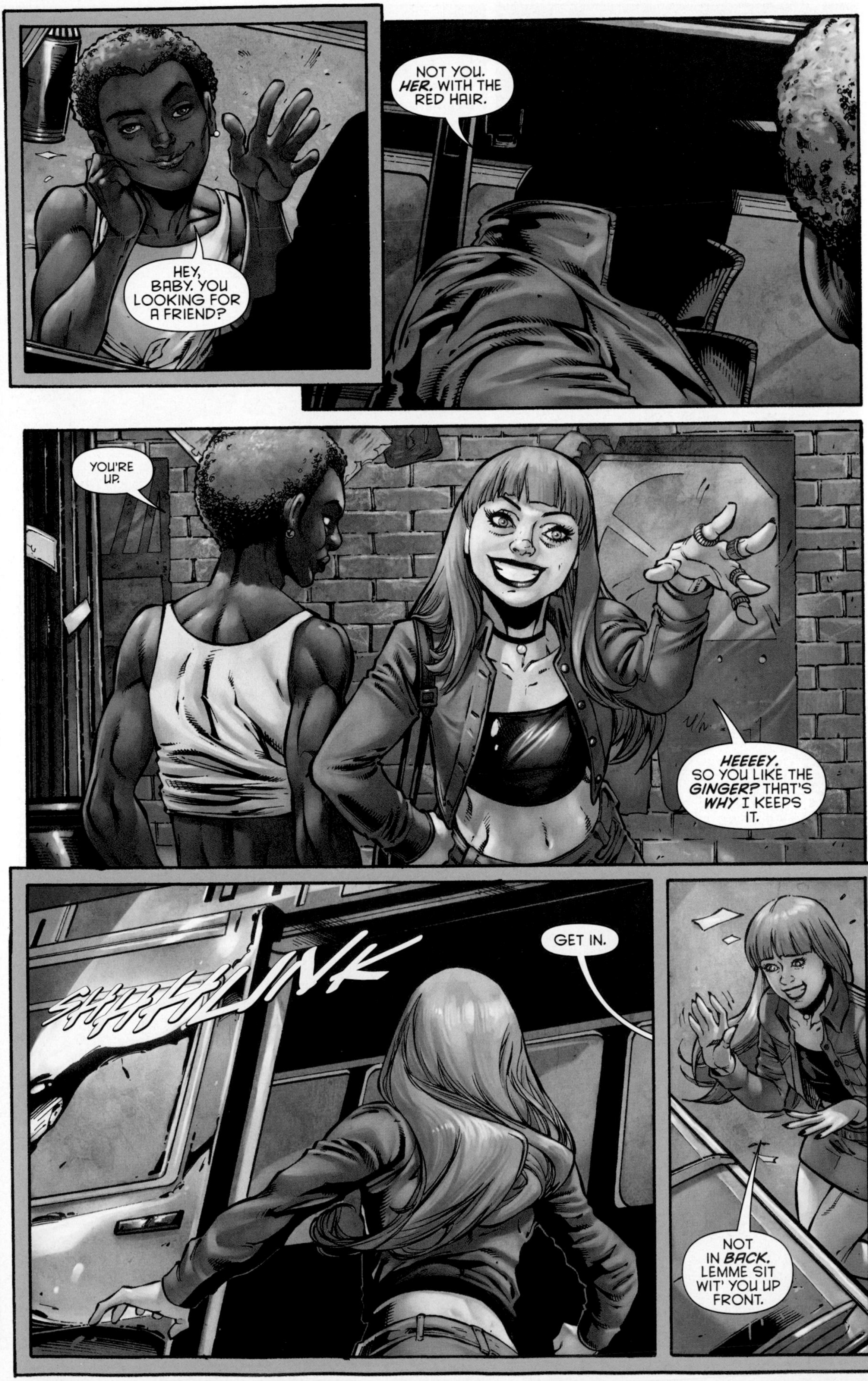
HEY, BABY. YOU LOOKING FOR A FRIEND?
NOT YOU. HER. WITH THE RED HAIR.
YOU'RE UP.
HEEEEY. SO YOU LIKE THE GINGER? THAT'S WHY I KEEPS IT.
SHHHHLUNK
GET IN.
NOT IN BACK. LEMME SIT WIT' YOU UP FRONT.

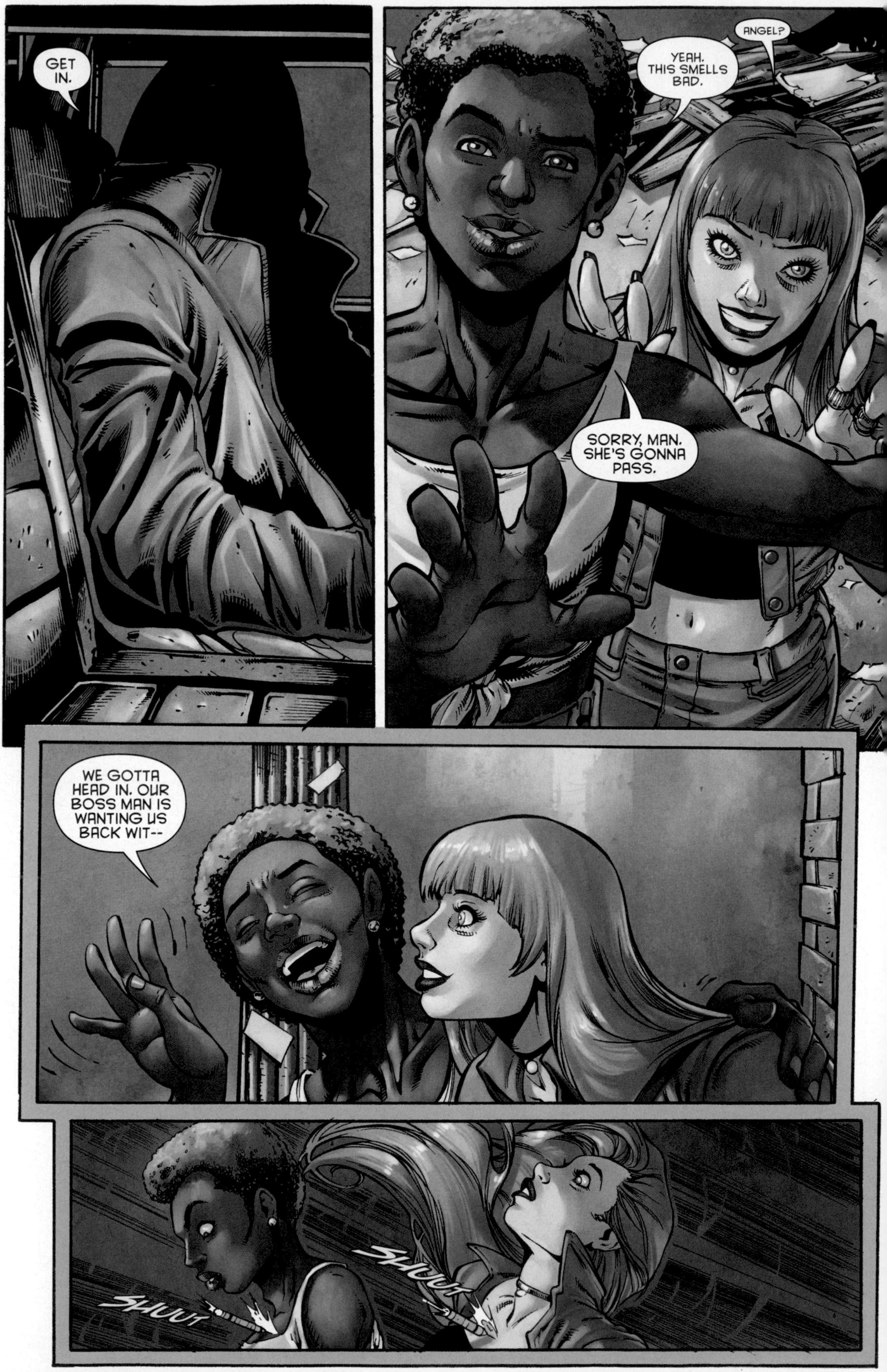
GET IN.
ANGEL?
YEAH. THIS SMELLS BAD.
SORRY, MAN. SHE'S GONNA PASS.
WE GOTTA HEAD IN. OUR BOSS MAN IS WANTING US BACK WIT--
SHUUT
SHUUT

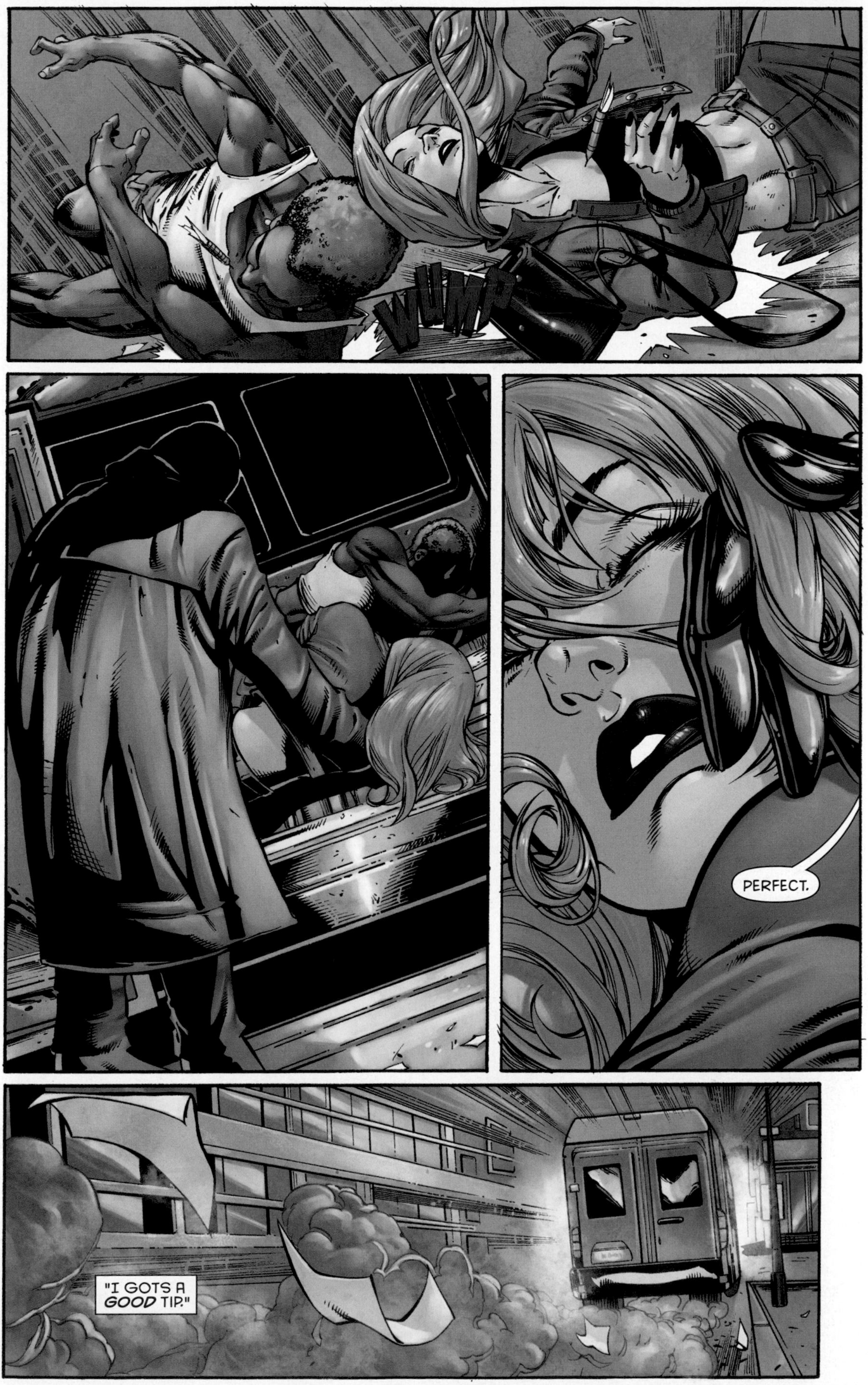
WUMP
PERFECT.
"I GOTS A GOOD TIP."

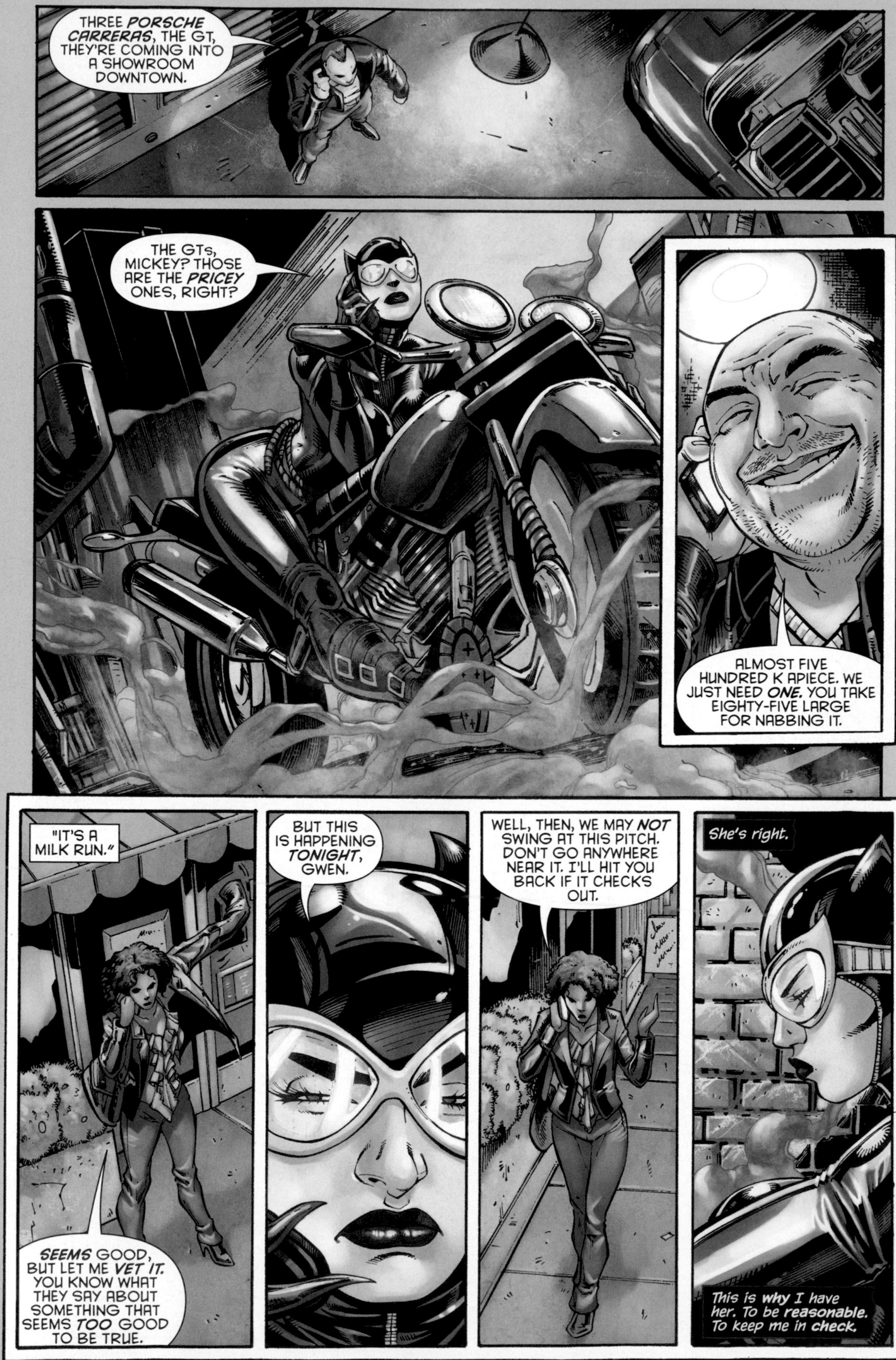
THREE PORSCHE CARRERAS, THE GT, THEY'RE COMING INTO A SHOWROOM DOWNTOWN.
THE GTs, MICKEY? THOSE ARE THE PRICEY ONES, RIGHT?
ALMOST FIVE HUNDRED K APIECE. WE JUST NEED ONE. YOU TAKE EIGHTY-FIVE LARGE FOR NABBING IT.
"IT'S A MILK RUN."
SEEMS GOOD, BUT LET ME VET IT. YOU KNOW WHAT THEY SAY ABOUT SOMETHING THAT SEEMS TOO GOOD TO BE TRUE.
BUT THIS IS HAPPENING TONIGHT, GWEN.
WELL, THEN, WE MAY NOT SWING AT THIS PITCH. DON'T GO ANYWHERE NEAR IT. I'LL HIT YOU BACK IF IT CHECKS OUT.
She's right.
This is why I have her. To be reasonable. To keep me in check.

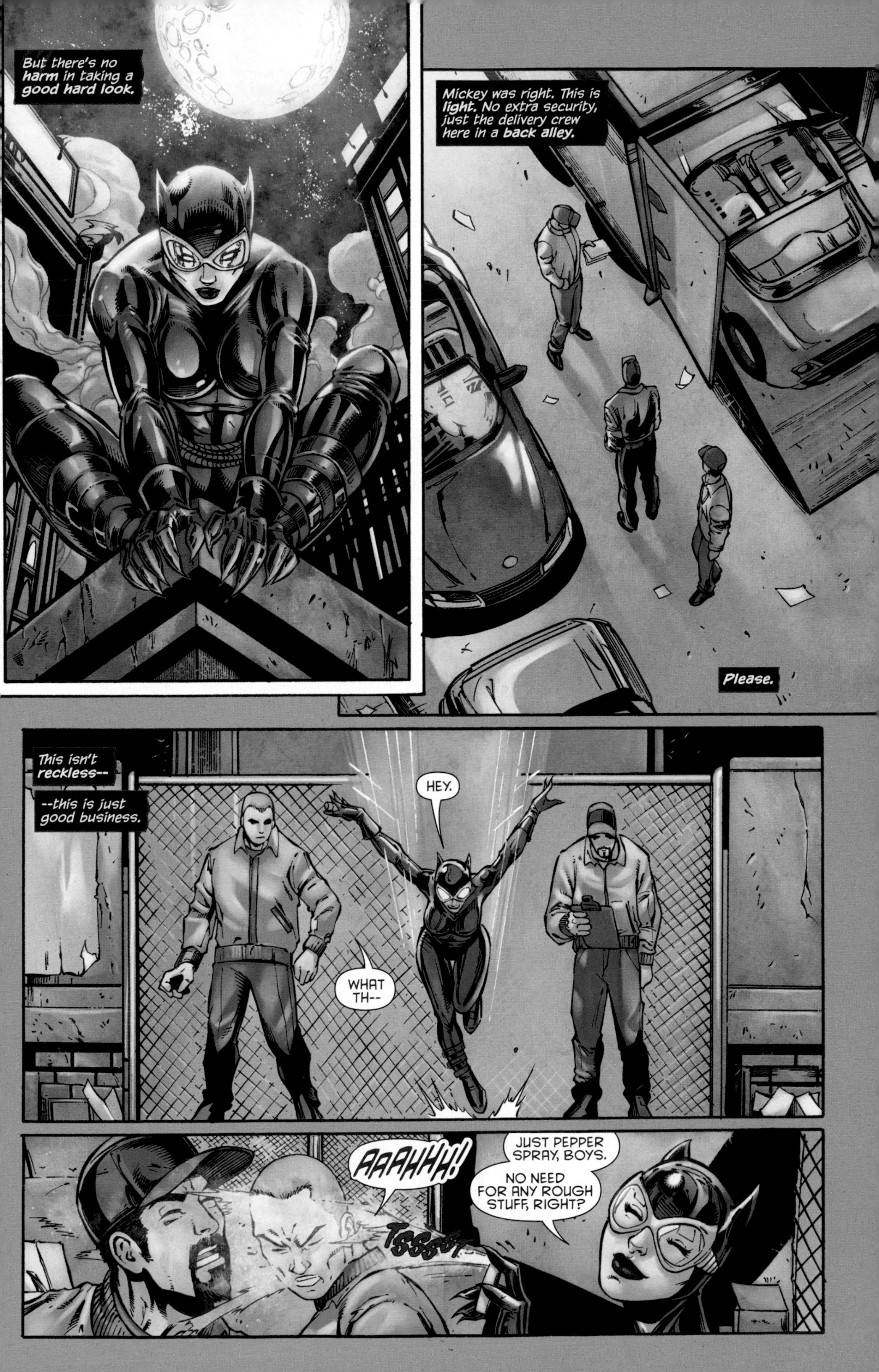

But there's no harm in taking a good hard look.
Mickey was right. This is light. No extra security, just the delivery crew here in a back alley.
Please.
This isn't reckless--
--this is just good business.
HEY.
WHAT TH--
AAAHHH!
TSSSST!
JUST PEPPER SPRAY, BOYS.
NO NEED FOR ANY ROUGH STUFF, RIGHT?

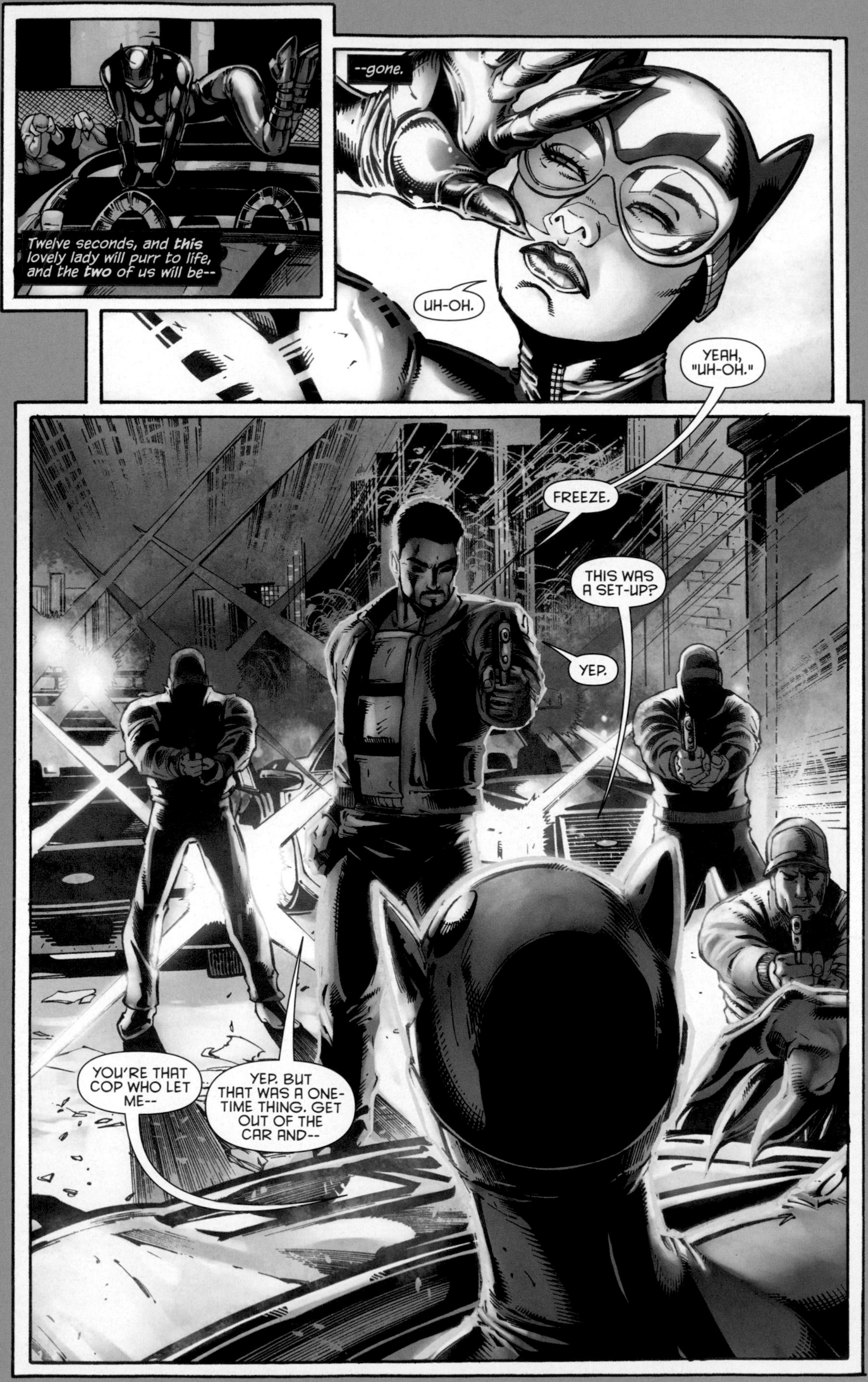

Twelve seconds, and **this** lovely lady will purr to life, and the **two** of us will be--
--gone.
UH-OH.
YEAH, "UH-OH."
FREEZE.
THIS WAS A SET-UP?
YEP.
YOU'RE THAT COP WHO LET ME--
YEP. BUT THAT WAS A ONE-TIME THING. GET OUT OF THE CAR AND--

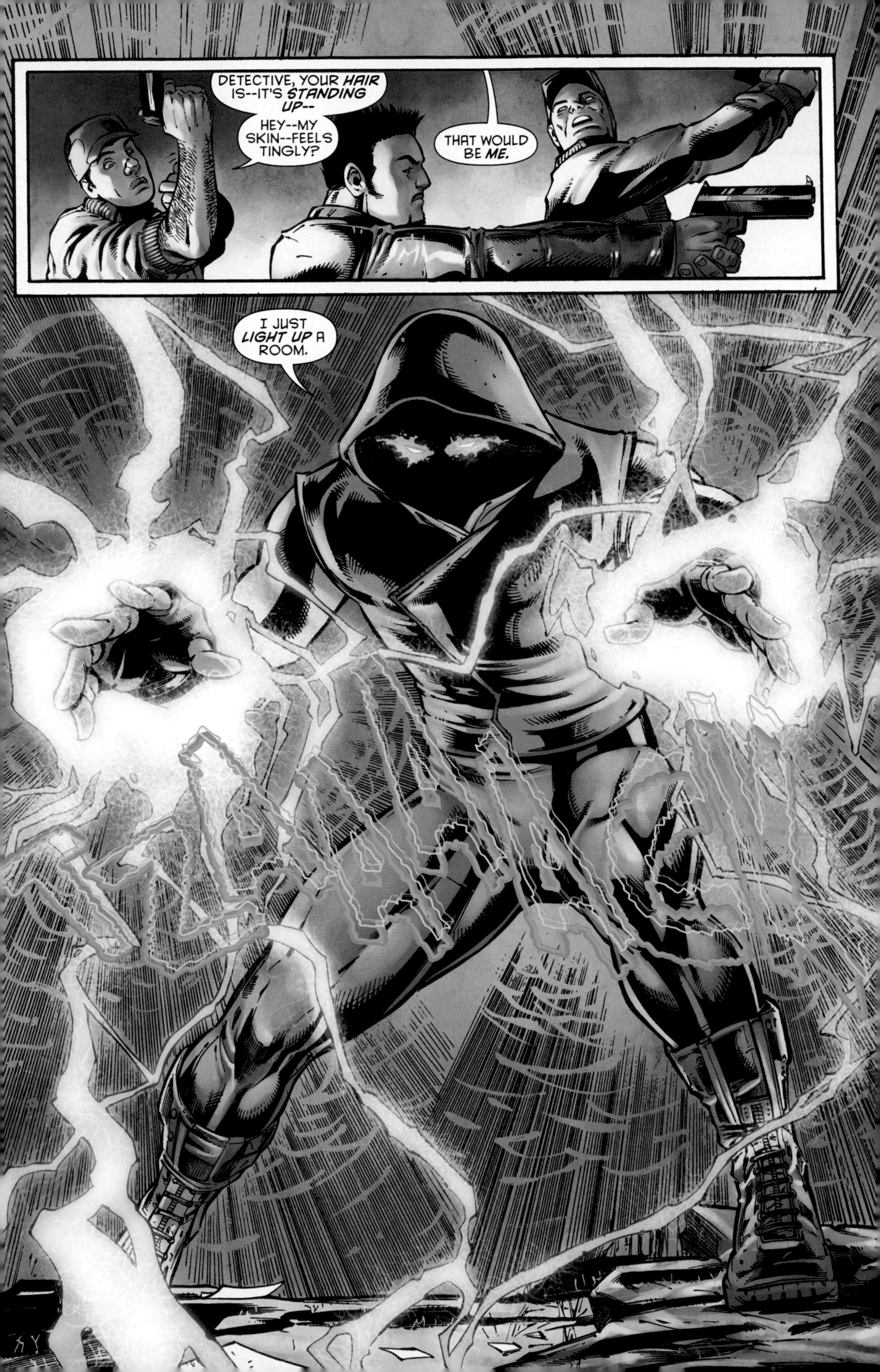
DETECTIVE, YOUR HAIR IS--IT'S STANDING UP--
HEY--MY SKIN--FEELS TINGLY?
THAT WOULD BE ME.
I JUST LIGHT UP A ROOM.

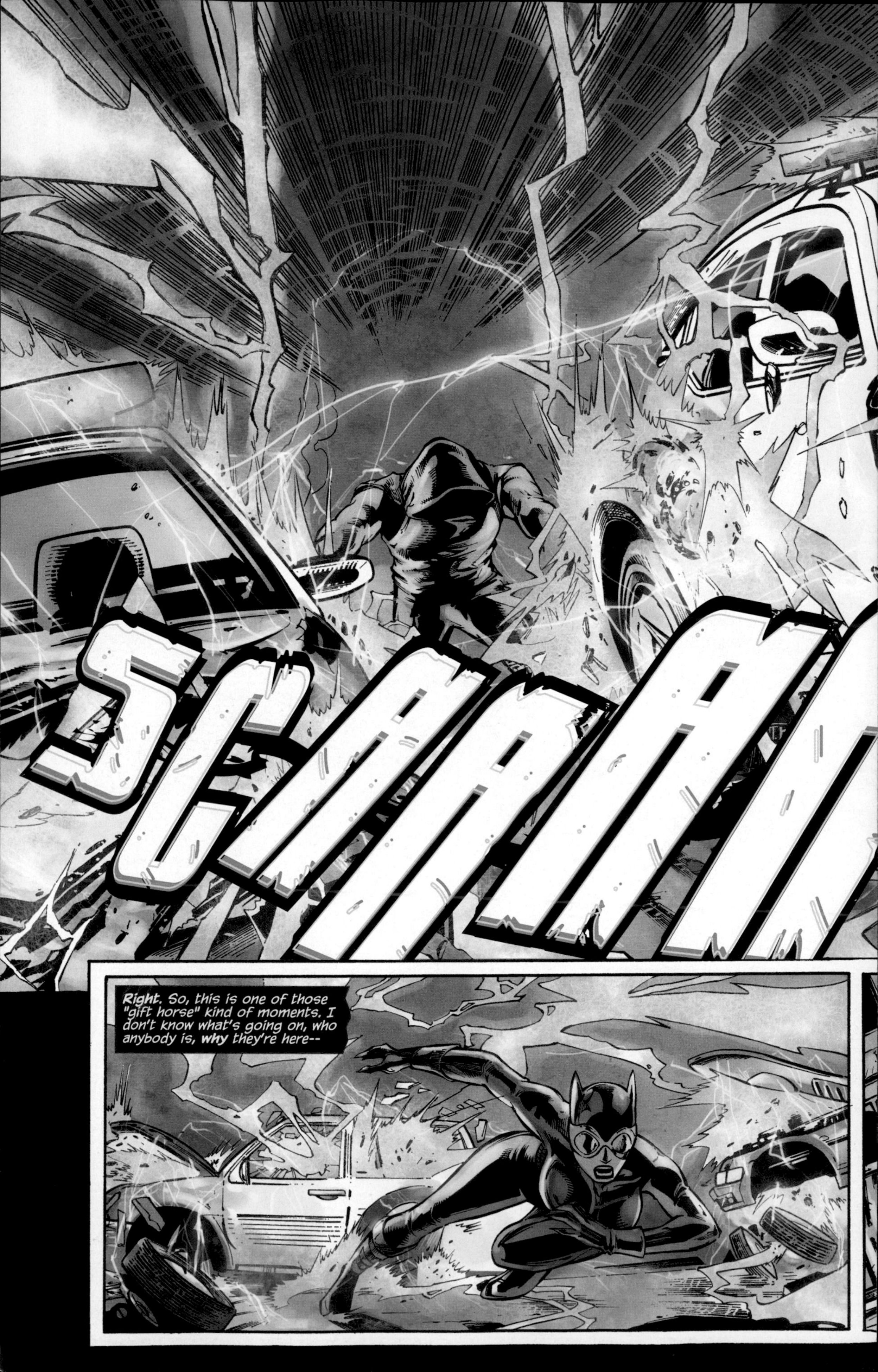
SCRAAAK
Right. So, this is one of those "gift horse" kind of moments. I don't know what's going on, who anybody is, why they're here--

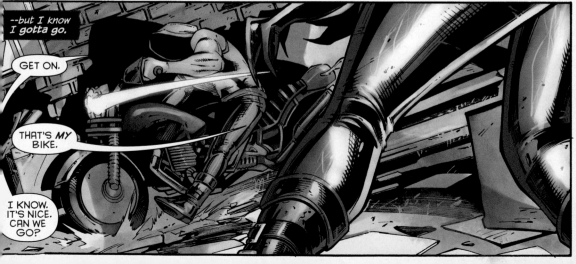

--but I know I gotta go.

GET ON.

THAT'S *MY* BIKE.

I KNOW. IT'S NICE. CAN WE GO?

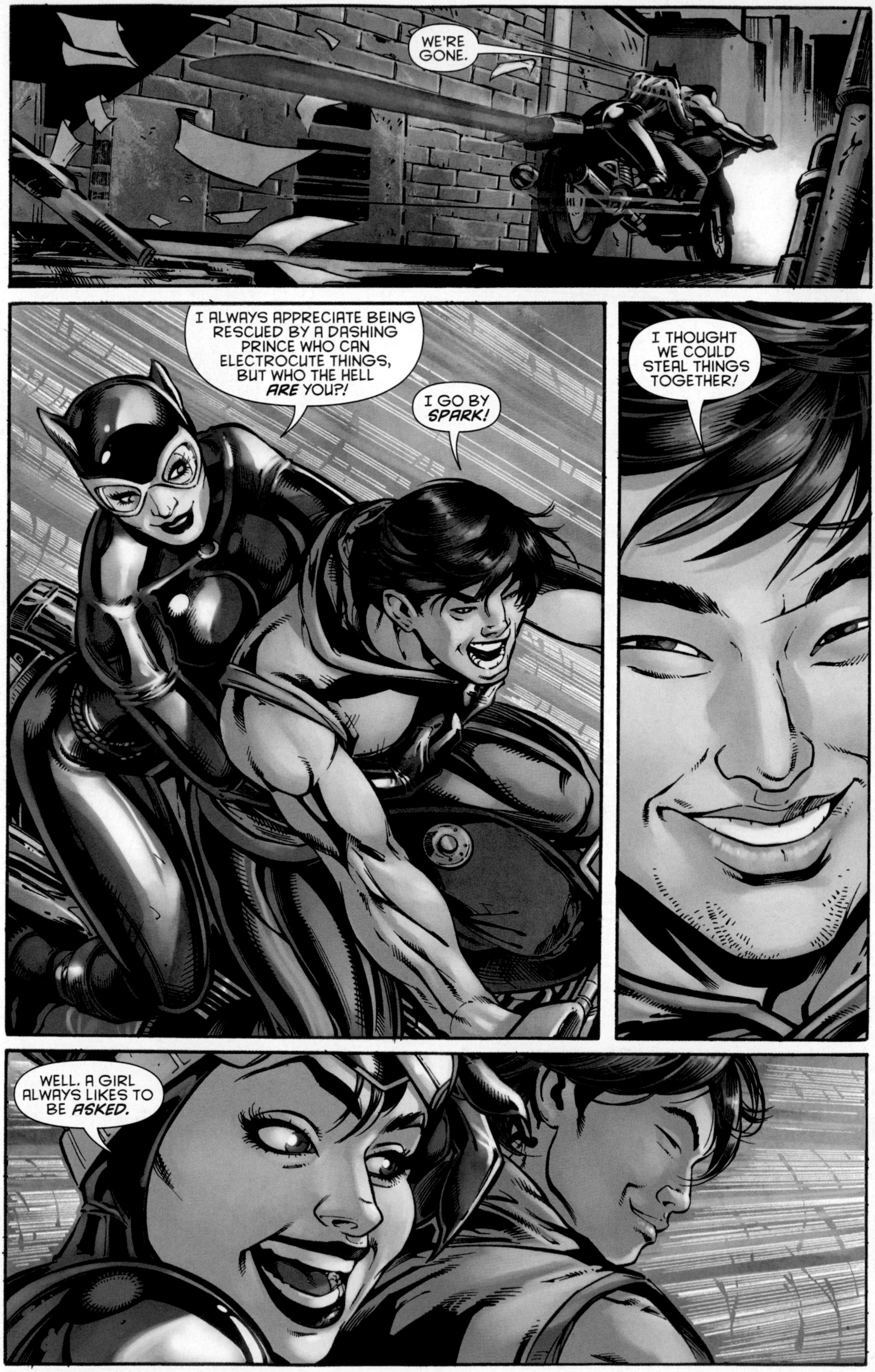
WE'RE GONE.
I ALWAYS APPRECIATE BEING RESCUED BY A DASHING PRINCE WHO CAN ELECTROCUTE THINGS, BUT WHO THE HELL ARE YOU?!
I GO BY SPARK!
I THOUGHT WE COULD STEAL THINGS TOGETHER!
WELL. A GIRL ALWAYS LIKES TO BE ASKED.

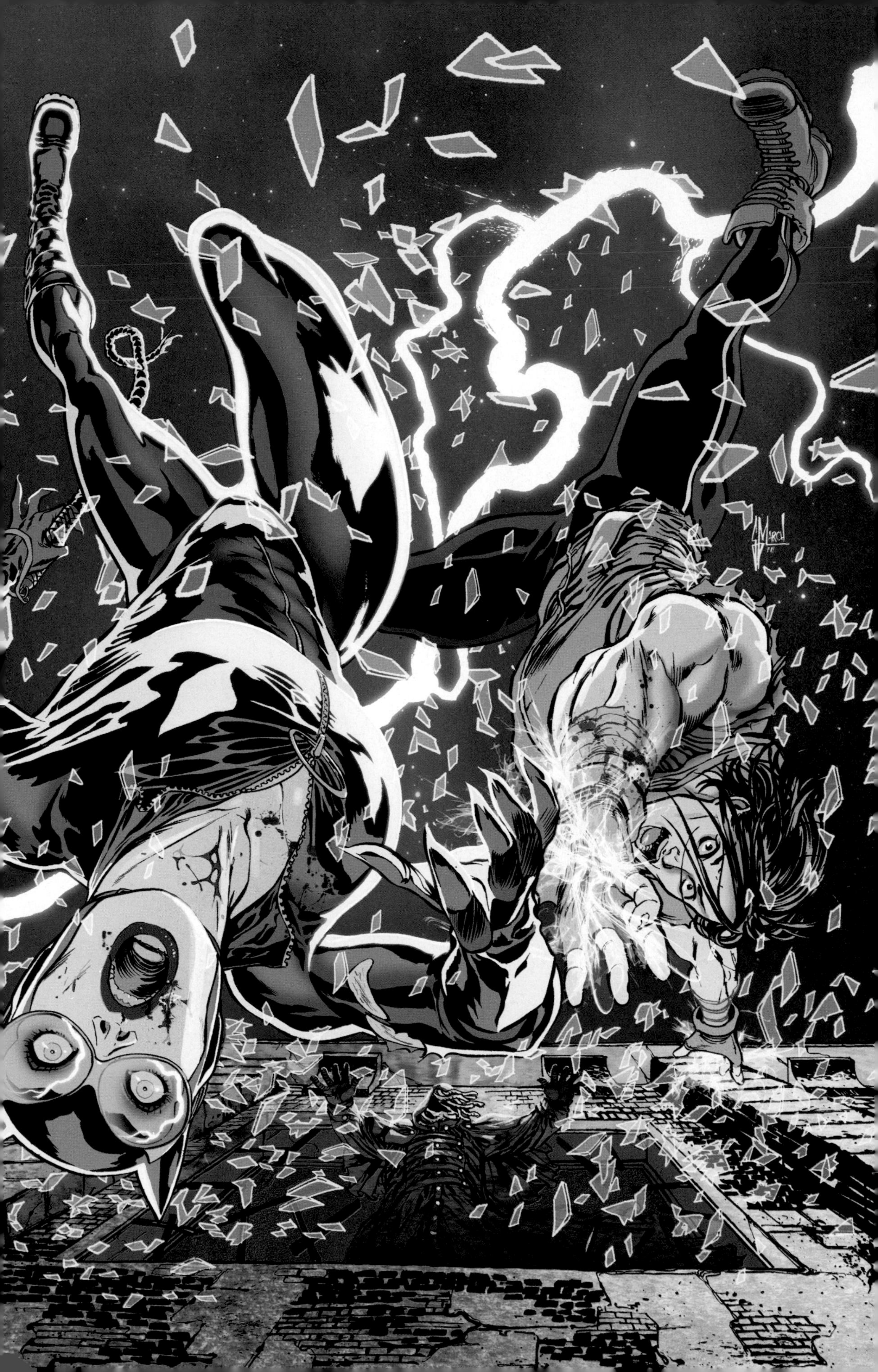

JUDD WINICK writer ADRIANA MELO penciller MARIAH BENES & JULIO FERREIRA inkers

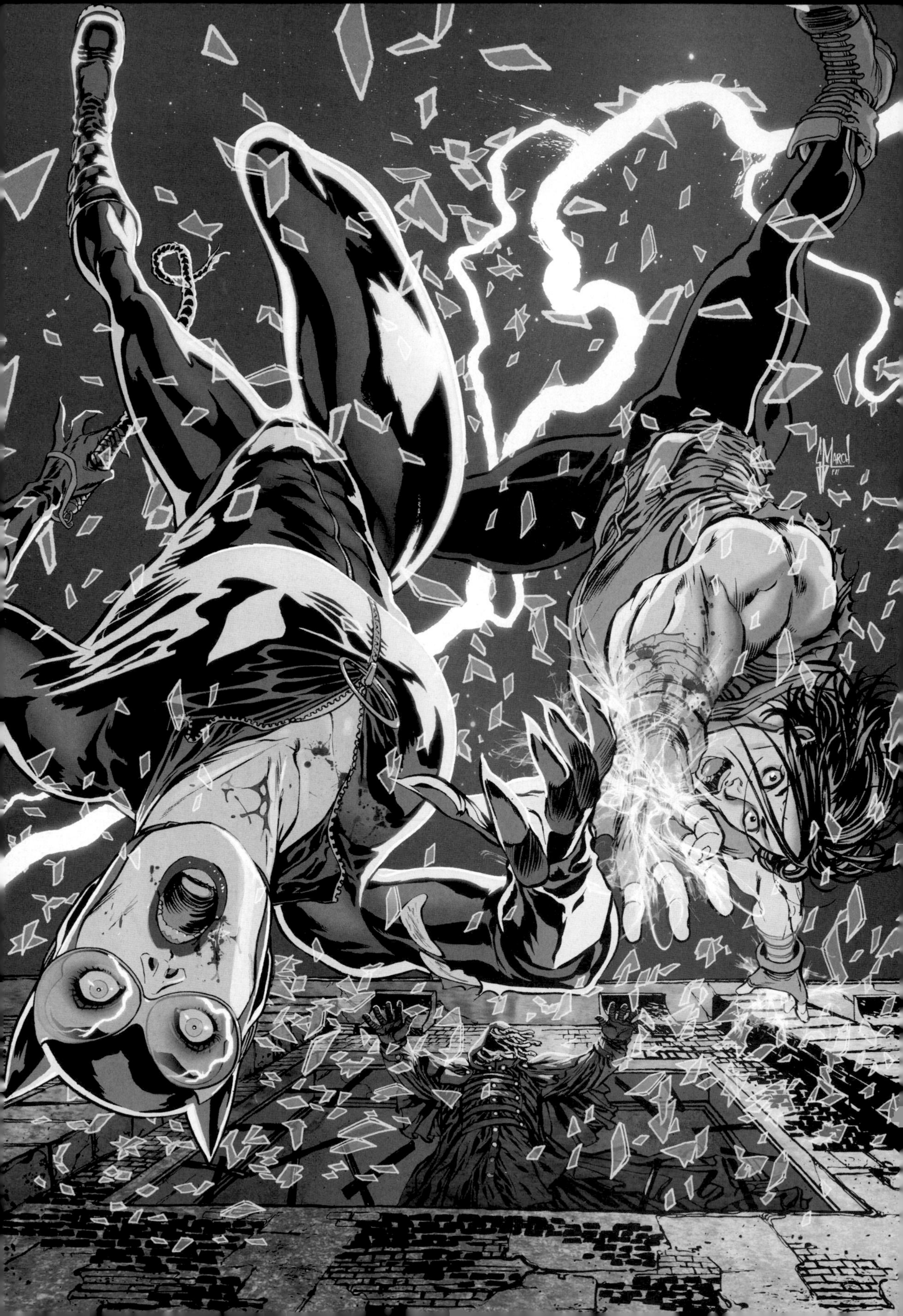

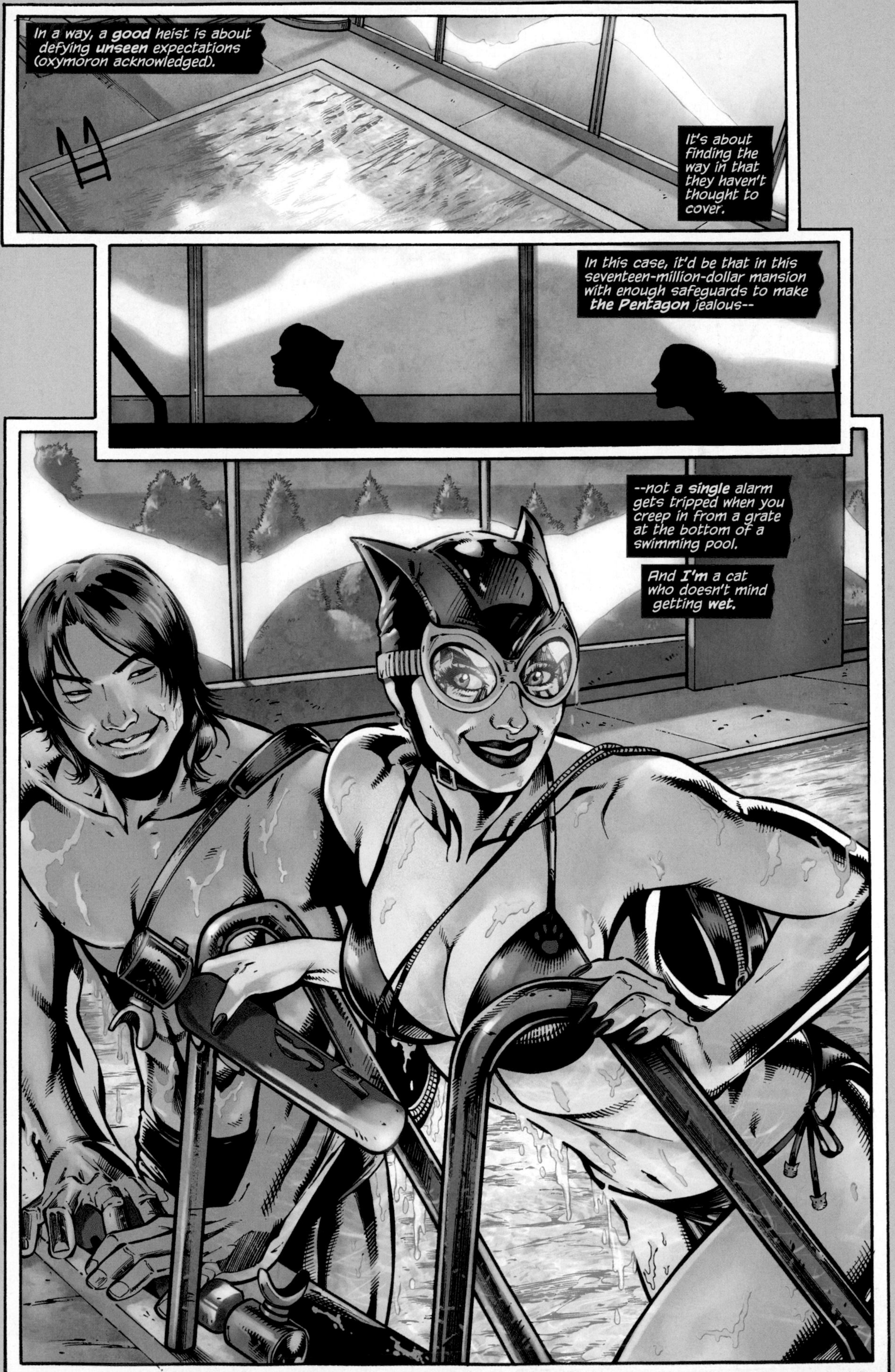
In a way, a **good** heist is about defying **unseen** expectations (oxymoron acknowledged).
It's about finding the way in that they haven't thought to cover.
In this case, it'd be that in this seventeen-million-dollar mansion with enough safeguards to make **the Pentagon** jealous--
--not a **single** alarm gets tripped when you creep in from a grate at the bottom of a swimming pool.
And **I'm** a cat who doesn't mind getting **wet.**

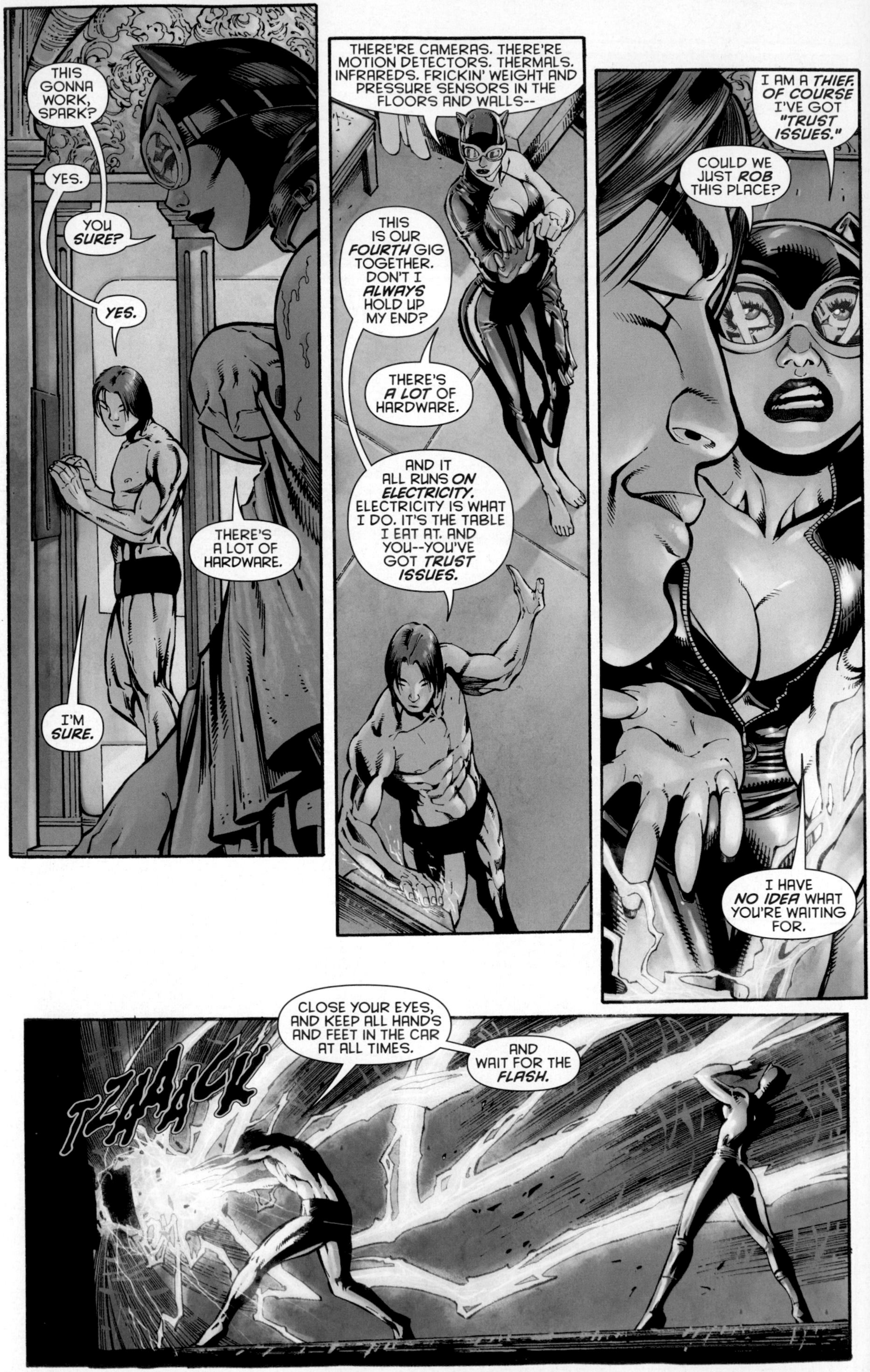
THIS GONNA WORK, SPARK?
YES.
YOU SURE?
YES.
I'M SURE.
THERE'S A LOT OF HARDWARE.
THERE'RE CAMERAS. THERE'RE MOTION DETECTORS. THERMALS. INFRAREDS. FRICKIN' WEIGHT AND PRESSURE SENSORS IN THE FLOORS AND WALLS--
THIS IS OUR FOURTH GIG TOGETHER. DON'T I ALWAYS HOLD UP MY END?
THERE'S A LOT OF HARDWARE.
AND IT ALL RUNS ON ELECTRICITY. ELECTRICITY IS WHAT I DO. IT'S THE TABLE I EAT AT. AND YOU--YOU'VE GOT TRUST ISSUES.
I AM A THIEF. OF COURSE I'VE GOT "TRUST ISSUES."
COULD WE JUST ROB THIS PLACE?
I HAVE NO IDEA WHAT YOU'RE WAITING FOR.
CLOSE YOUR EYES, AND KEEP ALL HANDS AND FEET IN THE CAR AT ALL TIMES.
AND WAIT FOR THE FLASH.
TZAAACK

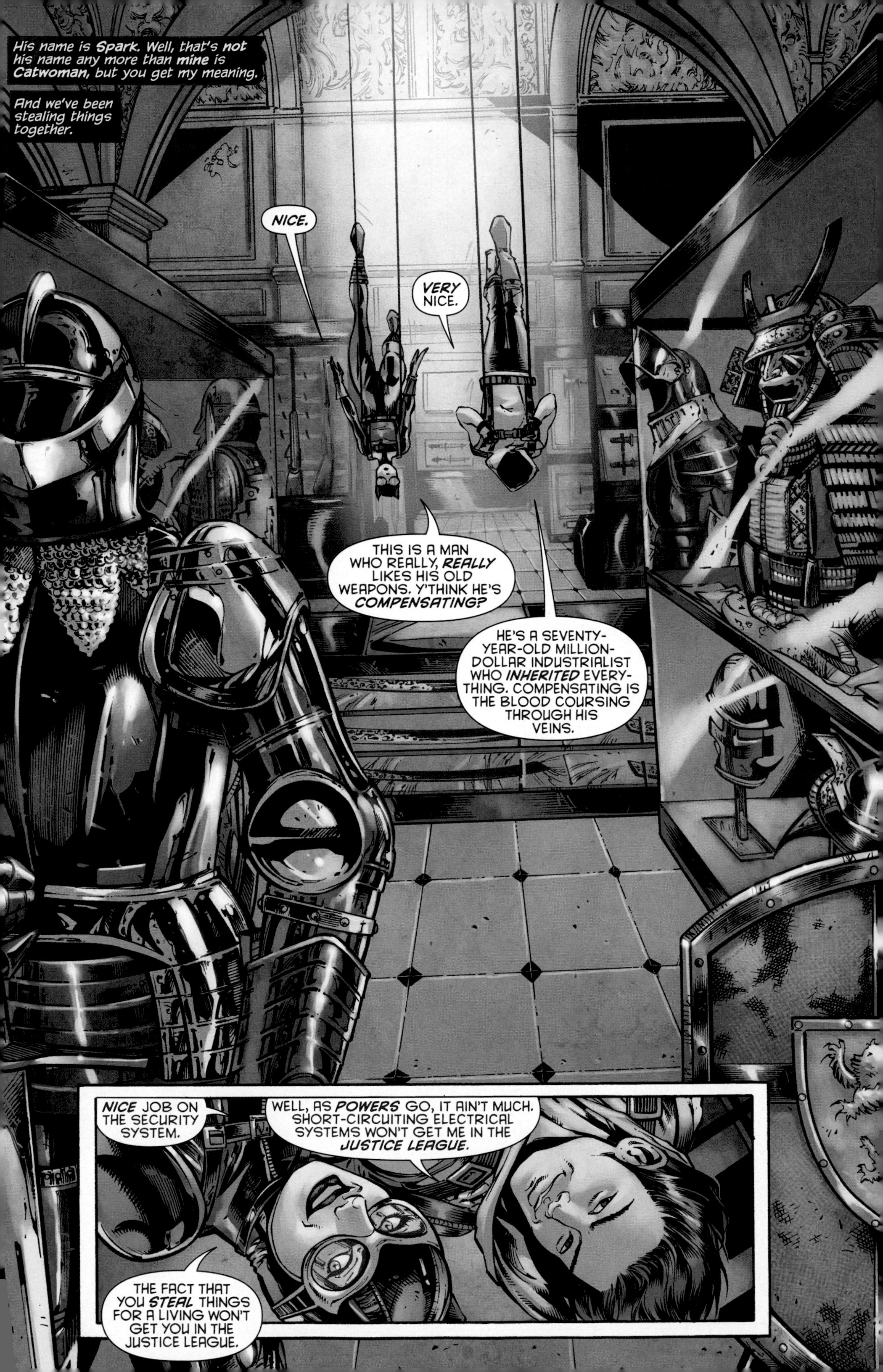
His name is **Spark**. Well, that's **not** his name any more than **mine** is **Catwoman**, but you get my meaning.
And we've been stealing things together.
NICE.
VERY NICE.
THIS IS A MAN WHO REALLY, *REALLY* LIKES HIS OLD WEAPONS. Y'THINK HE'S *COMPENSATING?*
HE'S A SEVENTY-YEAR-OLD MILLION-DOLLAR INDUSTRIALIST WHO *INHERITED* EVERYTHING. COMPENSATING IS THE BLOOD COURSING THROUGH HIS VEINS.
NICE JOB ON THE SECURITY SYSTEM.
WELL, AS *POWERS* GO, IT AIN'T MUCH. SHORT-CIRCUITING ELECTRICAL SYSTEMS WON'T GET ME IN THE *JUSTICE LEAGUE*.
THE FACT THAT YOU *STEAL* THINGS FOR A LIVING WON'T GET YOU IN THE JUSTICE LEAGUE.

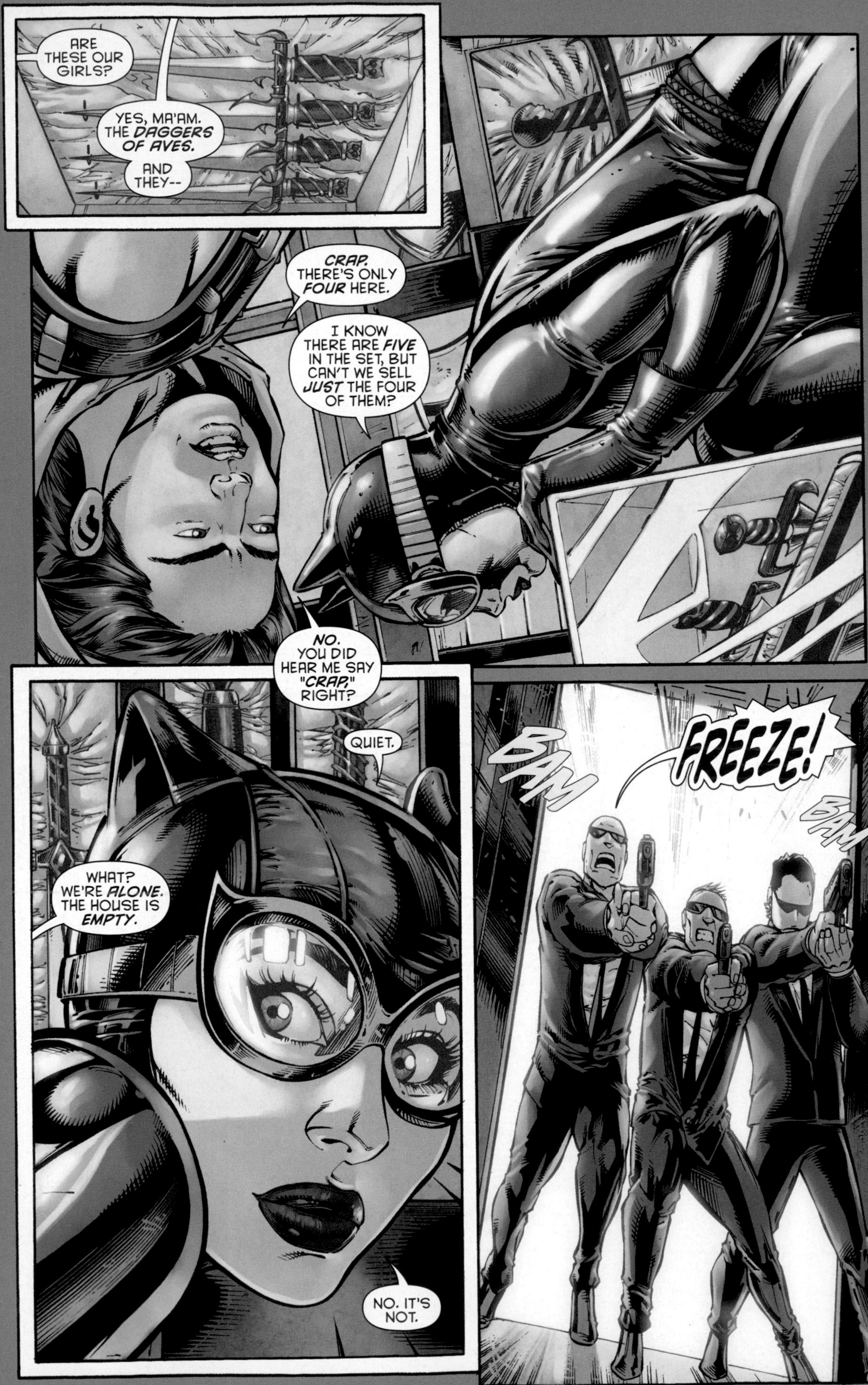
ARE THESE OUR GIRLS?
YES, MA'AM. THE *DAGGERS OF AVES.*
AND THEY--
CRAP. THERE'S ONLY *FOUR* HERE.
I KNOW THERE ARE *FIVE* IN THE SET, BUT CAN'T WE SELL *JUST* THE FOUR OF THEM?
NO. YOU DID HEAR ME SAY "*CRAP,*" RIGHT?
QUIET.
WHAT? WE'RE *ALONE*. THE HOUSE IS *EMPTY*.
NO. IT'S NOT.
BAM
FREEZE!
BAM

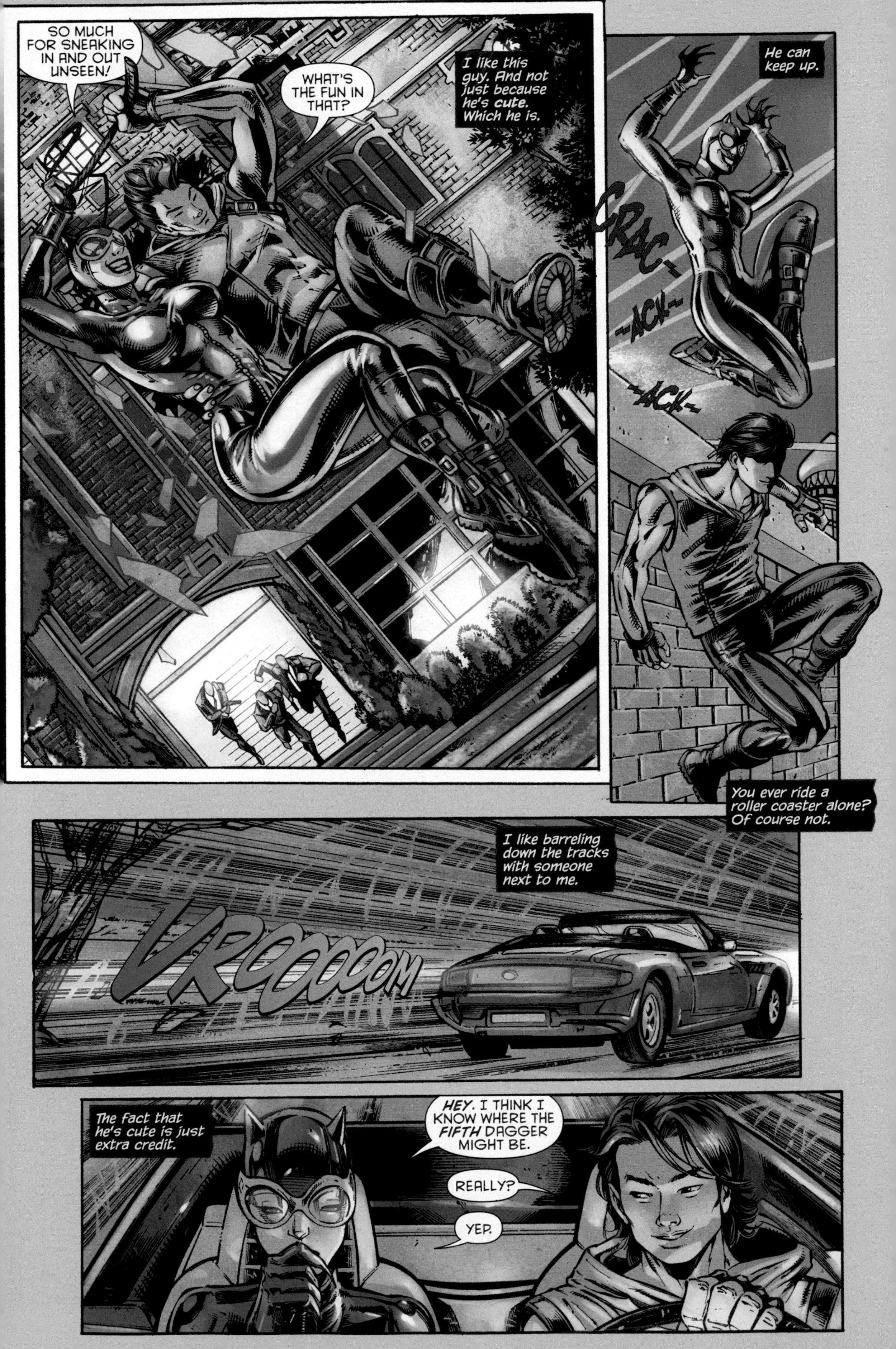
SO MUCH FOR SNEAKING IN AND OUT UNSEEN!
WHAT'S THE FUN IN THAT?
I like this guy. And not just because he's **cute**. Which he is.
He can keep up.
CRAC-
-ACK-
-ACK-
You ever ride a roller coaster alone? Of course not.
I like barreling down the tracks with someone next to me.
VROOOOOOM
The fact that he's cute is just extra credit.
HEY. I THINK I KNOW WHERE THE ***FIFTH*** DAGGER MIGHT BE.
REALLY?
YEP.

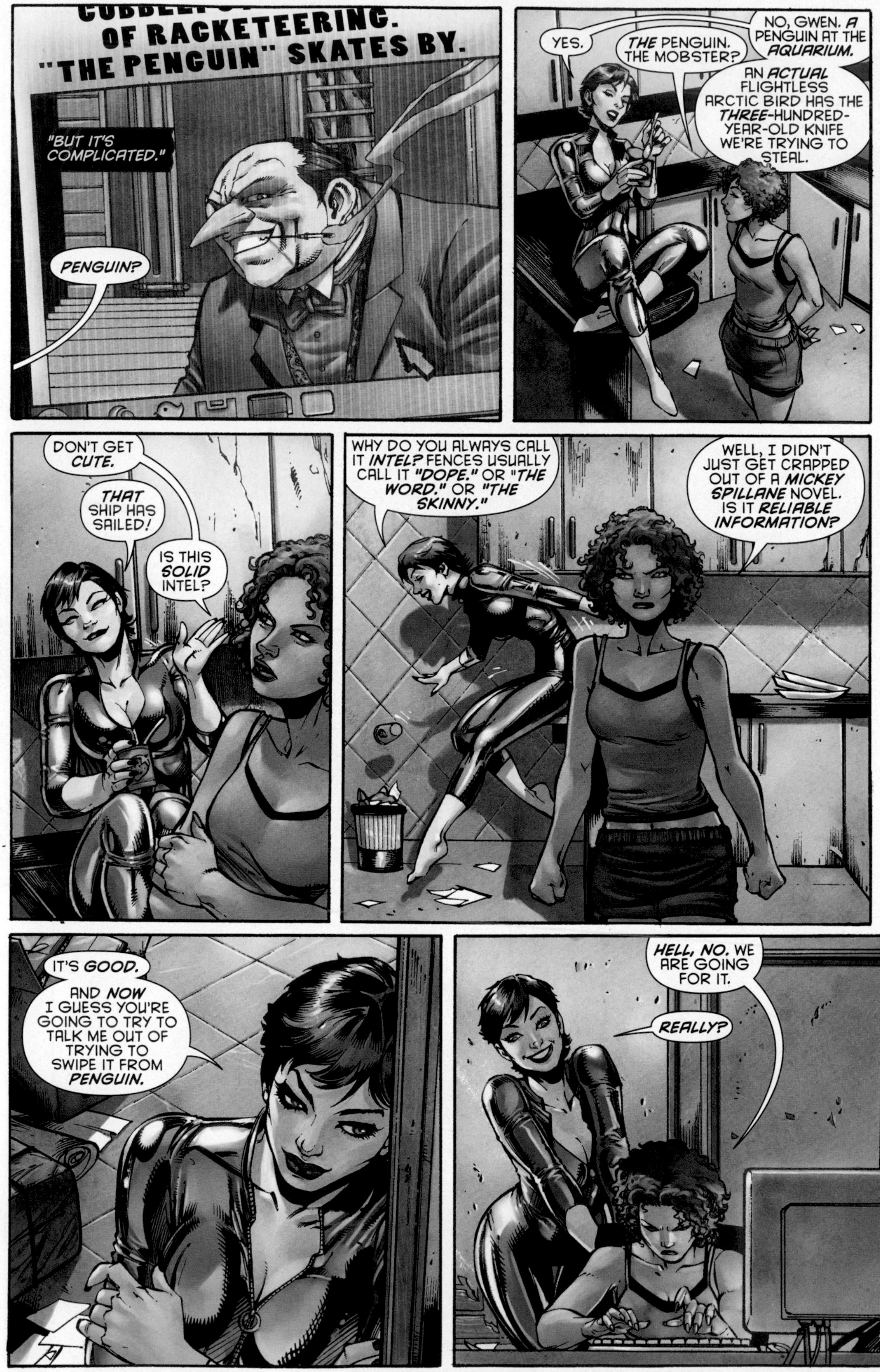
COBBLEP... OF RACKETEERING. "THE PENGUIN" SKATES BY.
"BUT IT'S COMPLICATED."
PENGUIN?
YES.
THE PENGUIN. THE MOBSTER?
NO, GWEN. A PENGUIN AT THE AQUARIUM.
AN ACTUAL FLIGHTLESS ARCTIC BIRD HAS THE THREE-HUNDRED-YEAR-OLD KNIFE WE'RE TRYING TO STEAL.
DON'T GET CUTE.
THAT SHIP HAS SAILED!
IS THIS SOLID INTEL?
WHY DO YOU ALWAYS CALL IT INTEL? FENCES USUALLY CALL IT "DOPE." OR "THE WORD." OR "THE SKINNY."
WELL, I DIDN'T JUST GET CRAPPED OUT OF A MICKEY SPILLANE NOVEL. IS IT RELIABLE INFORMATION?
IT'S GOOD.
AND NOW I GUESS YOU'RE GOING TO TRY TO TALK ME OUT OF TRYING TO SWIPE IT FROM PENGUIN.
HELL, NO. WE ARE GOING FOR IT.
REALLY?

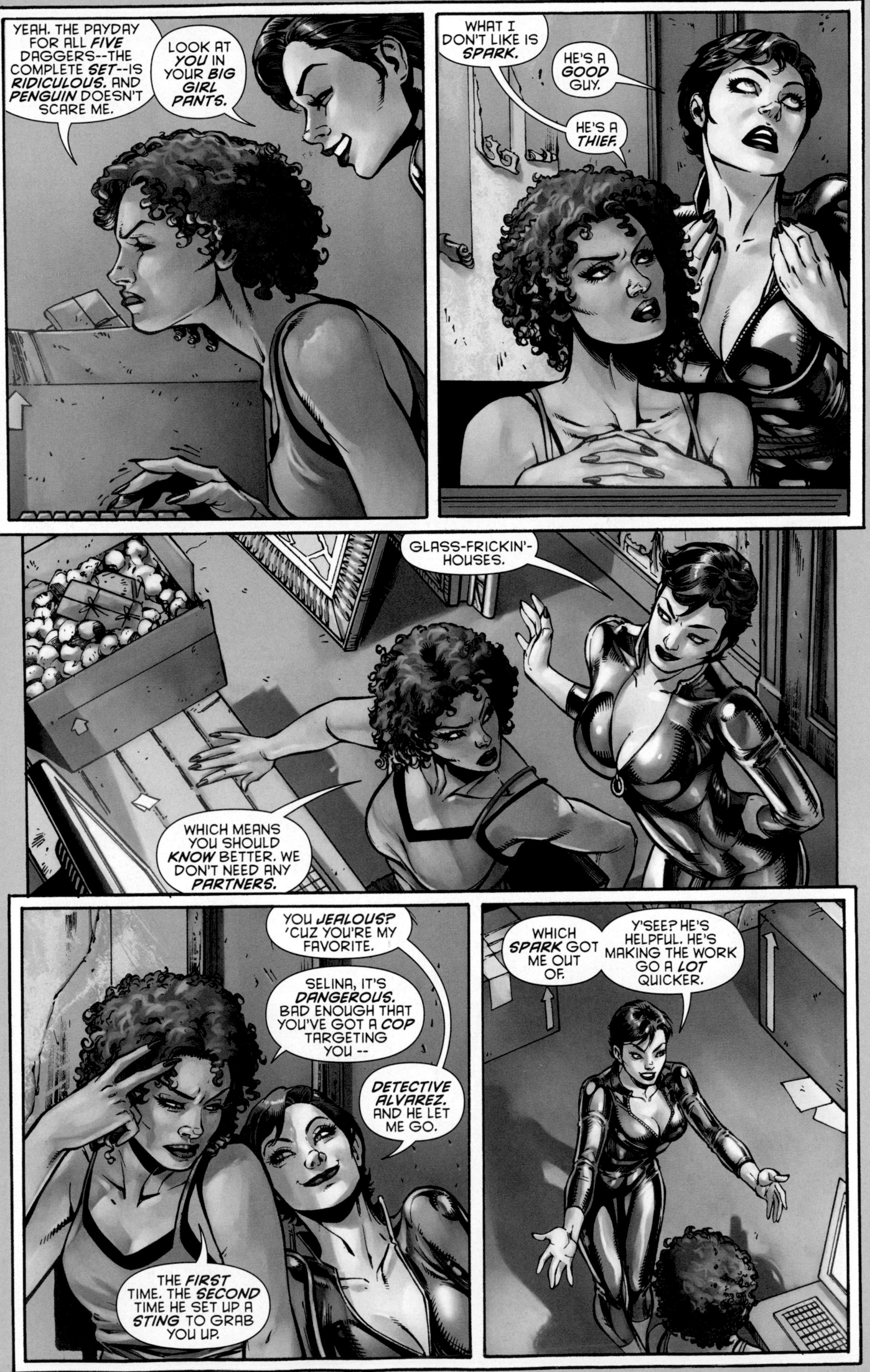
YEAH. THE PAYDAY FOR ALL FIVE DAGGERS--THE COMPLETE SET--IS RIDICULOUS. AND PENGUIN DOESN'T SCARE ME.
LOOK AT YOU IN YOUR BIG GIRL PANTS.
WHAT I DON'T LIKE IS SPARK.
HE'S A GOOD GUY.
HE'S A THIEF.
GLASS-FRICKIN'-HOUSES.
WHICH MEANS YOU SHOULD KNOW BETTER. WE DON'T NEED ANY PARTNERS.
YOU JEALOUS? 'CUZ YOU'RE MY FAVORITE.
SELINA, IT'S DANGEROUS. BAD ENOUGH THAT YOU'VE GOT A COP TARGETING YOU --
DETECTIVE ALVAREZ. AND HE LET ME GO.
THE FIRST TIME. THE SECOND TIME HE SET UP A STING TO GRAB YOU UP.
WHICH SPARK GOT ME OUT OF.
Y'SEE? HE'S HELPFUL. HE'S MAKING THE WORK GO A LOT QUICKER.

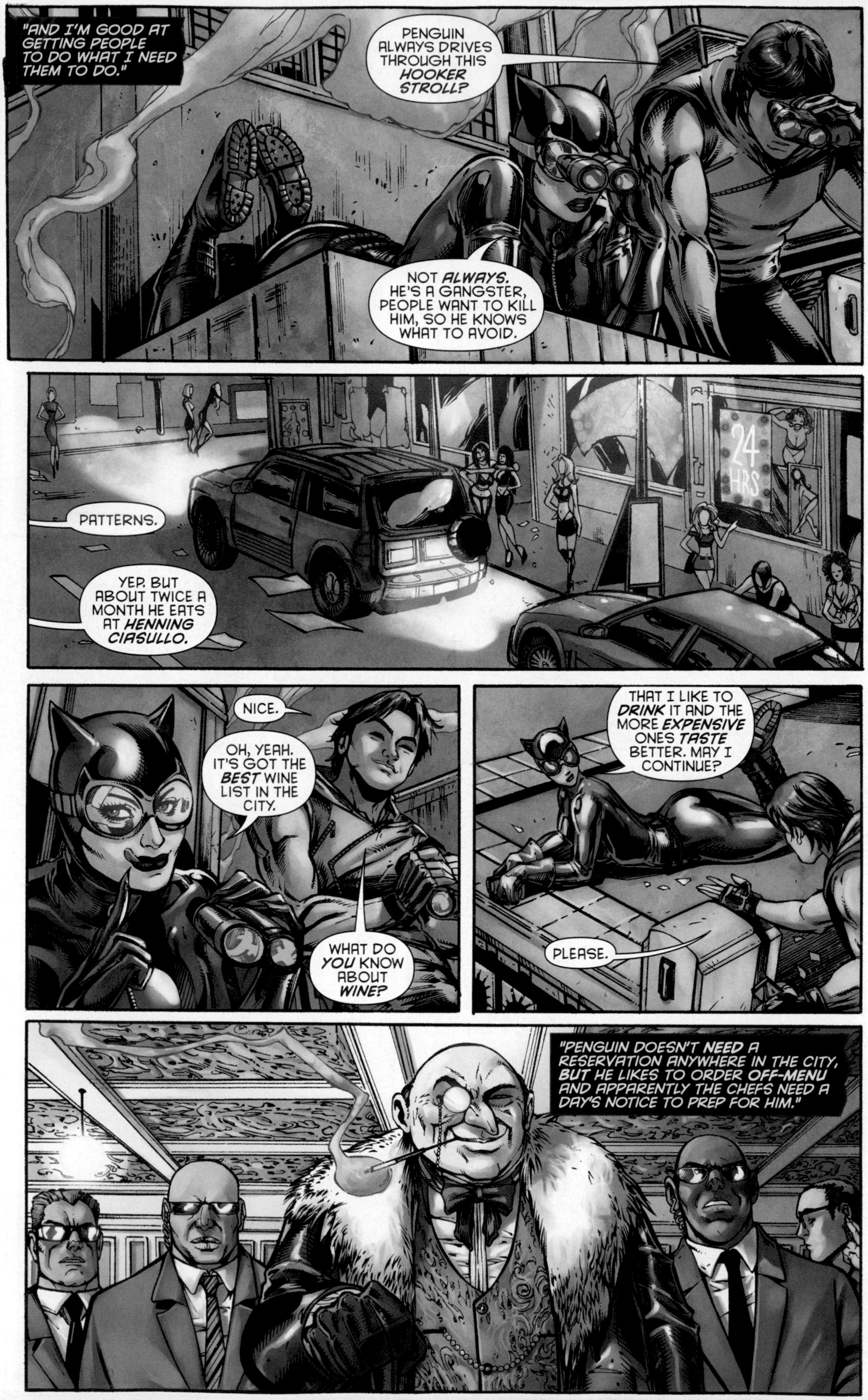
"AND I'M GOOD AT GETTING PEOPLE TO DO WHAT I NEED THEM TO DO."
PENGUIN ALWAYS DRIVES THROUGH THIS HOOKER STROLL?
NOT ALWAYS. HE'S A GANGSTER, PEOPLE WANT TO KILL HIM, SO HE KNOWS WHAT TO AVOID.
24 HRS
PATTERNS.
YEP. BUT ABOUT TWICE A MONTH HE EATS AT HENNING CIASULLO.
NICE.
OH, YEAH. IT'S GOT THE BEST WINE LIST IN THE CITY.
WHAT DO YOU KNOW ABOUT WINE?
THAT I LIKE TO DRINK IT AND THE MORE EXPENSIVE ONES TASTE BETTER. MAY I CONTINUE?
PLEASE.
"PENGUIN DOESN'T NEED A RESERVATION ANYWHERE IN THE CITY, BUT HE LIKES TO ORDER OFF-MENU AND APPARENTLY THE CHEFS NEED A DAY'S NOTICE TO PREP FOR HIM."

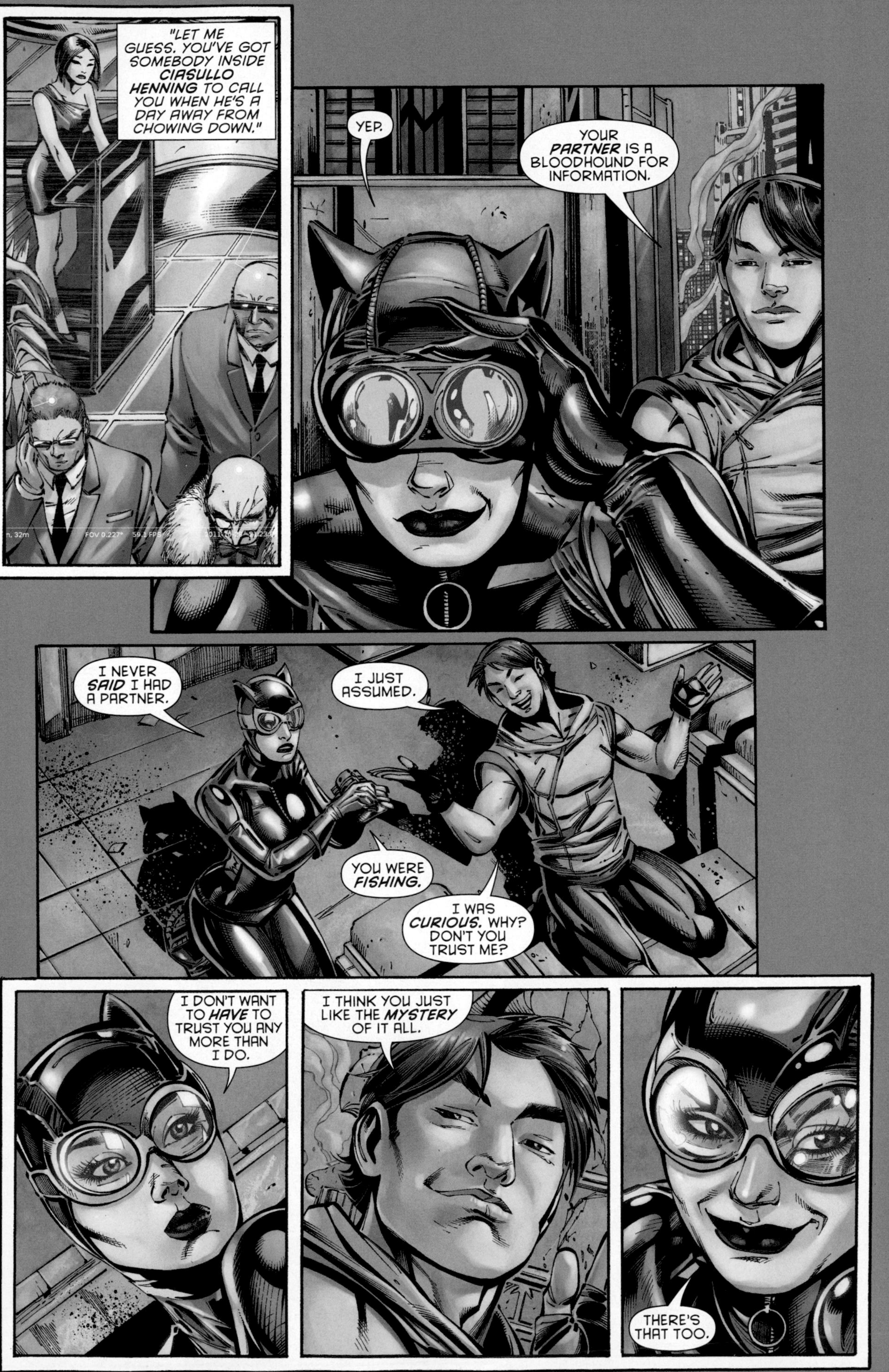
"LET ME GUESS. YOU'VE GOT SOMEBODY INSIDE CIASULLO HENNING TO CALL YOU WHEN HE'S A DAY AWAY FROM CHOWING DOWN."
YEP.
YOUR PARTNER IS A BLOODHOUND FOR INFORMATION.
I NEVER SAID I HAD A PARTNER.
I JUST ASSUMED.
YOU WERE FISHING.
I WAS CURIOUS. WHY? DON'T YOU TRUST ME?
I DON'T WANT TO HAVE TO TRUST YOU ANY MORE THAN I DO.
I THINK YOU JUST LIKE THE MYSTERY OF IT ALL.
THERE'S THAT TOO.

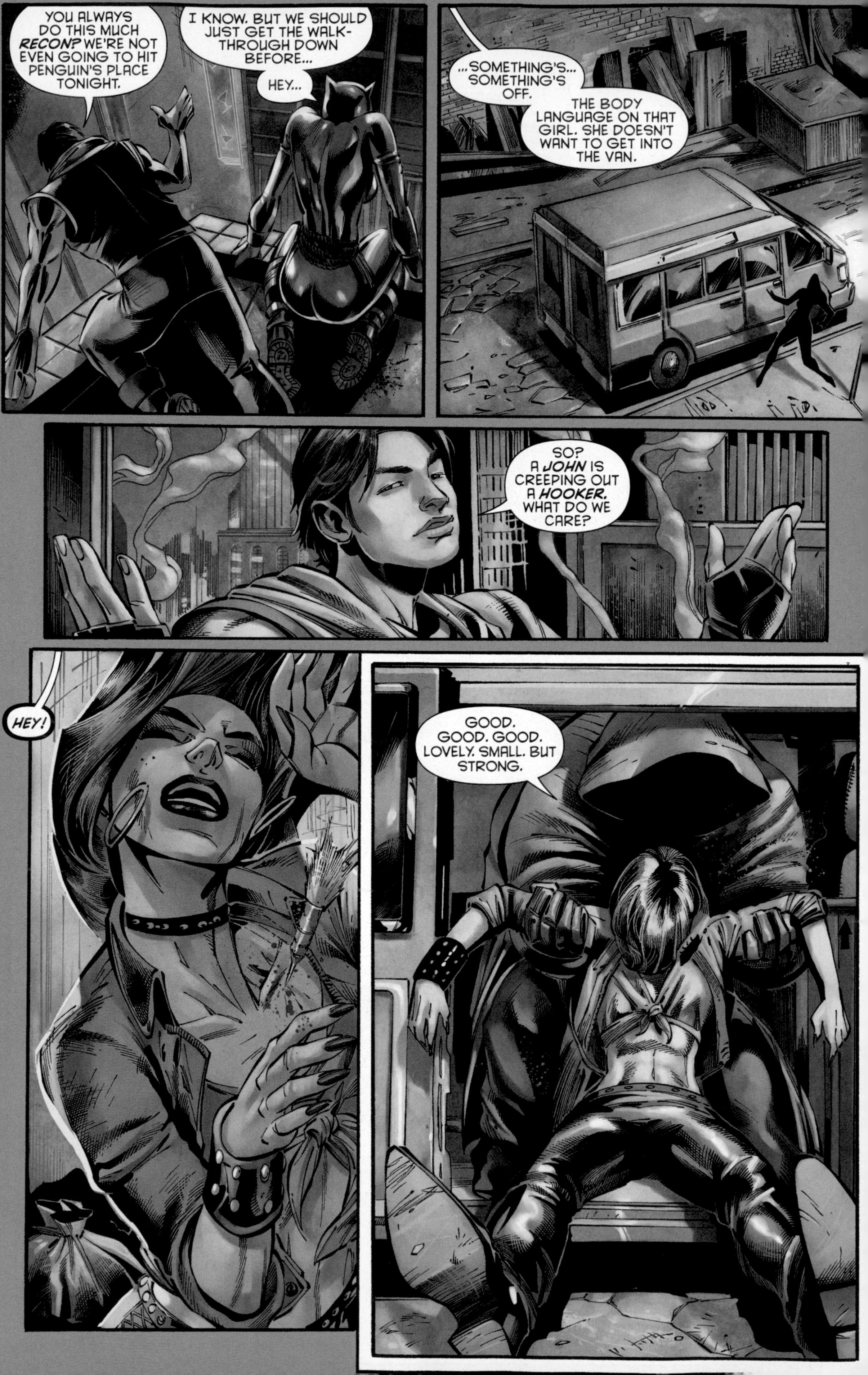
YOU ALWAYS DO THIS MUCH RECON? WE'RE NOT EVEN GOING TO HIT PENGUIN'S PLACE TONIGHT.
I KNOW. BUT WE SHOULD JUST GET THE WALK-THROUGH DOWN BEFORE...
HEY...
...SOMETHING'S... SOMETHING'S OFF.
THE BODY LANGUAGE ON THAT GIRL. SHE DOESN'T WANT TO GET INTO THE VAN.
SO? A JOHN IS CREEPING OUT A HOOKER. WHAT DO WE CARE?
HEY!
GOOD. GOOD. GOOD. LOVELY. SMALL. BUT STRONG.

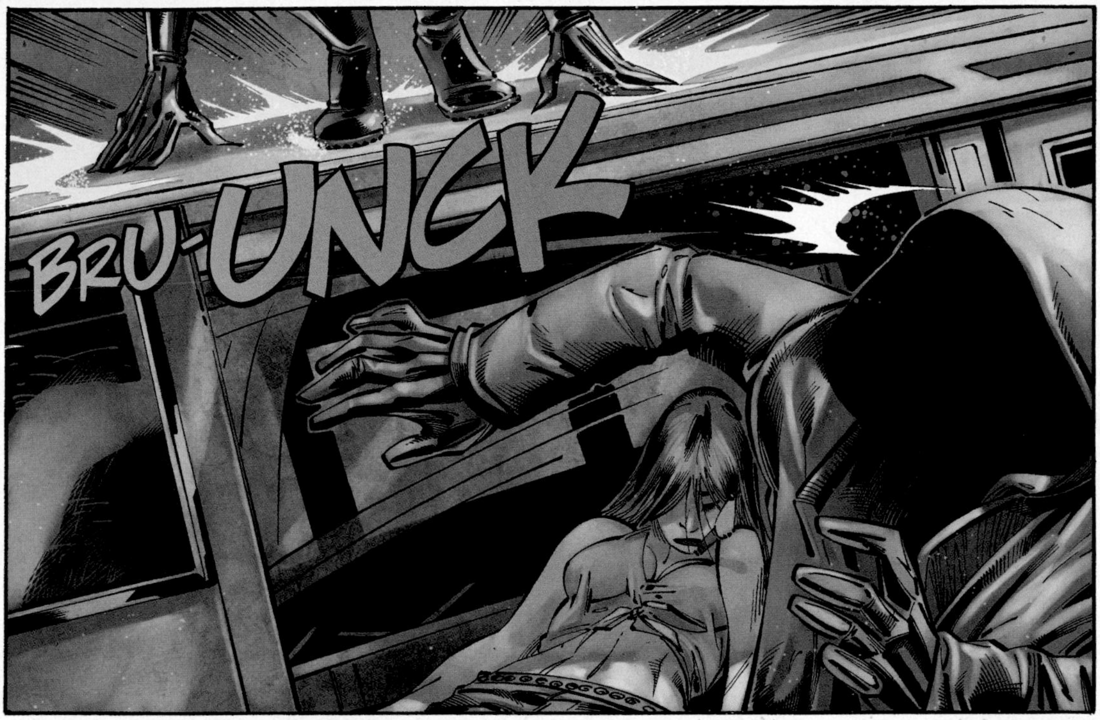
BRU-UNCK

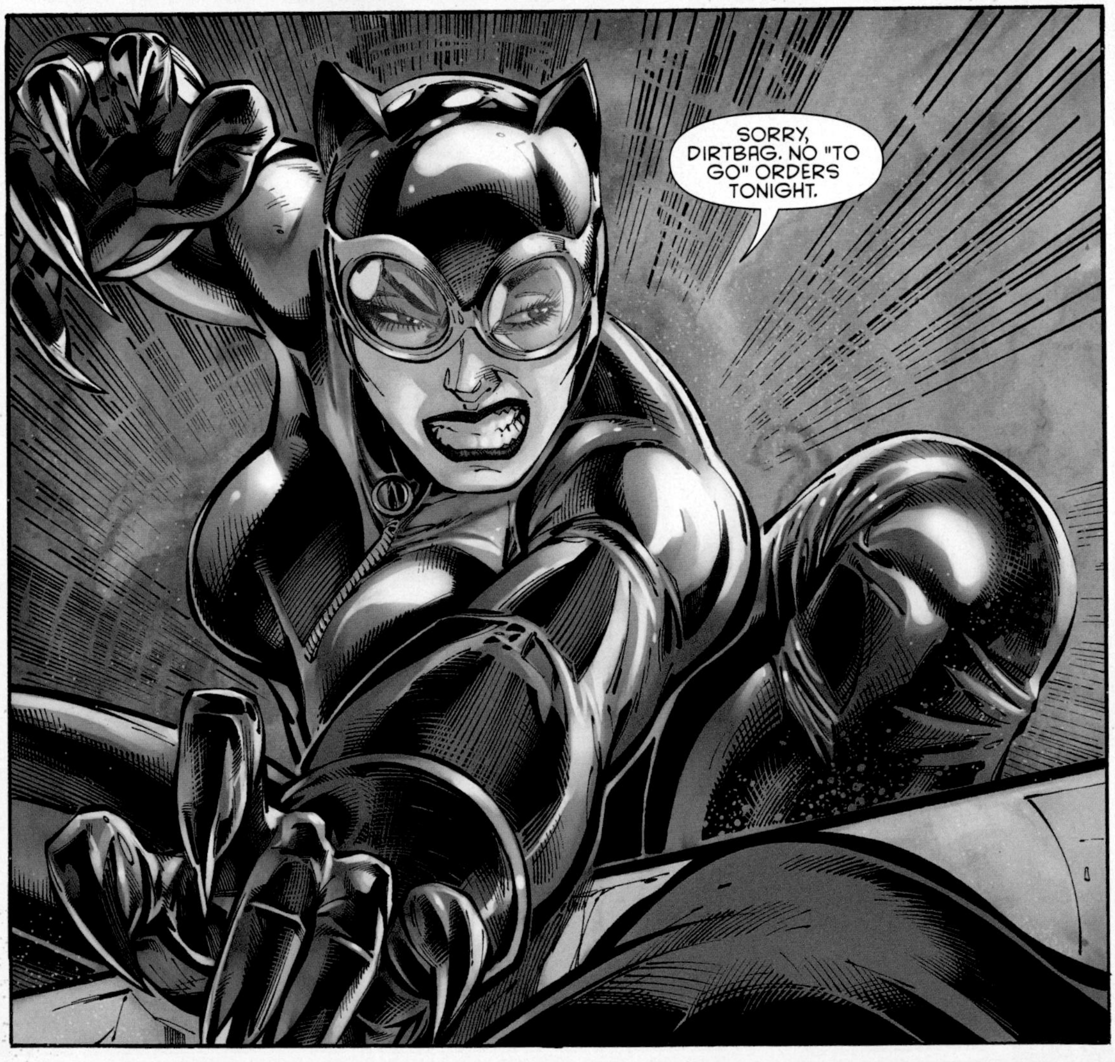
SORRY, DIRTBAG. NO "TO GO" ORDERS TONIGHT.

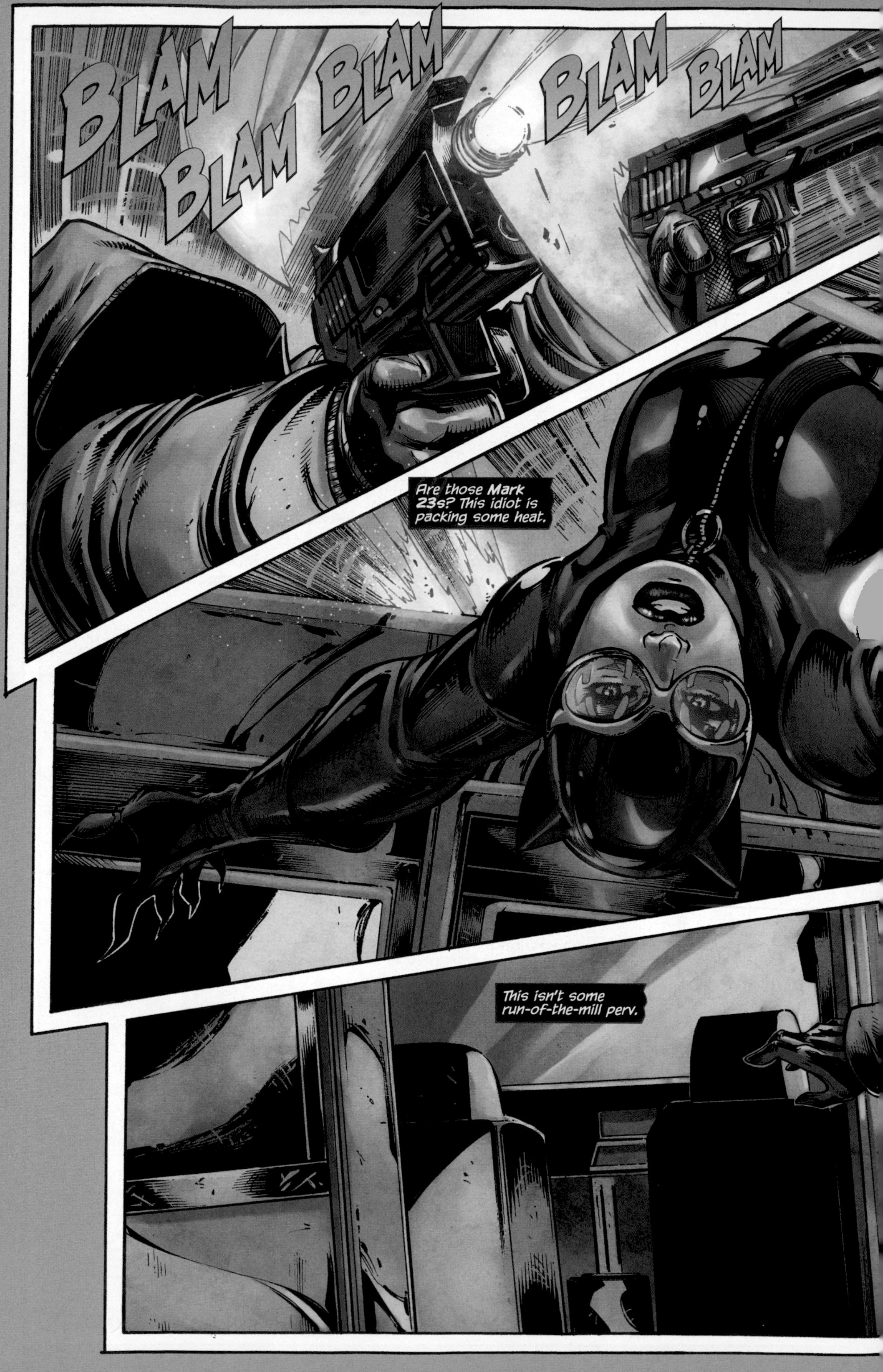
BLAM
BLAM
BLAM
BLAM
BLAM
Are those Mark 23s? This idiot is packing some heat.
This isn't some run-of-the-mill perv.

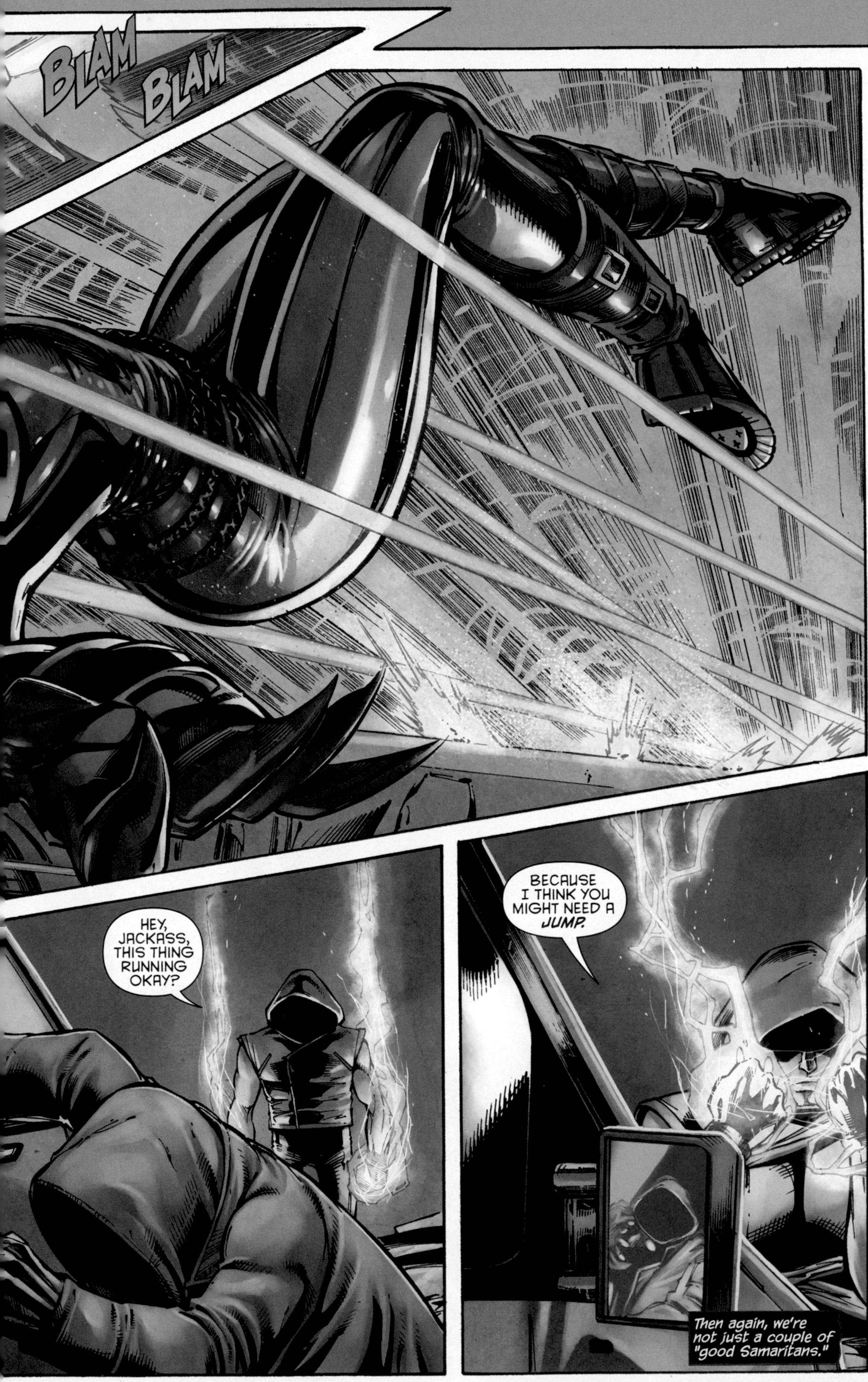
BLAM BLAM
HEY, JACKASS, THIS THING RUNNING OKAY?
BECAUSE I THINK YOU MIGHT NEED A JUMP.
Then again, we're not just a couple of "good Samaritans."

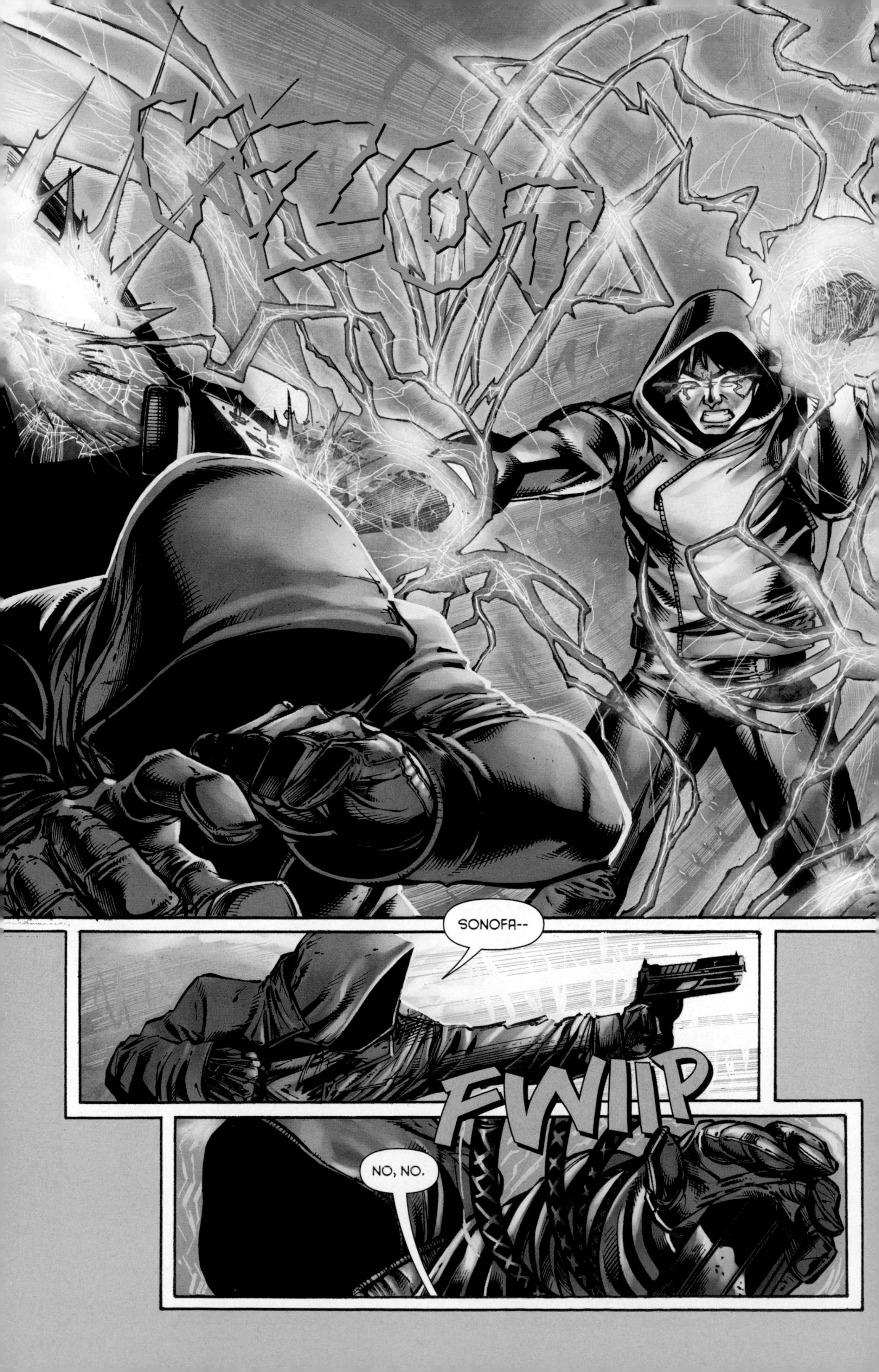

KZZOT
SONOFA--
FWIIP
NO, NO.

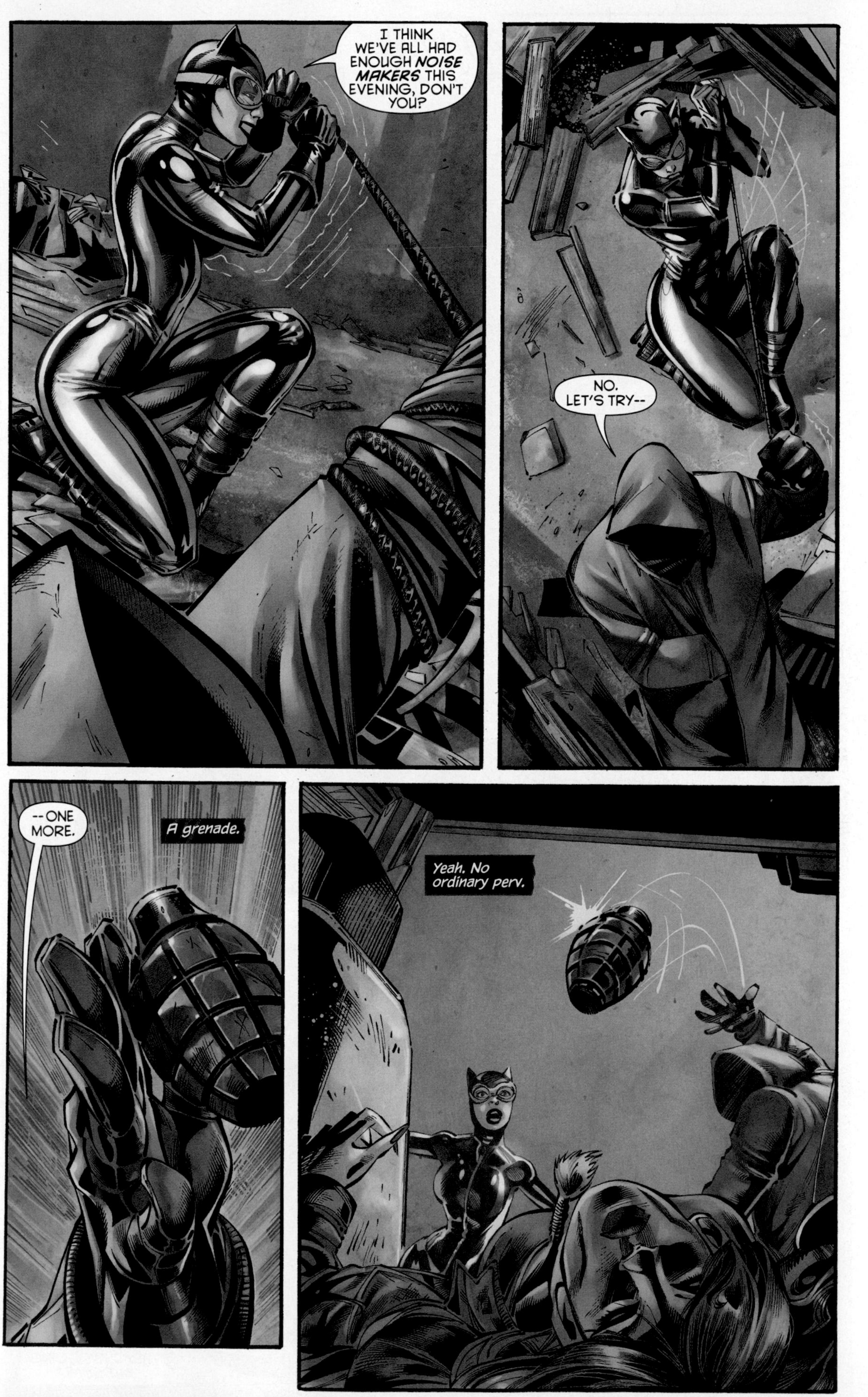
I THINK WE'VE ALL HAD ENOUGH NOISE MAKERS THIS EVENING, DON'T YOU?
NO. LET'S TRY--
--ONE MORE.
A grenade.
Yeah. No ordinary perv.

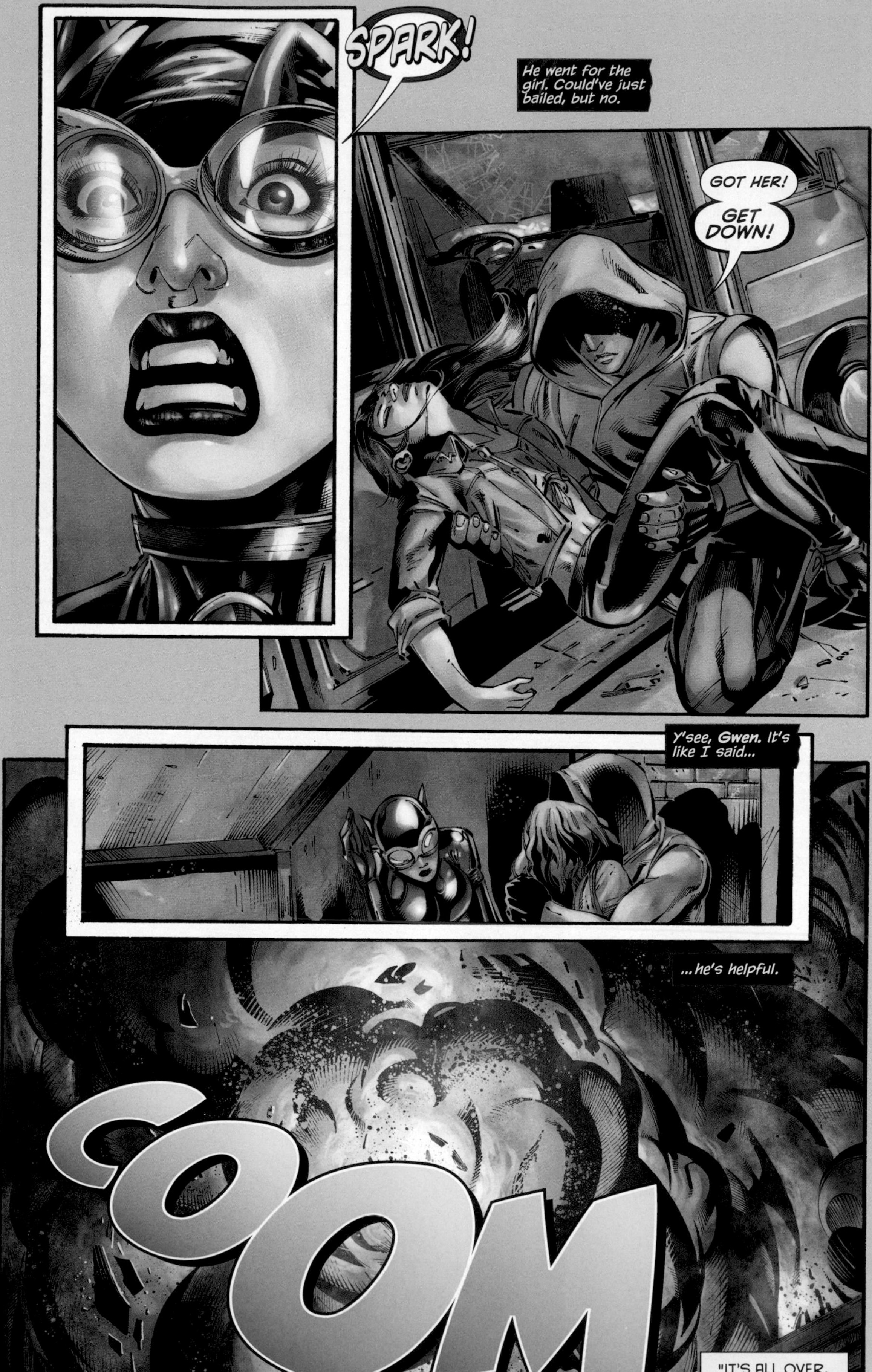
SPARK!
He went for the girl. Could've just bailed, but no.
GOT HER!
GET DOWN!
Y'see, Gwen. It's like I said...
...he's helpful.
COOM
"IT'S ALL OVER. THEY JUST GOING MISSING."

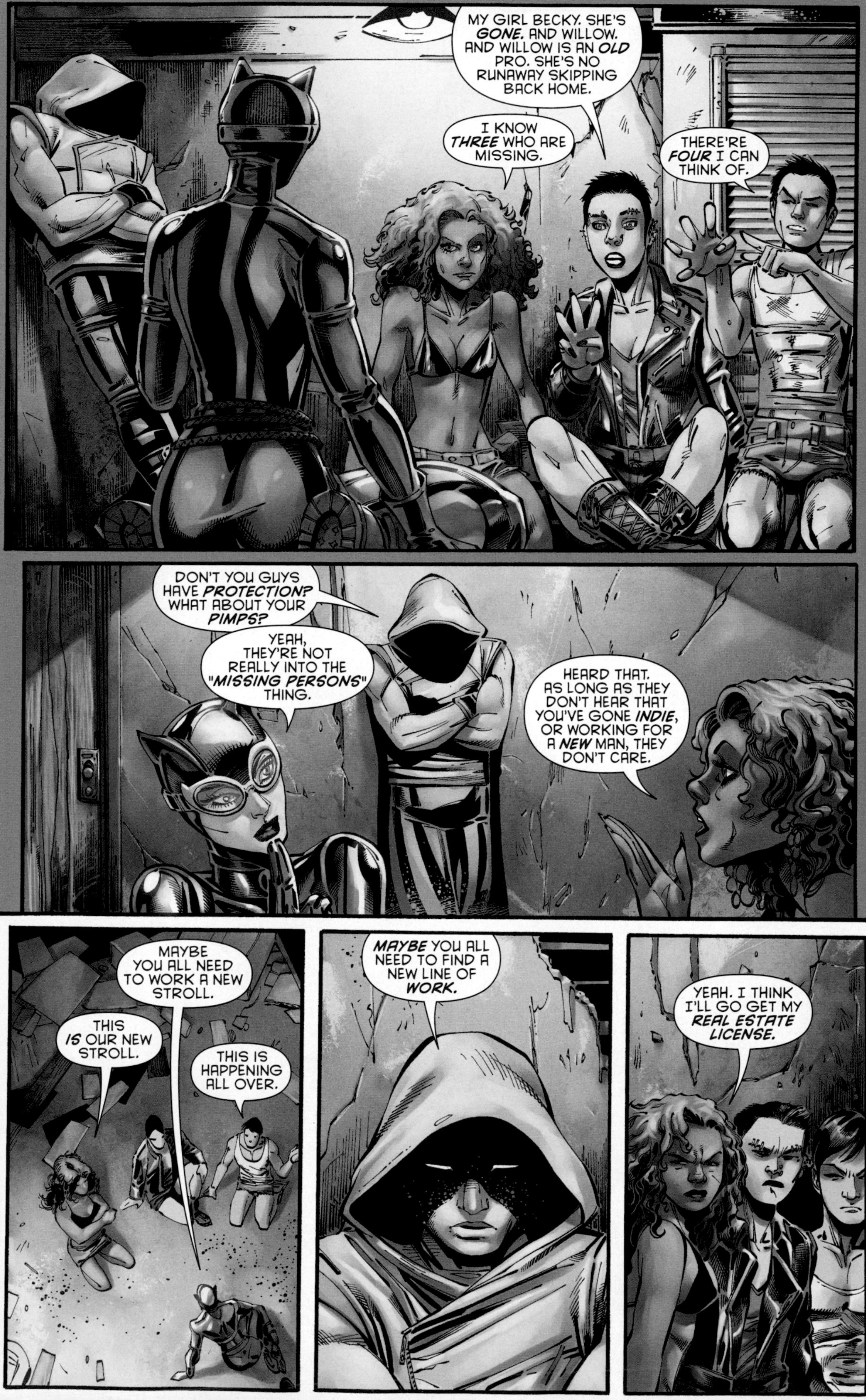
MY GIRL BECKY. SHE'S GONE. AND WILLOW. AND WILLOW IS AN OLD PRO. SHE'S NO RUNAWAY SKIPPING BACK HOME.
I KNOW THREE WHO ARE MISSING.
THERE'RE FOUR I CAN THINK OF.
DON'T YOU GUYS HAVE PROTECTION? WHAT ABOUT YOUR PIMPS?
YEAH, THEY'RE NOT REALLY INTO THE "MISSING PERSONS" THING.
HEARD THAT. AS LONG AS THEY DON'T HEAR THAT YOU'VE GONE INDIE, OR WORKING FOR A NEW MAN, THEY DON'T CARE.
MAYBE YOU ALL NEED TO WORK A NEW STROLL.
THIS IS OUR NEW STROLL.
THIS IS HAPPENING ALL OVER.
MAYBE YOU ALL NEED TO FIND A NEW LINE OF WORK.
YEAH. I THINK I'LL GO GET MY REAL ESTATE LICENSE.

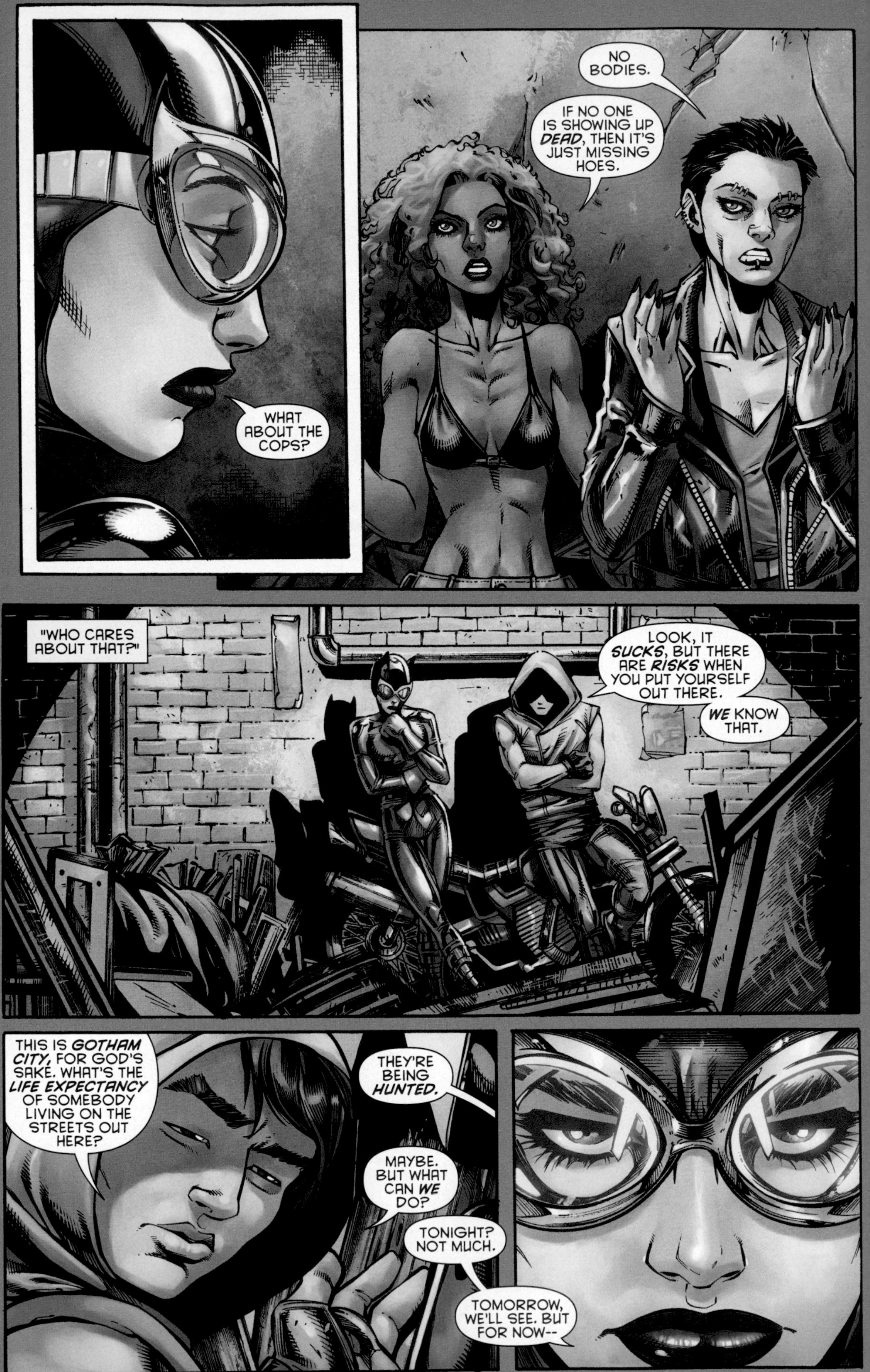
WHAT ABOUT THE COPS?
NO BODIES.
IF NO ONE IS SHOWING UP DEAD, THEN IT'S JUST MISSING HOES.
"WHO CARES ABOUT THAT?"
LOOK, IT SUCKS, BUT THERE ARE RISKS WHEN YOU PUT YOURSELF OUT THERE.
WE KNOW THAT.
THIS IS GOTHAM CITY, FOR GOD'S SAKE. WHAT'S THE LIFE EXPECTANCY OF SOMEBODY LIVING ON THE STREETS OUT HERE?
THEY'RE BEING HUNTED.
MAYBE. BUT WHAT CAN WE DO?
TONIGHT? NOT MUCH.
TOMORROW, WE'LL SEE. BUT FOR NOW--

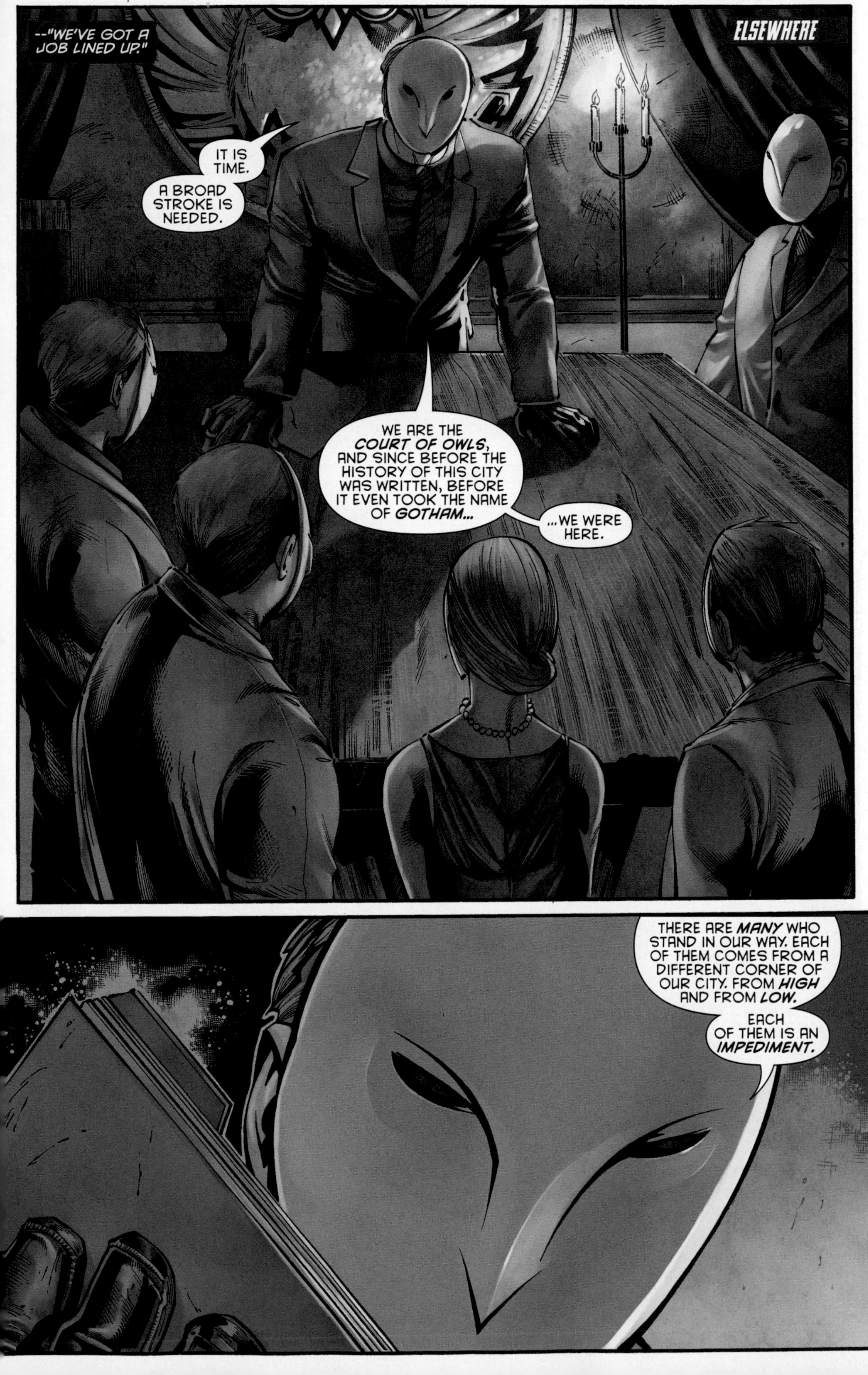
--"WE'VE GOT A JOB LINED UP."
ELSEWHERE
IT IS TIME.
A BROAD STROKE IS NEEDED.
WE ARE THE COURT OF OWLS, AND SINCE BEFORE THE HISTORY OF THIS CITY WAS WRITTEN, BEFORE IT EVEN TOOK THE NAME OF GOTHAM...
...WE WERE HERE.
THERE ARE MANY WHO STAND IN OUR WAY. EACH OF THEM COMES FROM A DIFFERENT CORNER OF OUR CITY. FROM HIGH AND FROM LOW.
EACH OF THEM IS AN IMPEDIMENT.

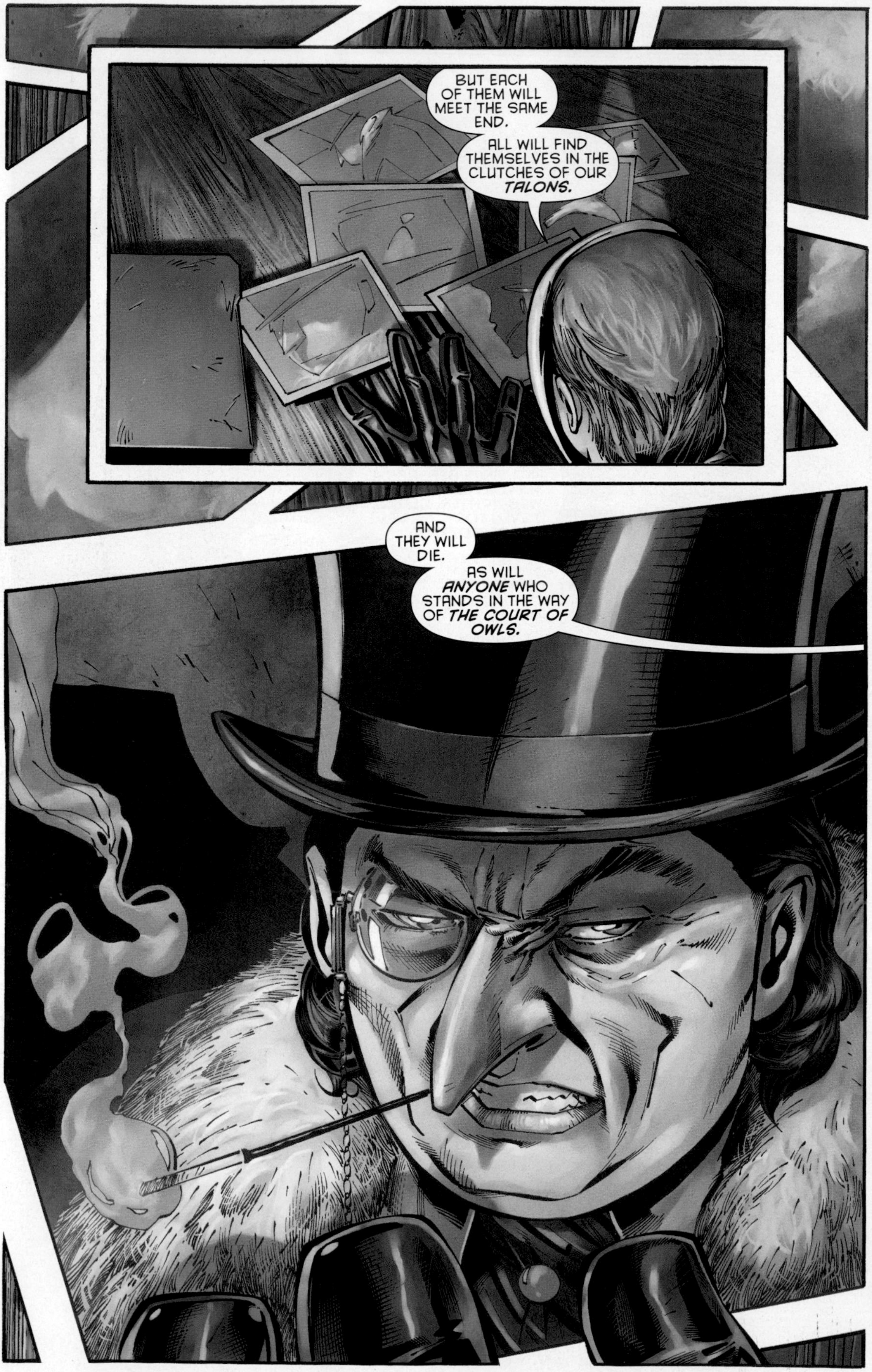

BUT EACH OF THEM WILL MEET THE SAME END.
ALL WILL FIND THEMSELVES IN THE CLUTCHES OF OUR *TALONS.*
AND THEY WILL DIE.
AS WILL *ANYONE* WHO STANDS IN THE WAY OF *THE COURT OF OWLS.*

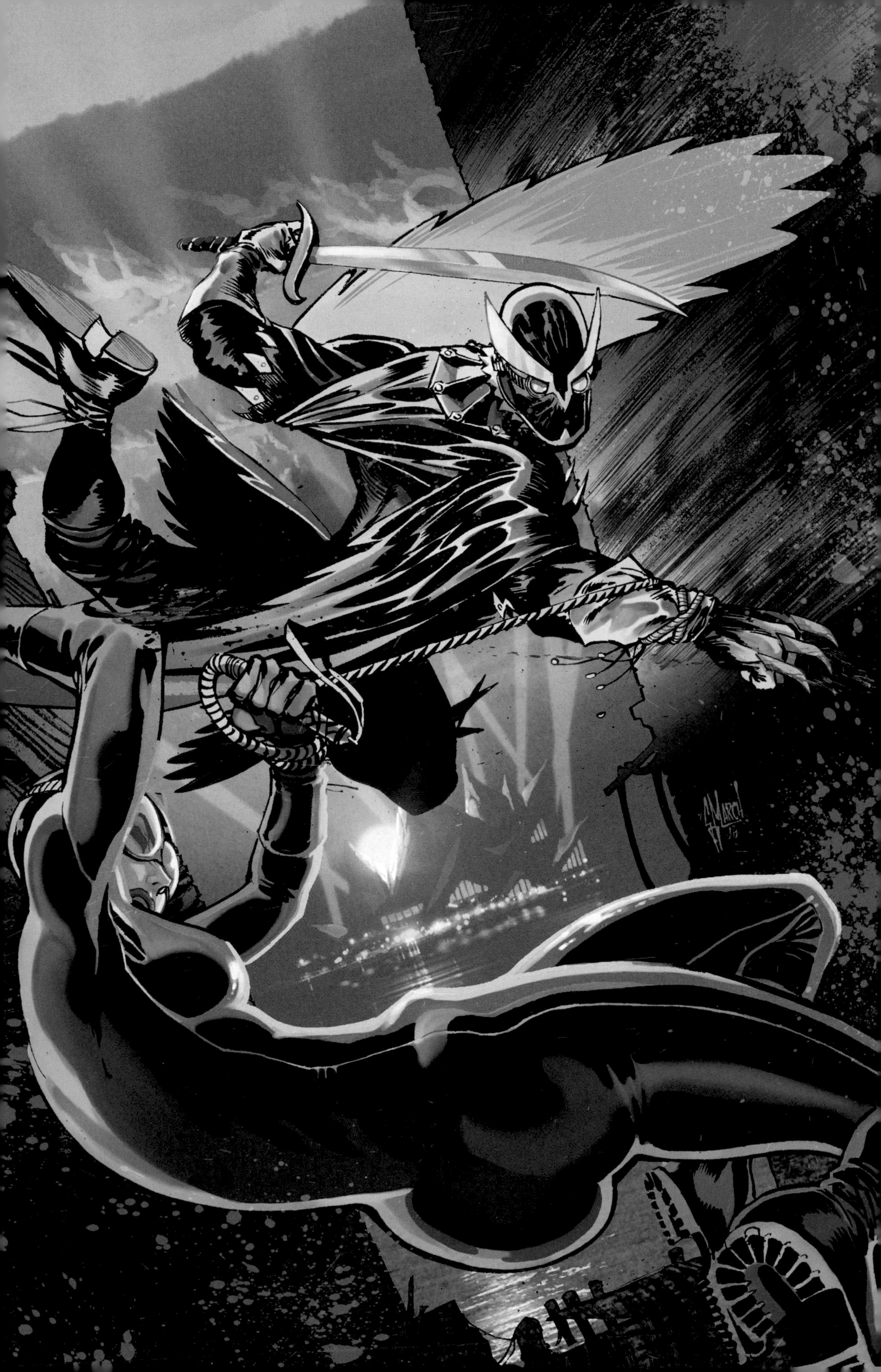

JUDD WINICK writer **GUILLEM MARCH** artist

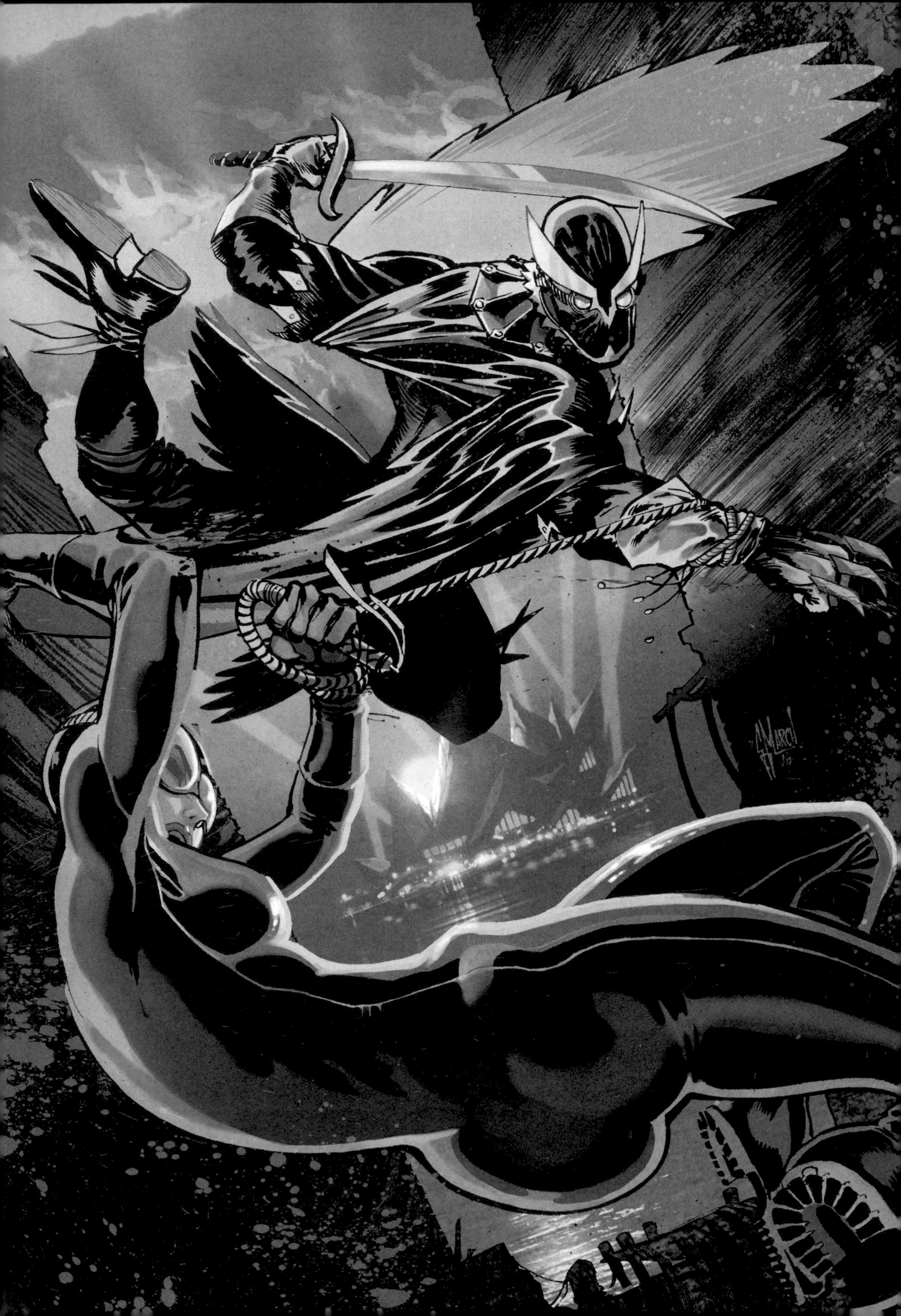

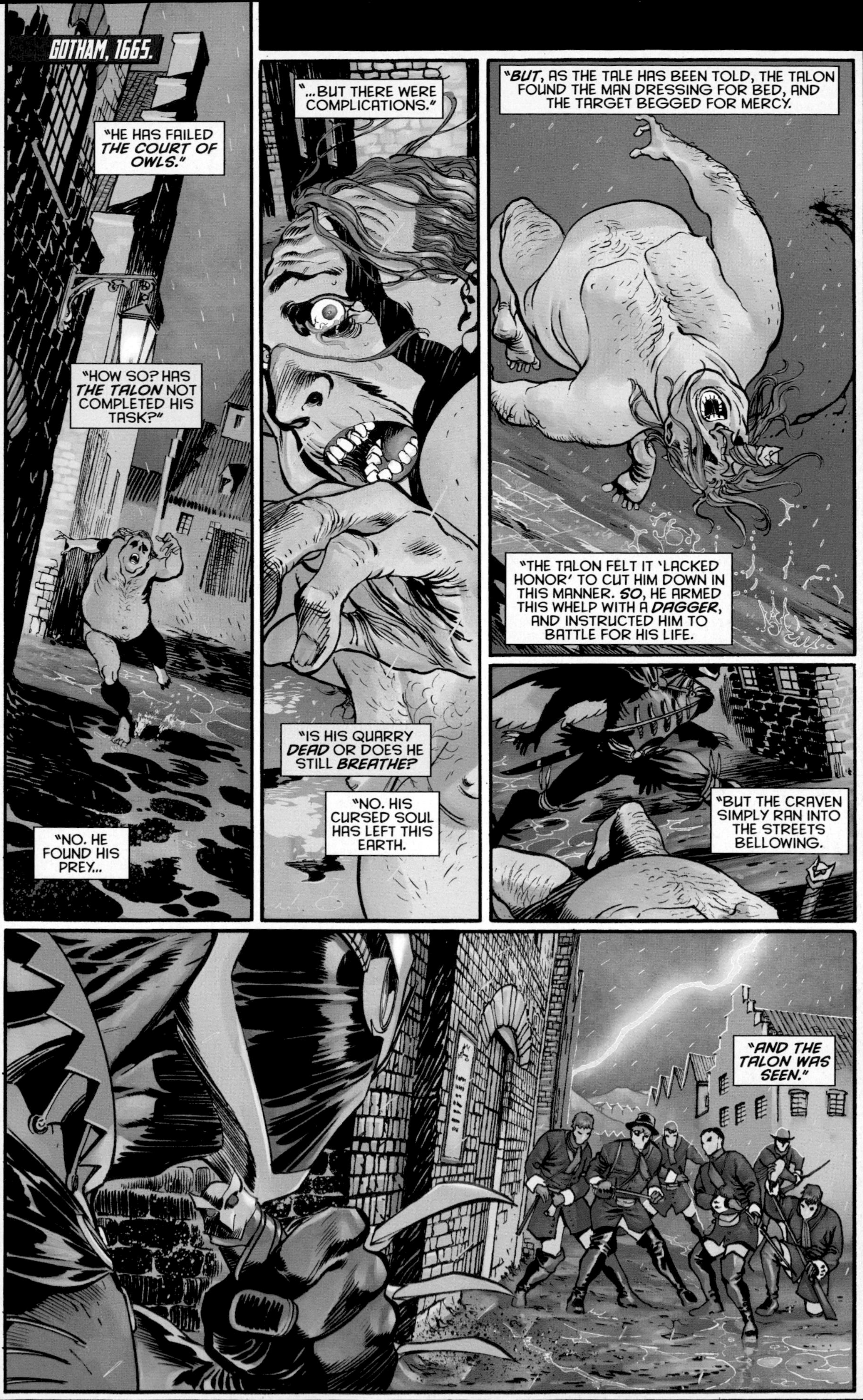
GOTHAM, 1665.
"HE HAS FAILED THE COURT OF OWLS."
"HOW SO? HAS THE TALON NOT COMPLETED HIS TASK?"
"NO. HE FOUND HIS PREY...
"...BUT THERE WERE COMPLICATIONS."
"IS HIS QUARRY DEAD OR DOES HE STILL BREATHE?
"NO. HIS CURSED SOUL HAS LEFT THIS EARTH.
"BUT, AS THE TALE HAS BEEN TOLD, THE TALON FOUND THE MAN DRESSING FOR BED, AND THE TARGET BEGGED FOR MERCY.
"THE TALON FELT IT 'LACKED HONOR' TO CUT HIM DOWN IN THIS MANNER. SO, HE ARMED THIS WHELP WITH A DAGGER, AND INSTRUCTED HIM TO BATTLE FOR HIS LIFE.
"BUT THE CRAVEN SIMPLY RAN INTO THE STREETS BELLOWING.
"AND THE TALON WAS SEEN."

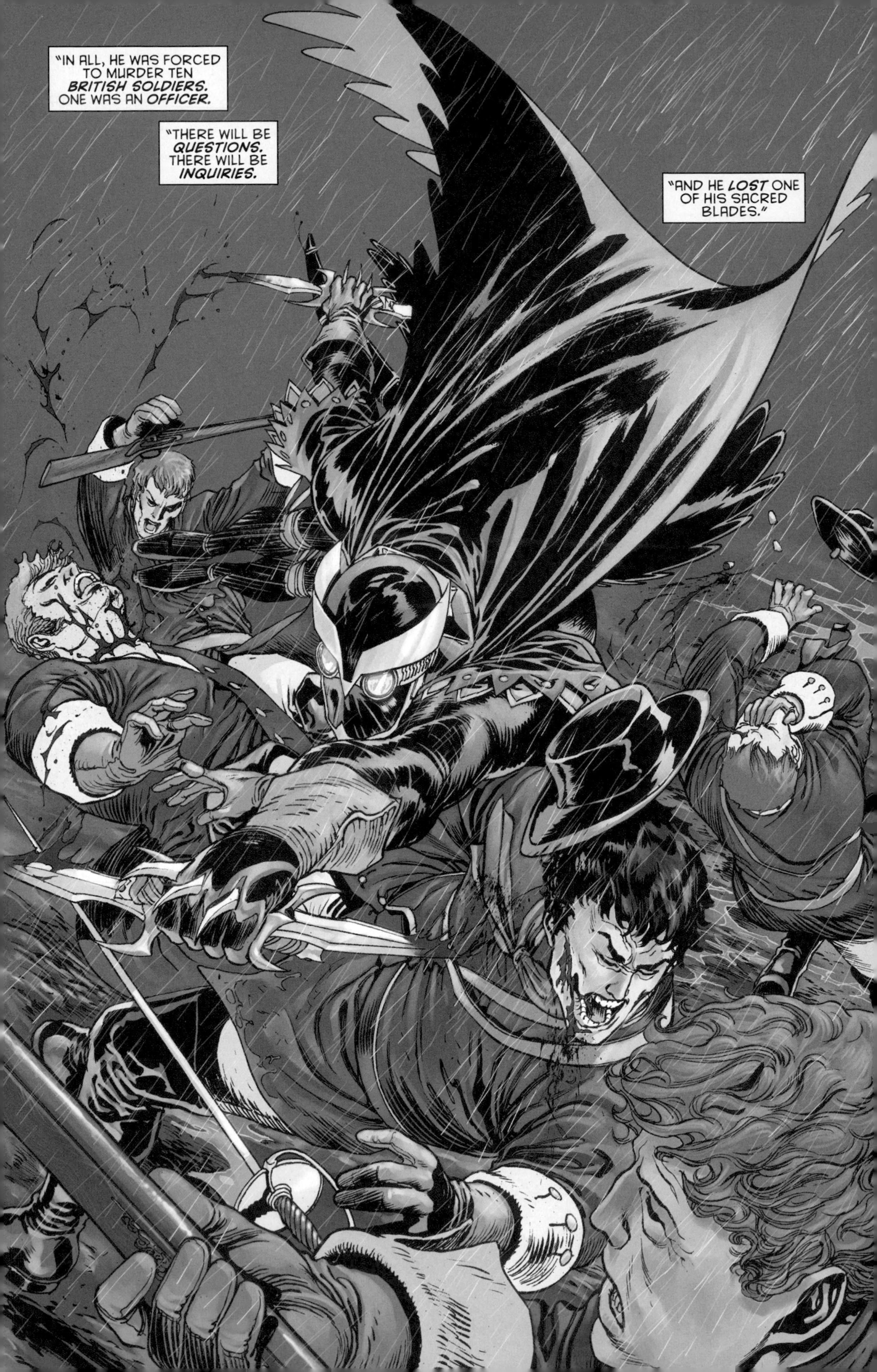
"IN ALL, HE WAS FORCED TO MURDER TEN BRITISH SOLDIERS. ONE WAS AN OFFICER.
"THERE WILL BE QUESTIONS. THERE WILL BE INQUIRIES.
"AND HE LOST ONE OF HIS SACRED BLADES."

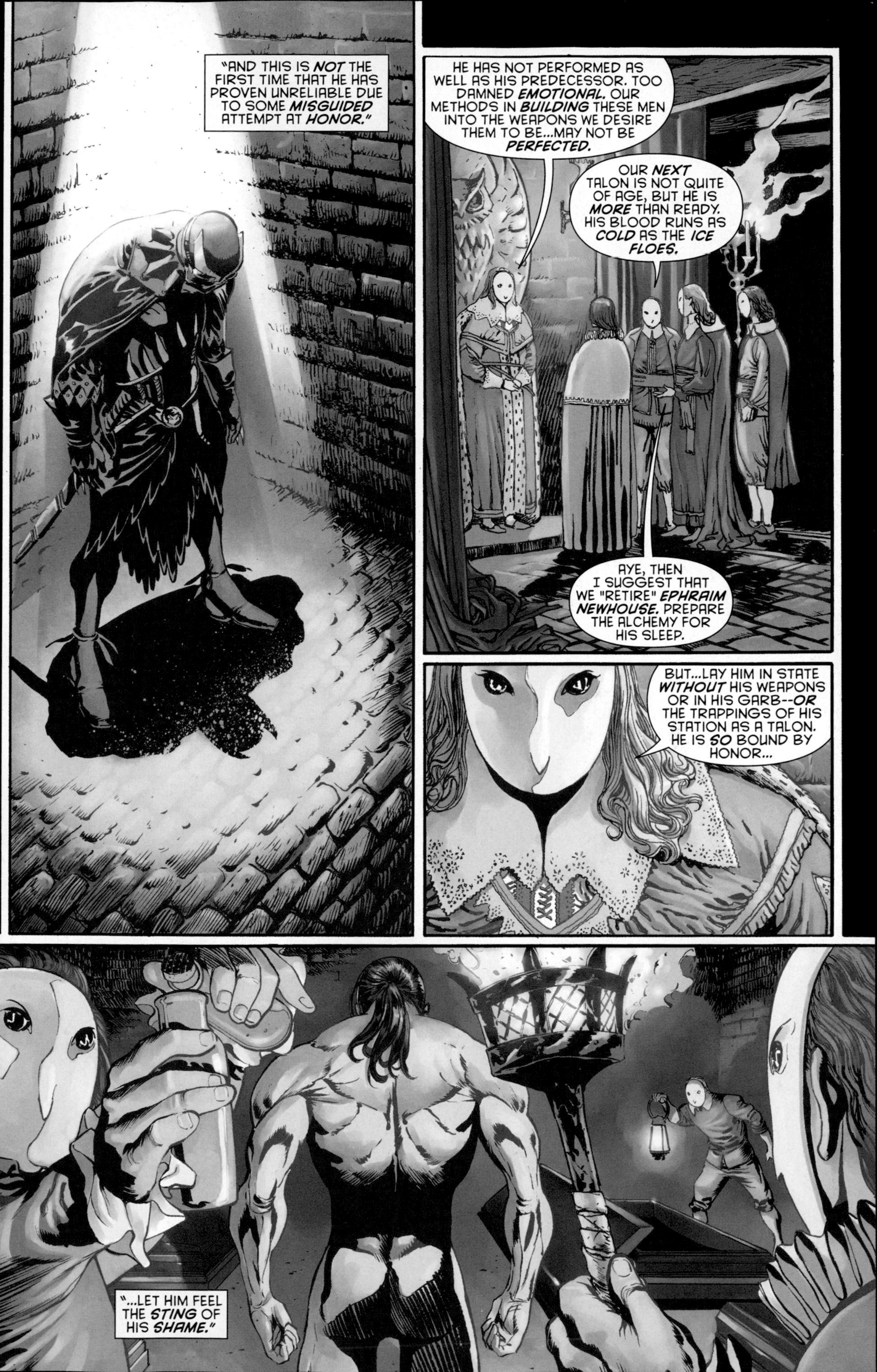
"AND THIS IS NOT THE FIRST TIME THAT HE HAS PROVEN UNRELIABLE DUE TO SOME MISGUIDED ATTEMPT AT HONOR."
HE HAS NOT PERFORMED AS WELL AS HIS PREDECESSOR. TOO DAMNED EMOTIONAL. OUR METHODS IN BUILDING THESE MEN INTO THE WEAPONS WE DESIRE THEM TO BE...MAY NOT BE PERFECTED.
OUR NEXT TALON IS NOT QUITE OF AGE, BUT HE IS MORE THAN READY. HIS BLOOD RUNS AS COLD AS THE ICE FLOES.
AYE, THEN I SUGGEST THAT WE "RETIRE" EPHRAIM NEWHOUSE. PREPARE THE ALCHEMY FOR HIS SLEEP.
BUT...LAY HIM IN STATE WITHOUT HIS WEAPONS OR IN HIS GARB--OR THE TRAPPINGS OF HIS STATION AS A TALON. HE IS SO BOUND BY HONOR...
"...LET HIM FEEL THE STING OF HIS SHAME."

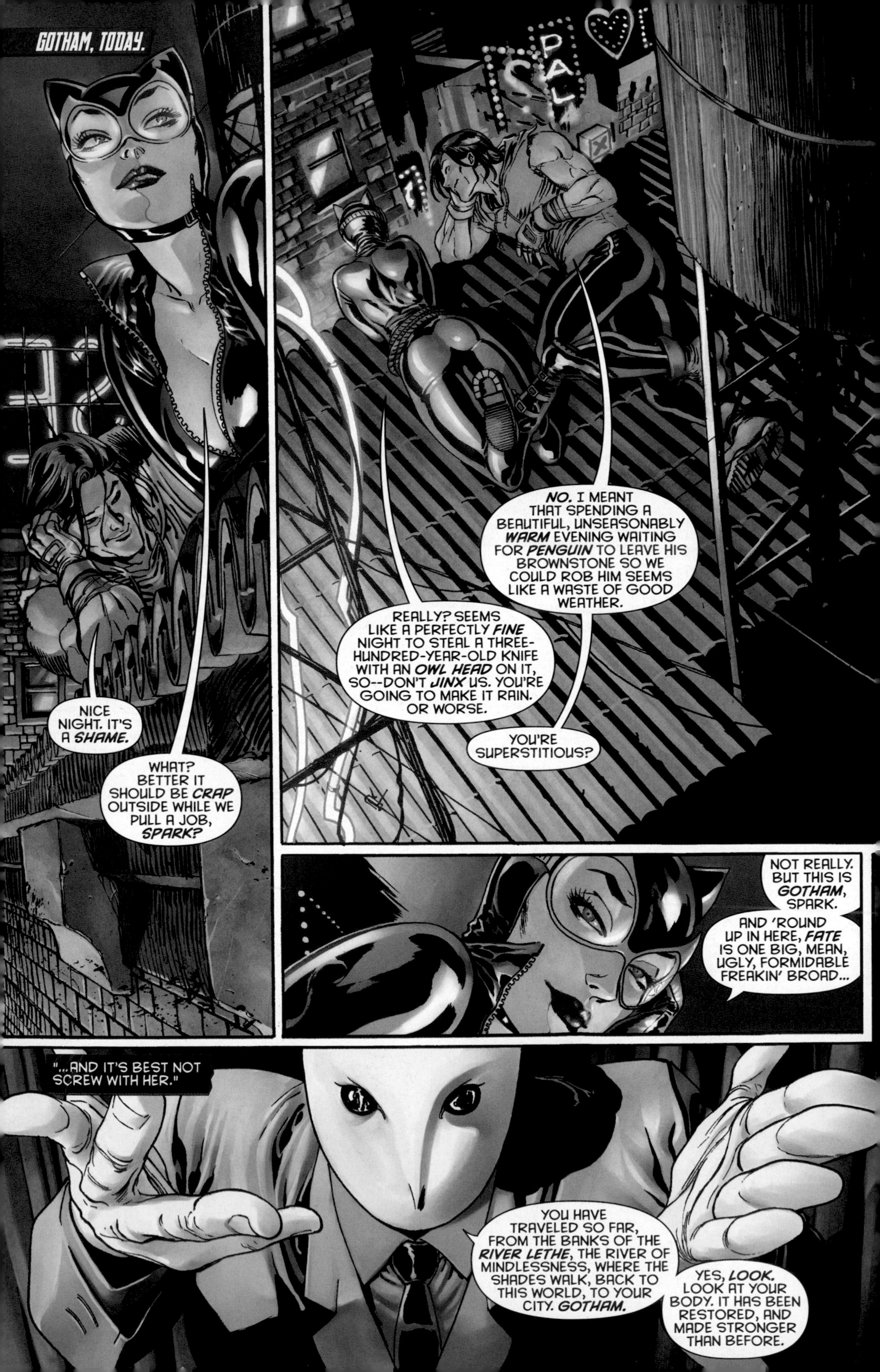
GOTHAM, TODAY.
NICE NIGHT. IT'S A SHAME.
WHAT? BETTER IT SHOULD BE CRAP OUTSIDE WHILE WE PULL A JOB, SPARK?
NO. I MEANT THAT SPENDING A BEAUTIFUL, UNSEASONABLY WARM EVENING WAITING FOR PENGUIN TO LEAVE HIS BROWNSTONE SO WE COULD ROB HIM SEEMS LIKE A WASTE OF GOOD WEATHER.
REALLY? SEEMS LIKE A PERFECTLY FINE NIGHT TO STEAL A THREE-HUNDRED-YEAR-OLD KNIFE WITH AN OWL HEAD ON IT, SO--DON'T JINX US. YOU'RE GOING TO MAKE IT RAIN. OR WORSE.
YOU'RE SUPERSTITIOUS?
NOT REALLY. BUT THIS IS GOTHAM, SPARK.
AND 'ROUND UP IN HERE, FATE IS ONE BIG, MEAN, UGLY, FORMIDABLE FREAKIN' BROAD...
"...AND IT'S BEST NOT SCREW WITH HER."
YOU HAVE TRAVELED SO FAR, FROM THE BANKS OF THE RIVER LETHE, THE RIVER OF MINDLESSNESS, WHERE THE SHADES WALK, BACK TO THIS WORLD, TO YOUR CITY. GOTHAM.
YES, LOOK. LOOK AT YOUR BODY. IT HAS BEEN RESTORED, AND MADE STRONGER THAN BEFORE.

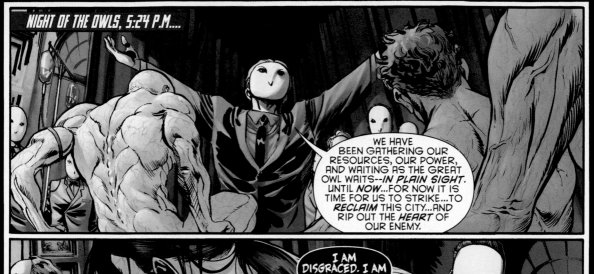

WE HAVE BEEN GATHERING OUR RESOURCES, OUR POWER, AND WAITING AS THE GREAT OWL WAITS--*IN PLAIN SIGHT*. UNTIL *NOW*...FOR NOW IT IS TIME FOR US TO STRIKE...TO *RECLAIM* THIS CITY...AND RIP OUT THE *HEART* OF OUR ENEMY.

I AM DISGRACED. I AM INCOMPLETE.

"DISGRACED"?

THERE'S SOME DOCUMENTATION ABOUT THAT ON THIS ONE. EPHRAIM NEWHOUSE. MORE *"DUTY-BOUND"* THAN NEEDED.

BUT HE WILL SERVE HIS PURPOSE.

YOU WILL BE BESTOWED WITH THE UNIFORM OF YOUR SERVICE AND STATION.

YOU ARE A *TALON*. COMPLETE THAT WHICH YOUR COURT ASKS OF YOU.

THIS ONE IS A BLIGHT UPON THE CITY. A SELF-APPOINTED *CZAR* OF THE SCUM THAT *FUELS* THE BODY OF GOTHAM.

REMOVE HIM...

...AND YOUR HONOR WILL BE RESTORED.

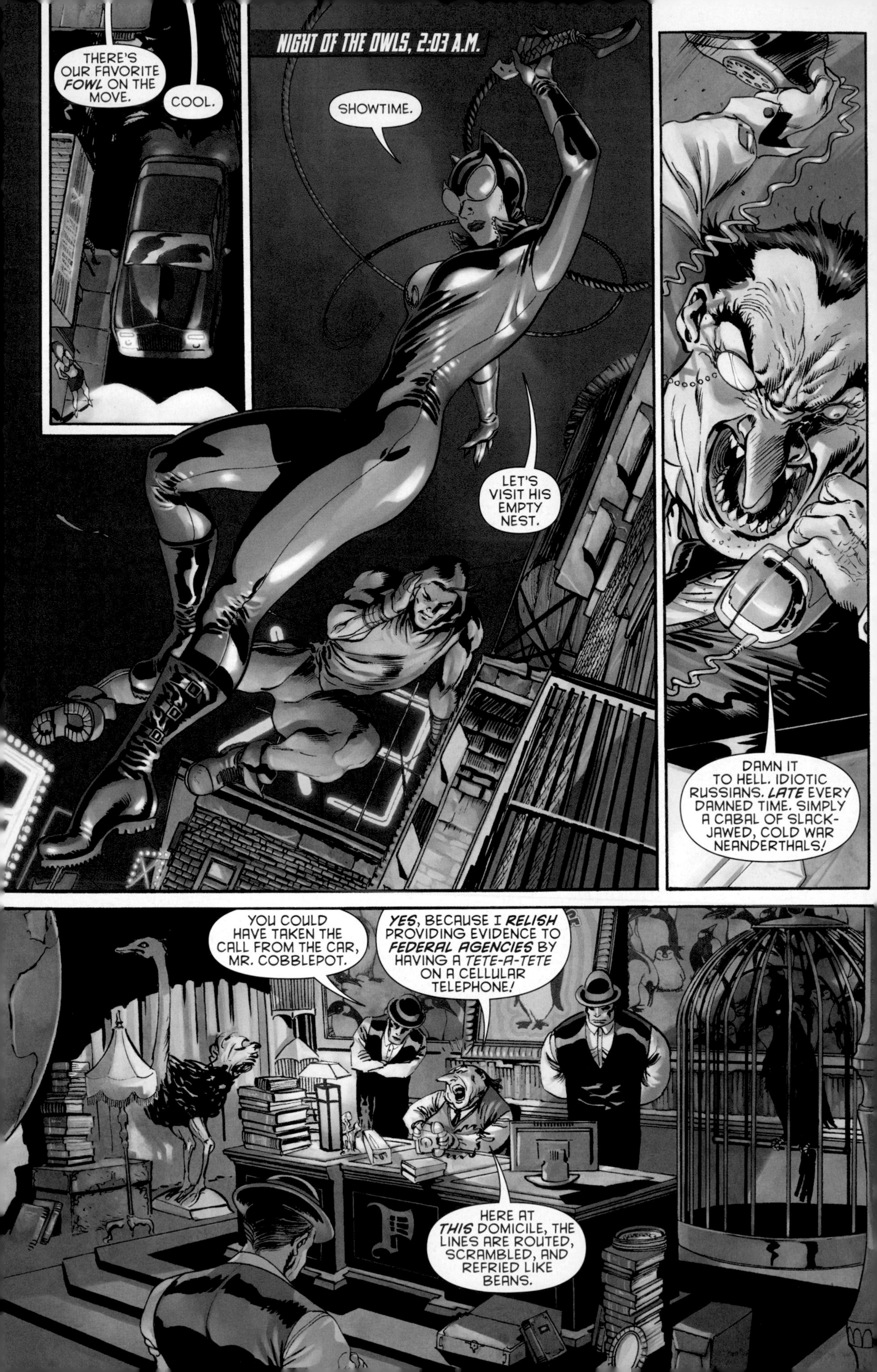
THERE'S OUR FAVORITE FOWL ON THE MOVE.
COOL.
NIGHT OF THE OWLS, 2:03 A.M.
SHOWTIME.
LET'S VISIT HIS EMPTY NEST.
DAMN IT TO HELL. IDIOTIC RUSSIANS. LATE EVERY DAMNED TIME. SIMPLY A CABAL OF SLACK-JAWED, COLD WAR NEANDERTHALS!
YOU COULD HAVE TAKEN THE CALL FROM THE CAR, MR. COBBLEPOT.
YES, BECAUSE I RELISH PROVIDING EVIDENCE TO FEDERAL AGENCIES BY HAVING A TETE-A-TETE ON A CELLULAR TELEPHONE!
HERE AT THIS DOMICILE, THE LINES ARE ROUTED, SCRAMBLED, AND REFRIED LIKE BEANS.

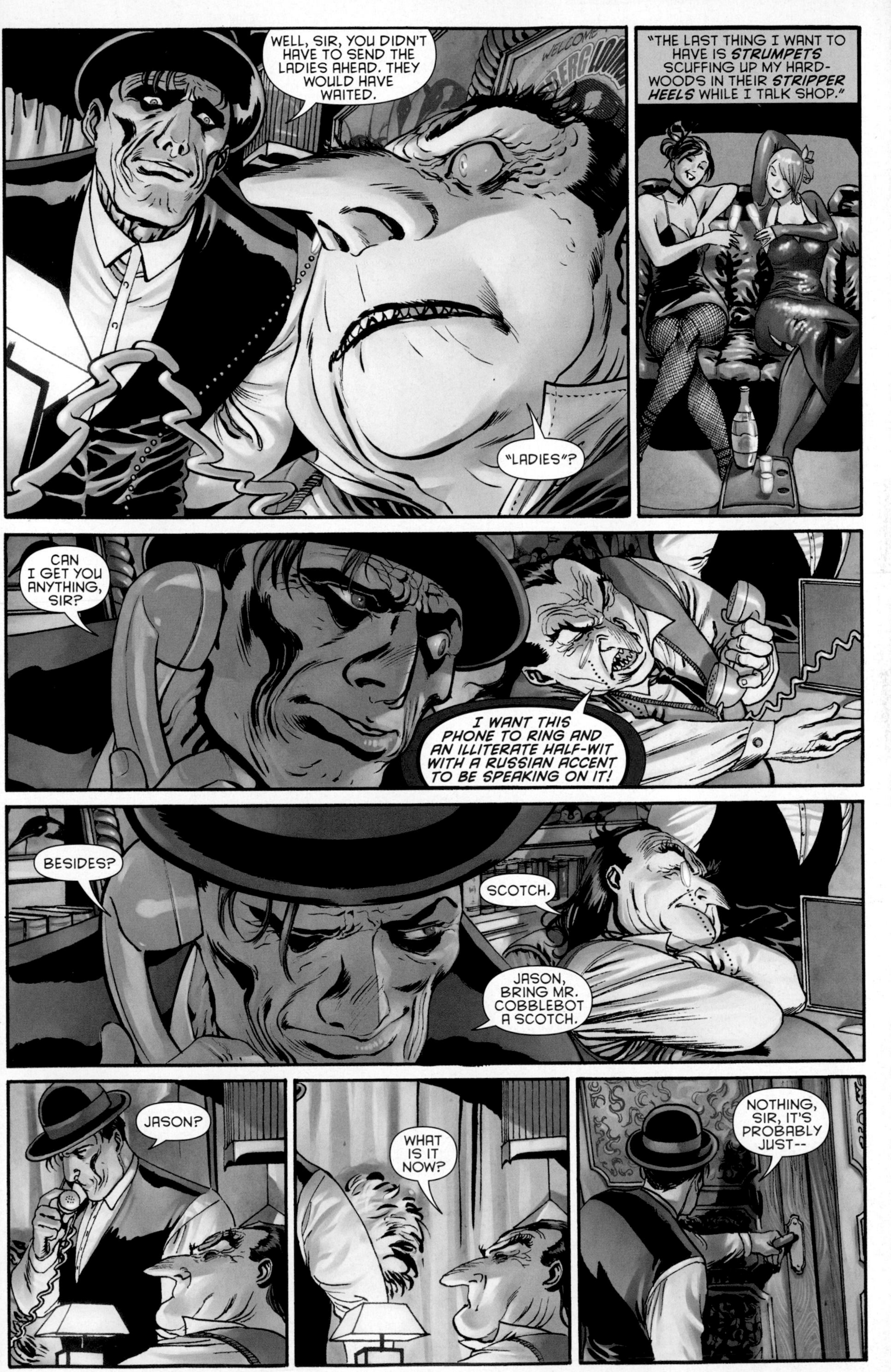
WELL, SIR, YOU DIDN'T HAVE TO SEND THE LADIES AHEAD. THEY WOULD HAVE WAITED.
"LADIES"?
"THE LAST THING I WANT TO HAVE IS STRUMPETS SCUFFING UP MY HARD-WOODS IN THEIR STRIPPER HEELS WHILE I TALK SHOP."
CAN I GET YOU ANYTHING, SIR?
I WANT THIS PHONE TO RING AND AN ILLITERATE HALF-WIT WITH A RUSSIAN ACCENT TO BE SPEAKING ON IT!
BESIDES?
SCOTCH.
JASON, BRING MR. COBBLEBOT A SCOTCH.
JASON?
WHAT IS IT NOW?
NOTHING, SIR, IT'S PROBABLY JUST--

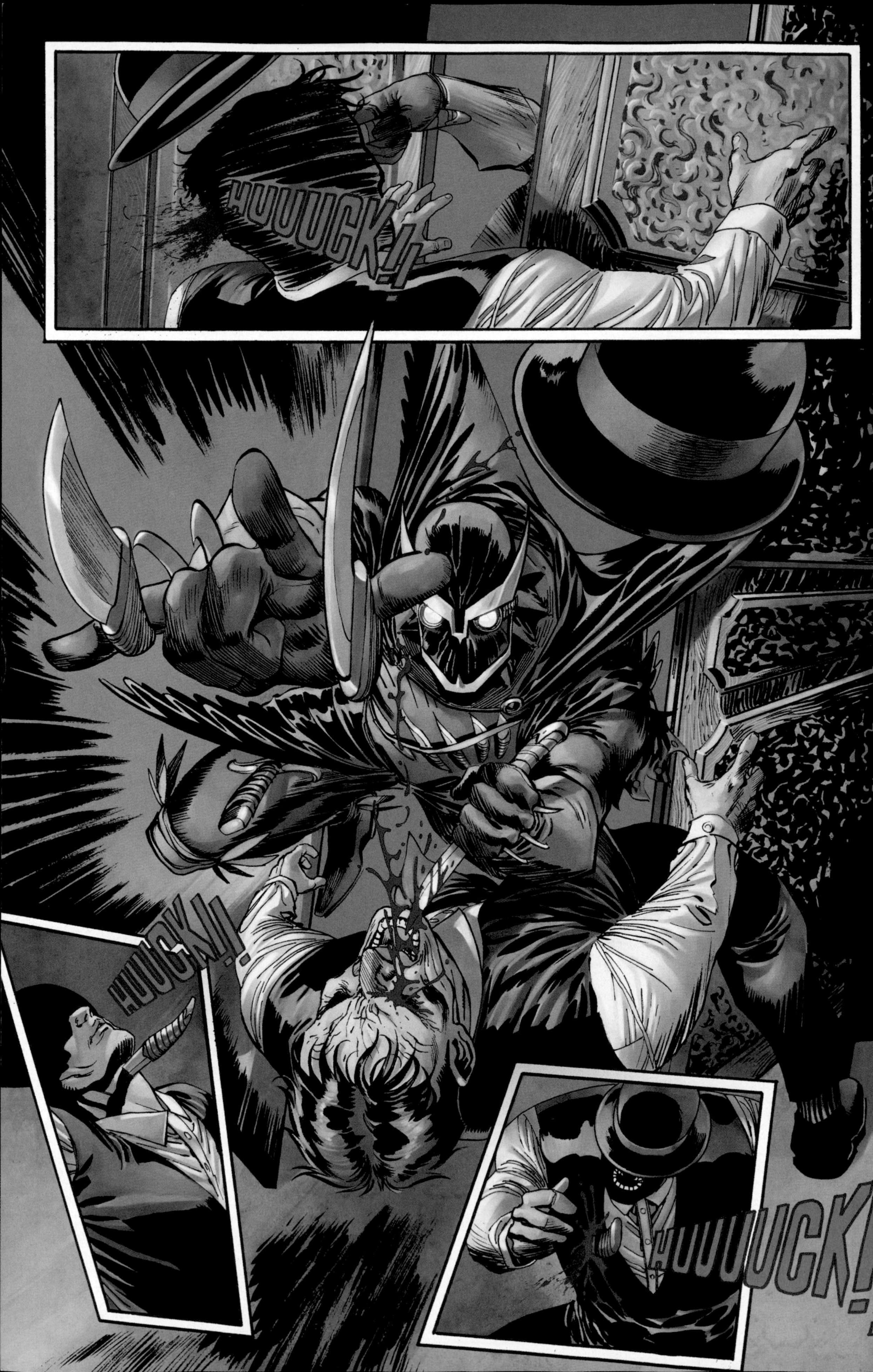
HUUUCK!!
HUUCK!!
HUUUUCK!!

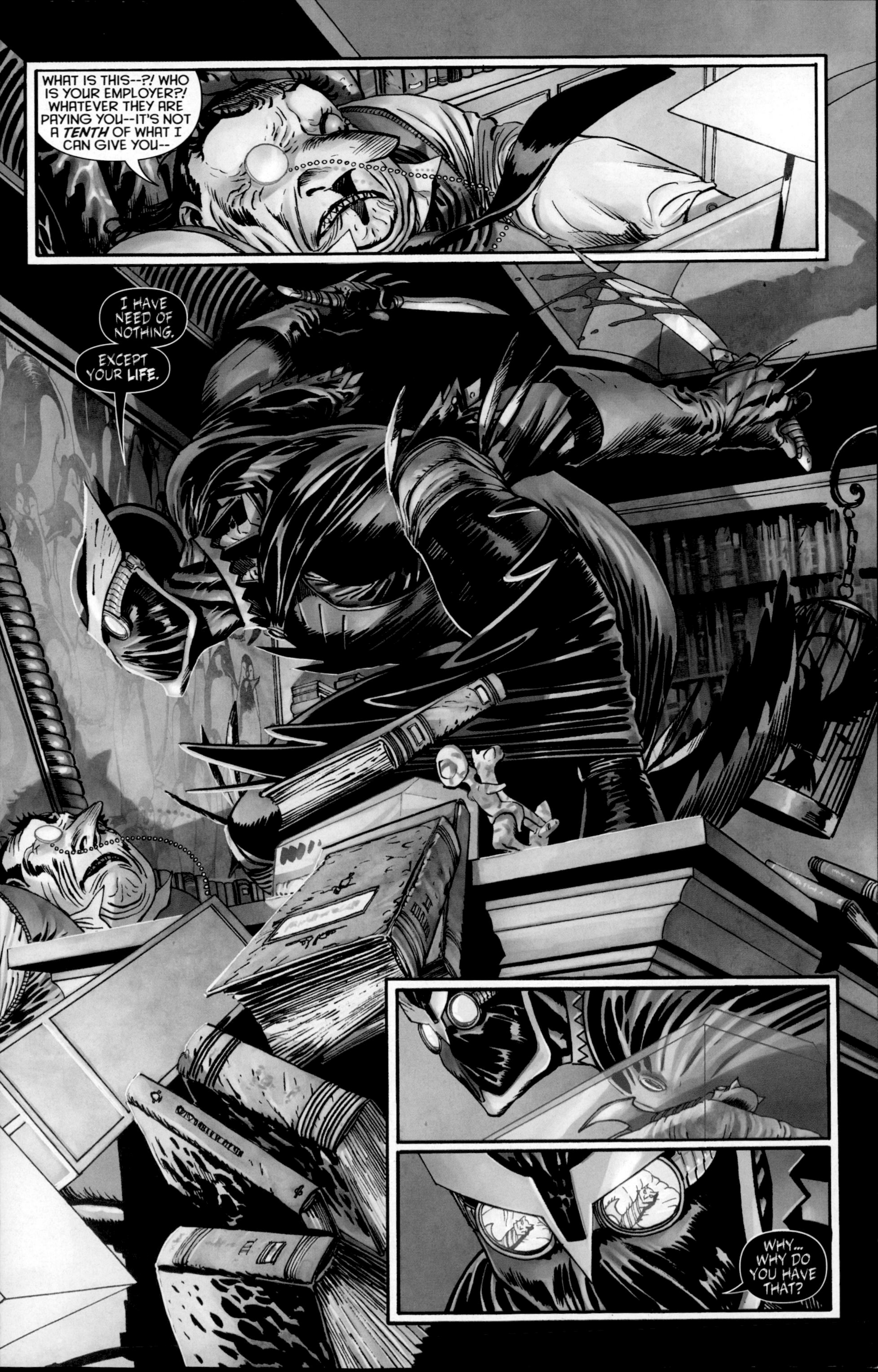
WHAT IS THIS--?! WHO IS YOUR EMPLOYER?! WHATEVER THEY ARE PAYING YOU--IT'S NOT A *TENTH* OF WHAT I CAN GIVE YOU--
I HAVE NEED OF NOTHING.
EXCEPT YOUR **LIFE**.
WHY... WHY DO YOU HAVE THAT?

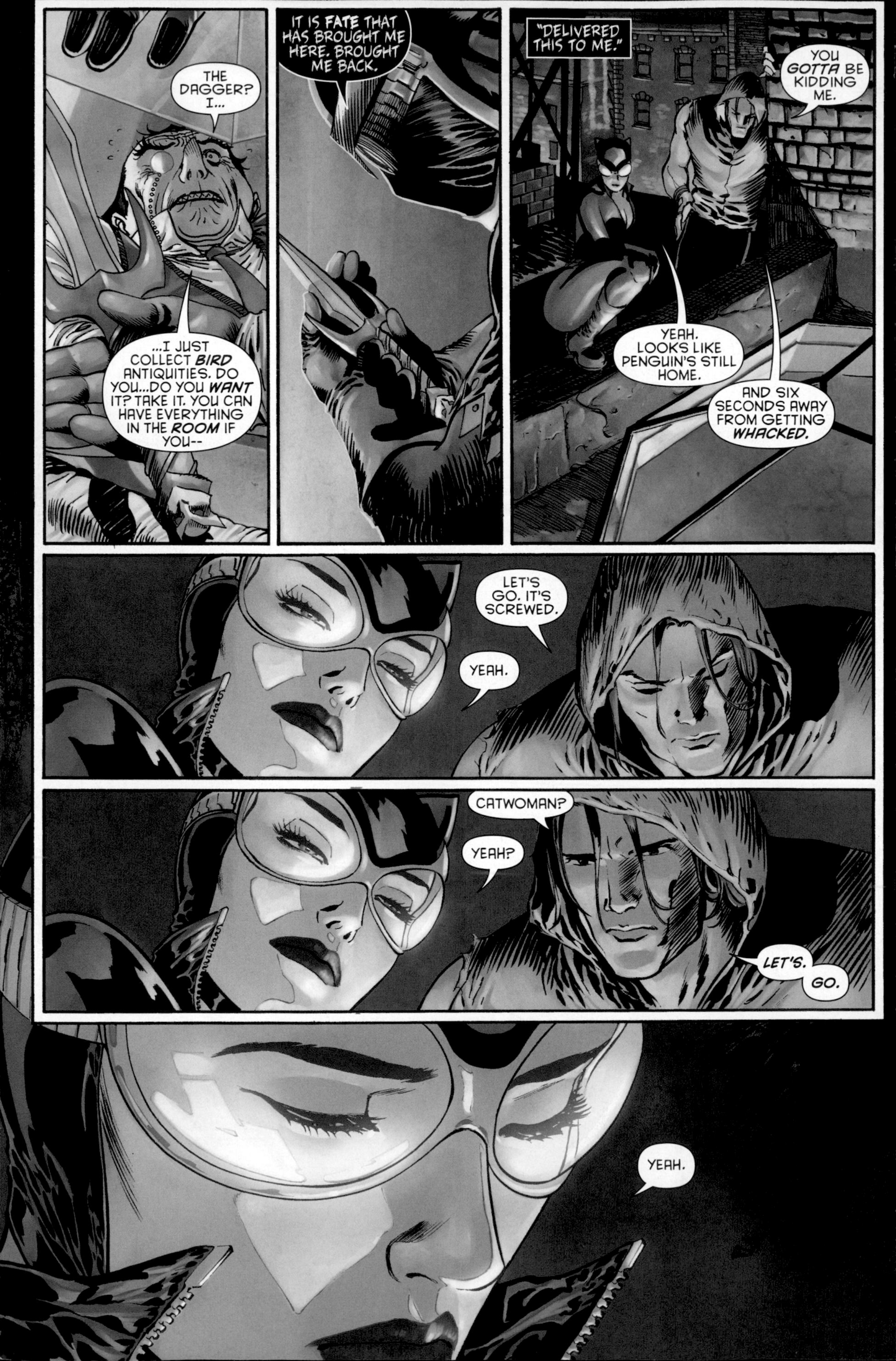
THE DAGGER? I...
...I JUST COLLECT BIRD ANTIQUITIES. DO YOU...DO YOU WANT IT? TAKE IT. YOU CAN HAVE EVERYTHING IN THE ROOM IF YOU--
IT IS FATE THAT HAS BROUGHT ME HERE. BROUGHT ME BACK.
"DELIVERED THIS TO ME."
YOU GOTTA BE KIDDING ME.
YEAH. LOOKS LIKE PENGUIN'S STILL HOME.
AND SIX SECONDS AWAY FROM GETTING WHACKED.
LET'S GO. IT'S SCREWED.
YEAH.
CATWOMAN?
YEAH?
LET'S. GO.
YEAH.

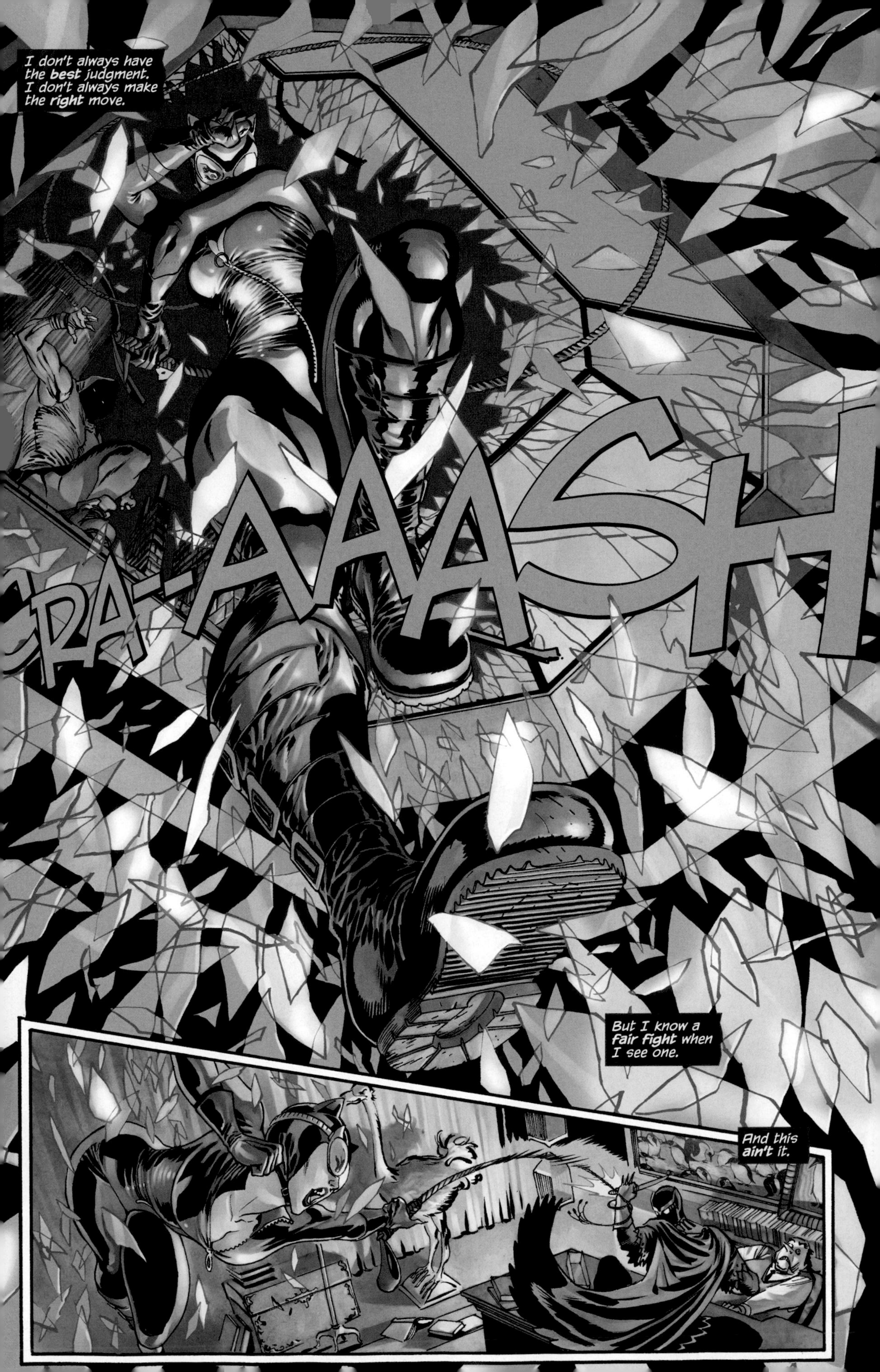
I don't always have the best judgment. I don't always make the right move.
CRA-AAASH!
But I know a fair fight when I see one.
And this ain't it.

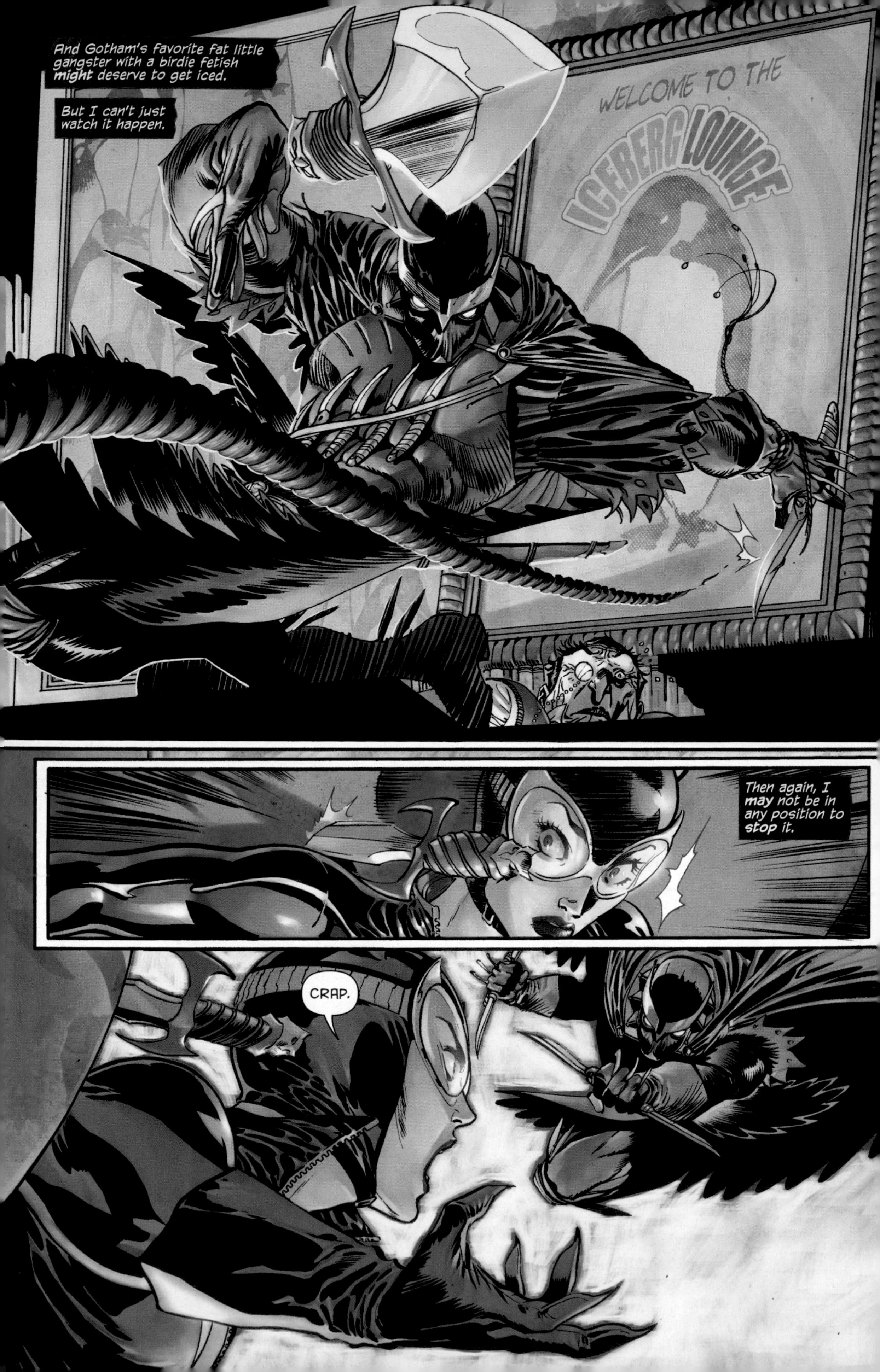
And Gotham's favorite fat little gangster with a birdie fetish **might** deserve to get iced.
But I can't just watch it happen.
WELCOME TO THE
ICEBERG LOUNGE
Then again, I **may** not be in any position to **stop** it.
CRAP.

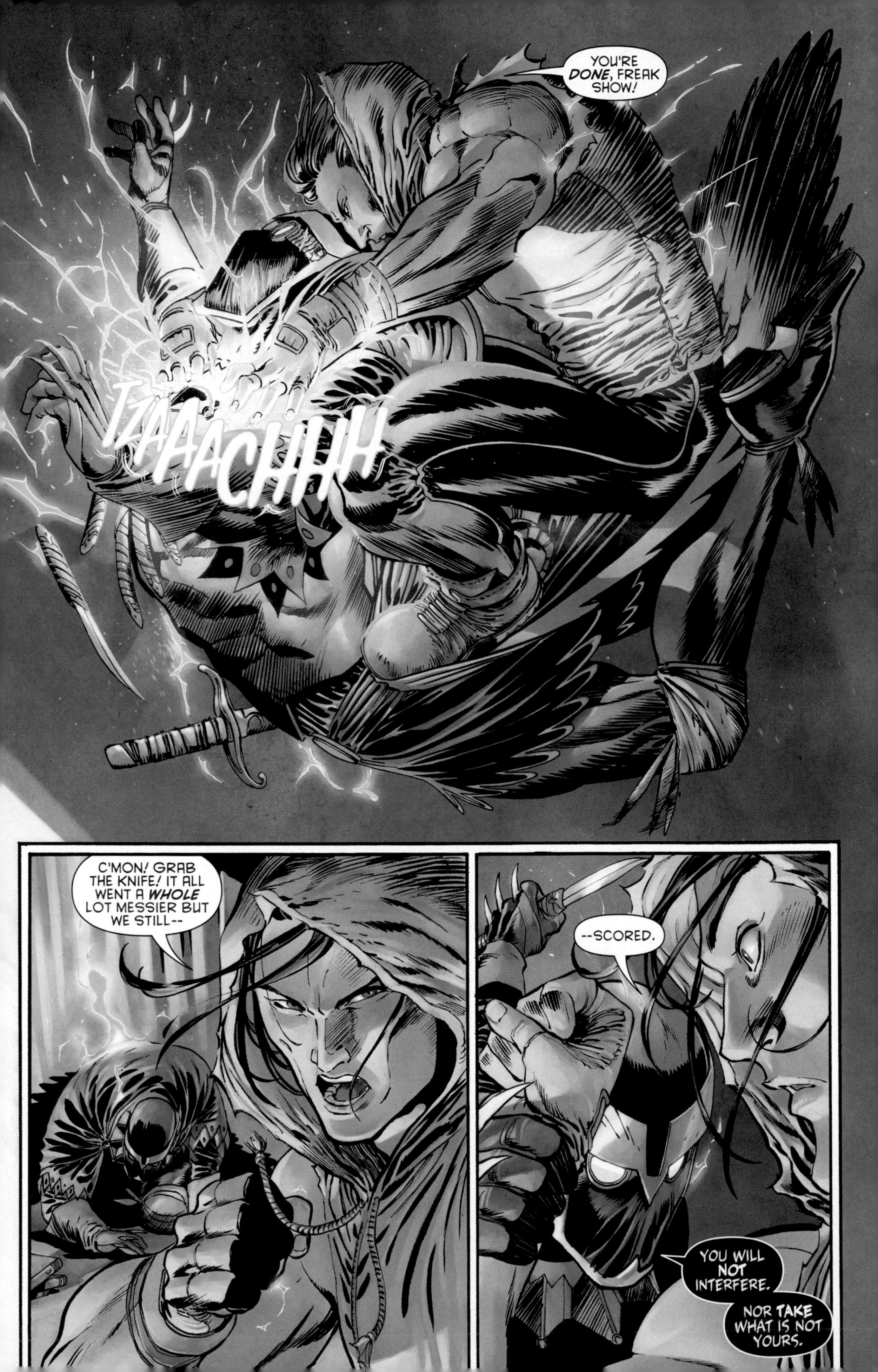
YOU'RE *DONE*, FREAK SHOW!
TZAAACHHH
C'MON! GRAB THE KNIFE! IT ALL WENT A *WHOLE* LOT MESSIER BUT WE STILL--
--SCORED.
YOU WILL **NOT** INTERFERE.
NOR **TAKE** WHAT IS NOT YOURS.

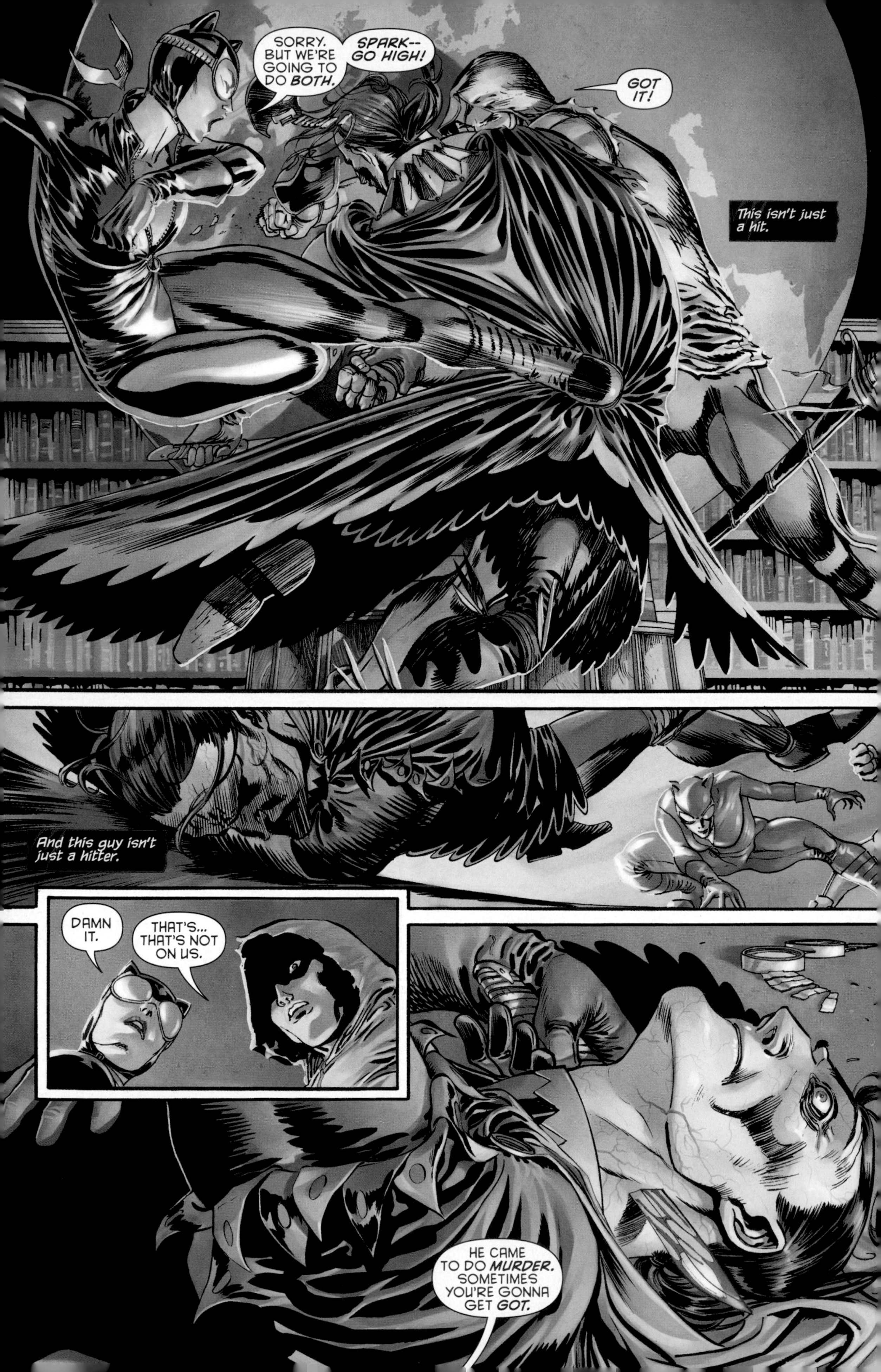
SORRY. BUT WE'RE GOING TO DO *BOTH*.
SPARK-- *GO HIGH!*
GOT IT!
This isn't just a hit.
And this guy isn't just a hitter.
DAMN IT.
THAT'S... THAT'S NOT ON US.
HE CAME TO DO *MURDER*. SOMETIMES YOU'RE GONNA GET *GOT*.

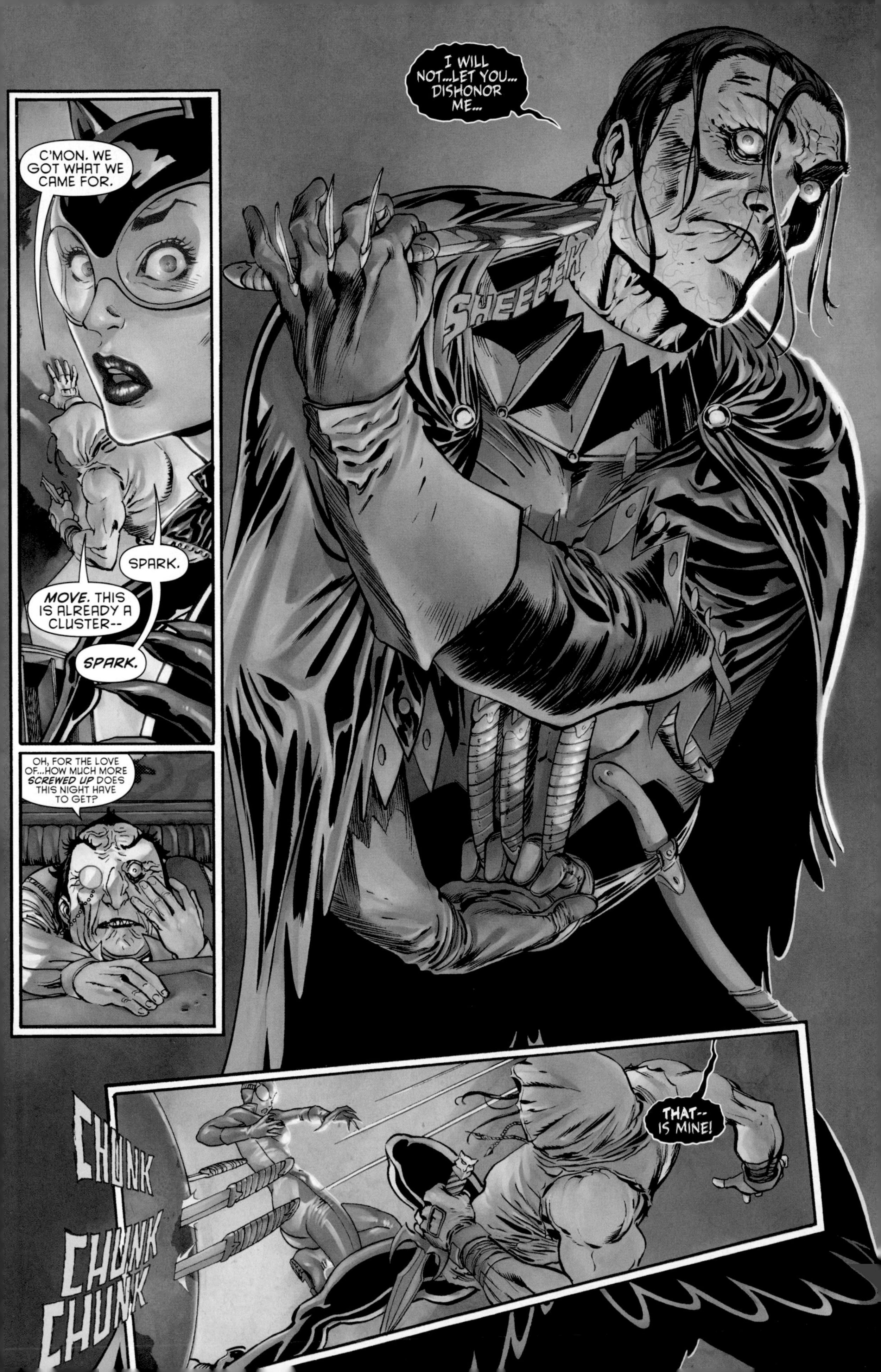
C'MON. WE GOT WHAT WE CAME FOR.
SPARK.
MOVE. THIS IS ALREADY A CLUSTER--
SPARK.
OH, FOR THE LOVE OF...HOW MUCH MORE SCREWED UP DOES THIS NIGHT HAVE TO GET?
I WILL NOT...LET YOU... DISHONOR ME...
SHEEEEEK
THAT-- IS MINE!
CHUNK
CHUNK
CHUNK

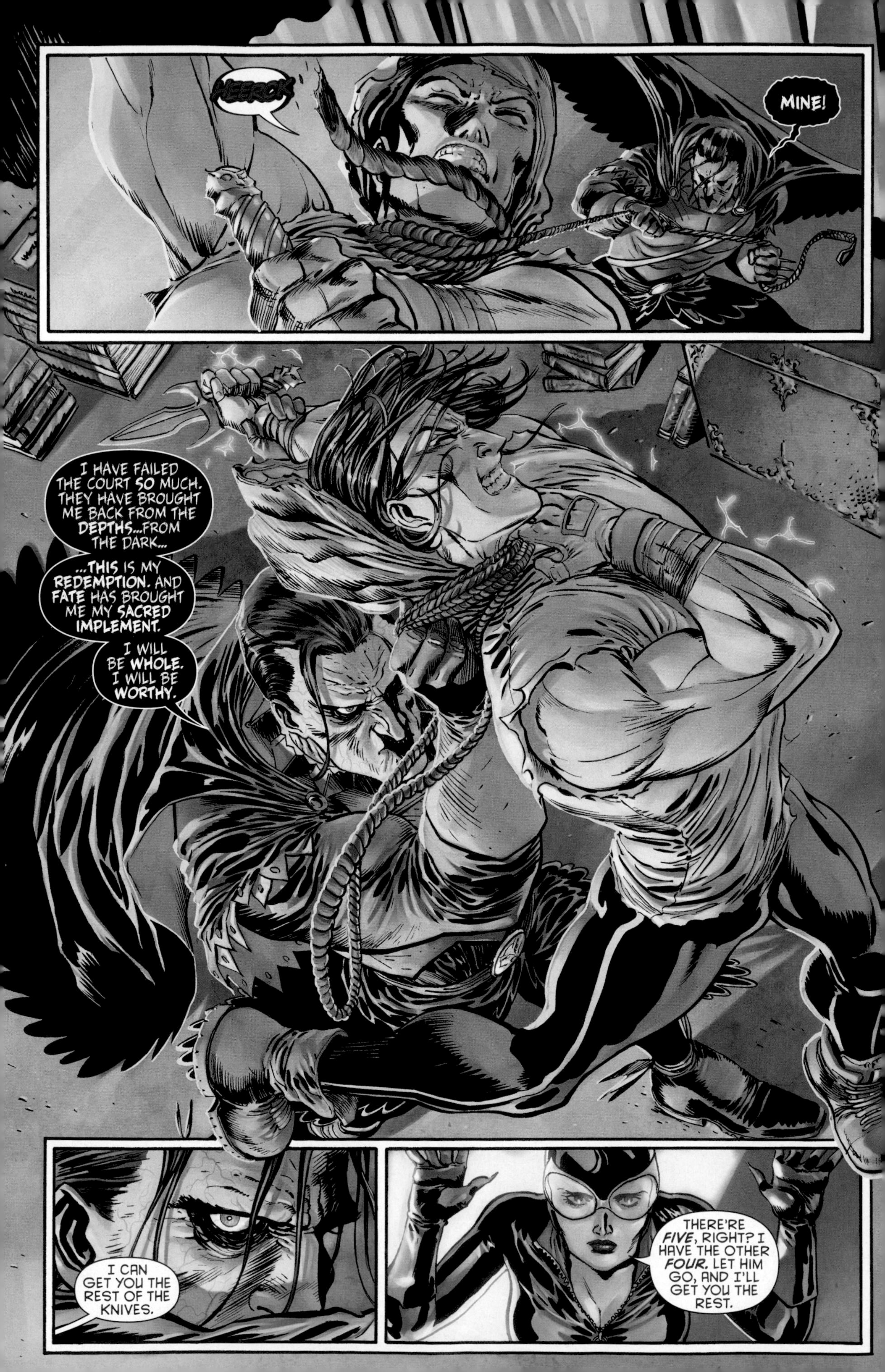
HEERCK
MINE!
I HAVE FAILED THE COURT SO MUCH. THEY HAVE BROUGHT ME BACK FROM THE DEPTHS...FROM THE DARK...
...THIS IS MY REDEMPTION. AND FATE HAS BROUGHT ME MY SACRED IMPLEMENT.
I WILL BE WHOLE. I WILL BE WORTHY.
I CAN GET YOU THE REST OF THE KNIVES.
THERE'RE FIVE, RIGHT? I HAVE THE OTHER FOUR. LET HIM GO, AND I'LL GET YOU THE REST.

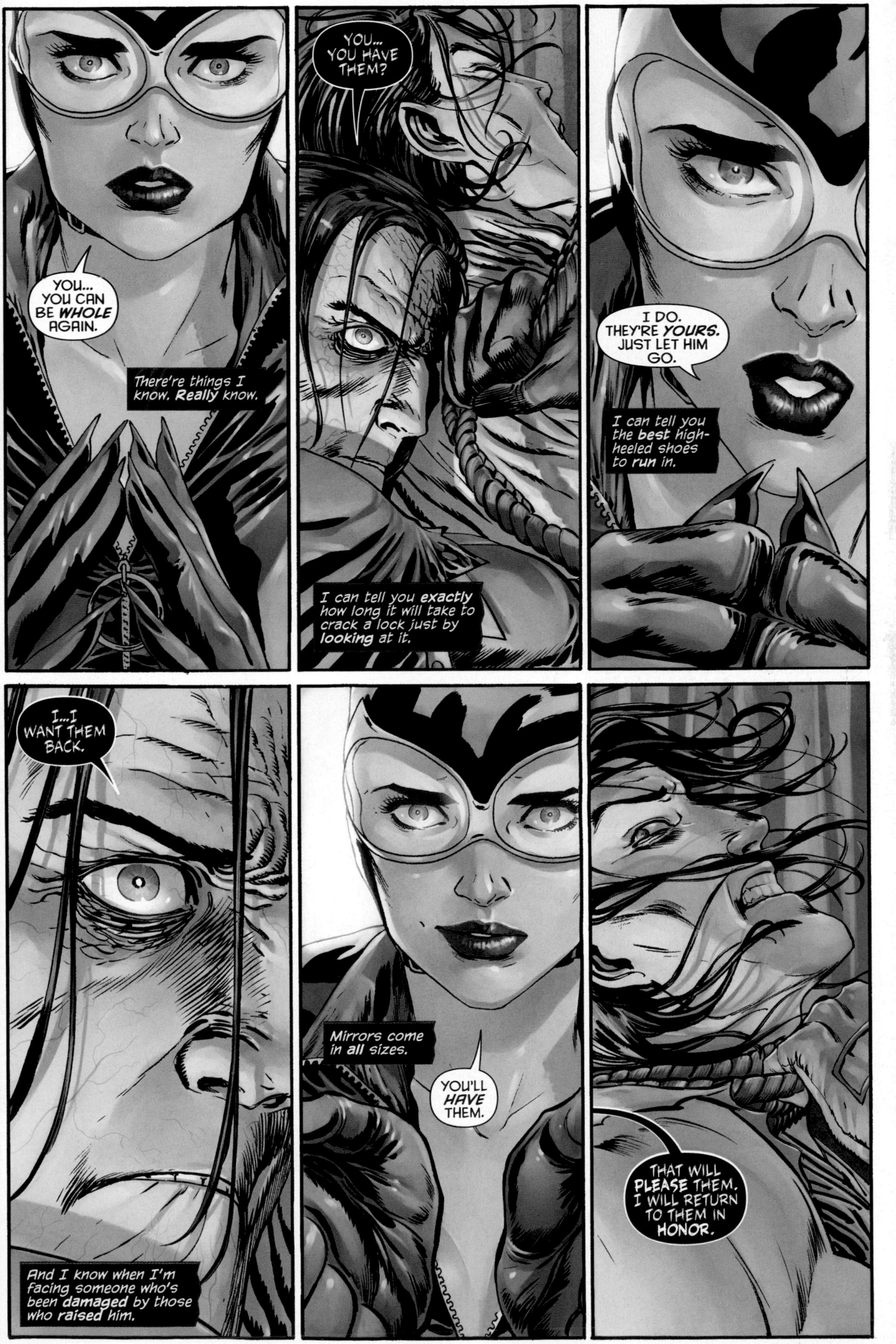
YOU... YOU CAN BE WHOLE AGAIN.
There're things I know. Really know.
YOU... YOU HAVE THEM?
I can tell you exactly how long it will take to crack a lock just by looking at it.
I DO. THEY'RE YOURS. JUST LET HIM GO.
I can tell you the best high-heeled shoes to run in.
I...I WANT THEM BACK.
And I know when I'm facing someone who's been damaged by those who raised him.
Mirrors come in all sizes.
YOU'LL HAVE THEM.
THAT WILL PLEASE THEM. I WILL RETURN TO THEM IN HONOR.

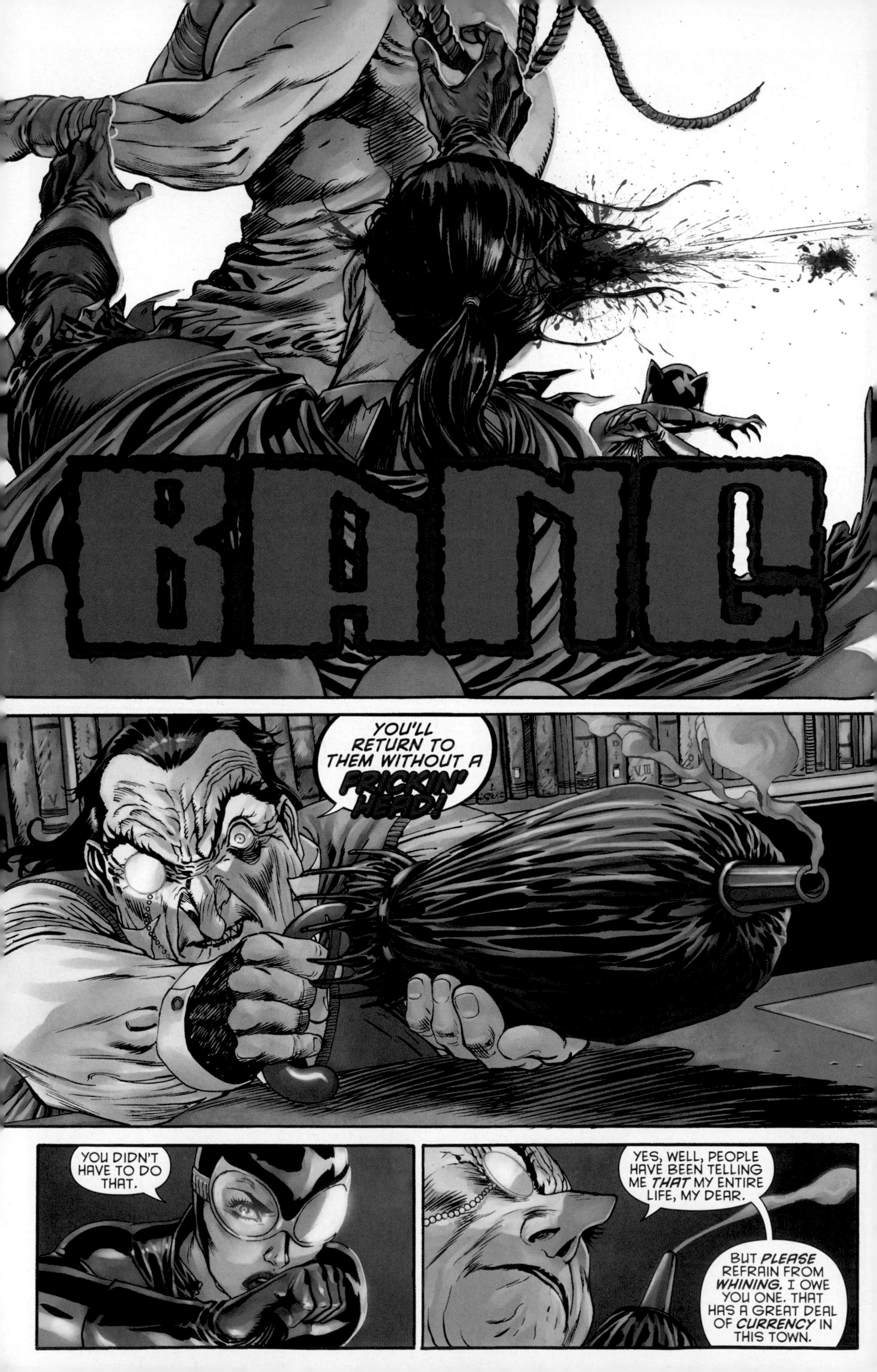
BANG
YOU'LL RETURN TO THEM WITHOUT A FRICKIN' HEAD!
YOU DIDN'T HAVE TO DO THAT.
YES, WELL, PEOPLE HAVE BEEN TELLING ME THAT MY ENTIRE LIFE, MY DEAR.
BUT PLEASE REFRAIN FROM WHINING. I OWE YOU ONE. THAT HAS A GREAT DEAL OF CURRENCY IN THIS TOWN.

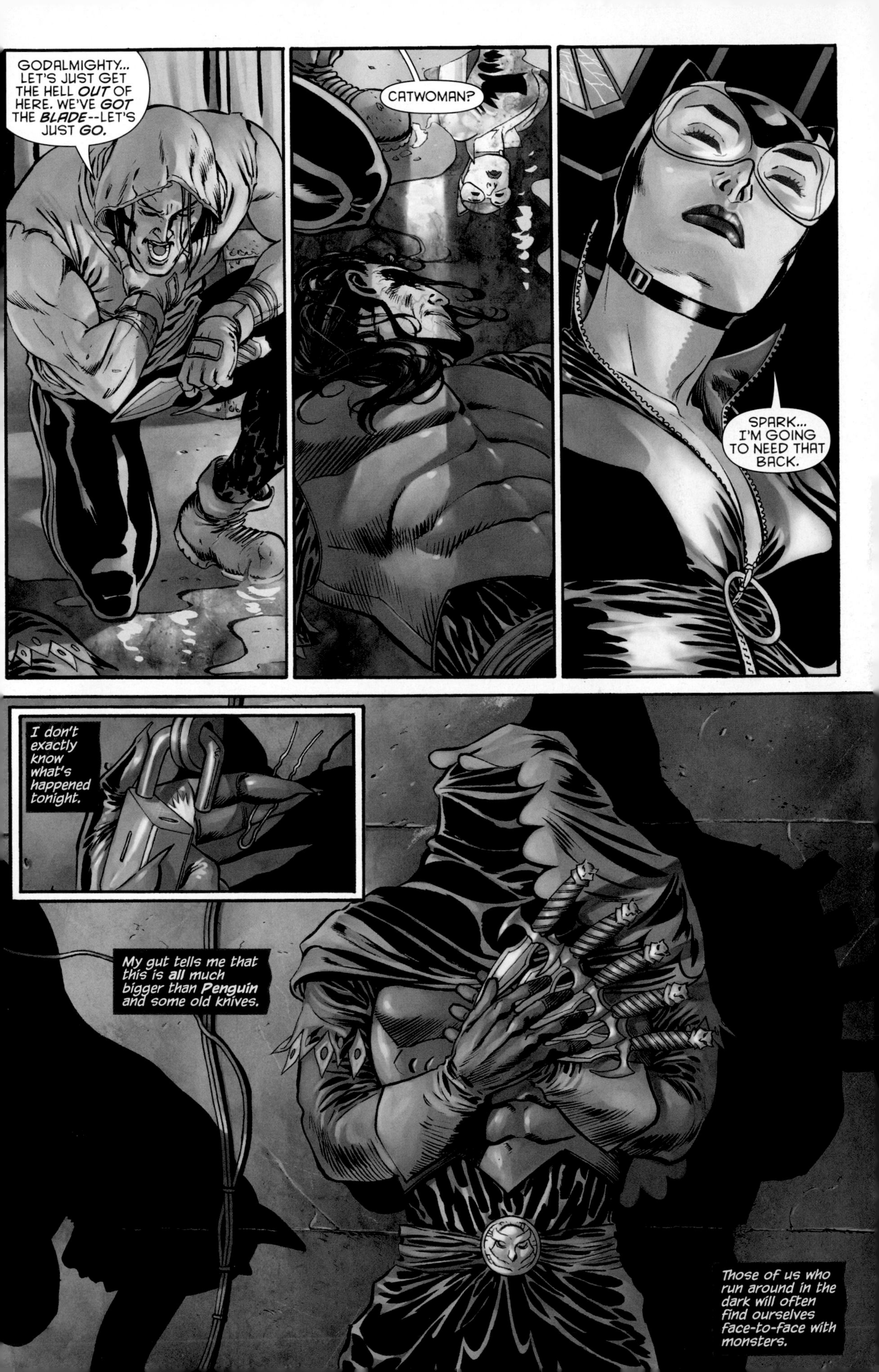
GODALMIGHTY... LET'S JUST GET THE HELL OUT OF HERE. WE'VE GOT THE BLADE--LET'S JUST GO.
CATWOMAN?
SPARK... I'M GOING TO NEED THAT BACK.
I don't exactly know what's happened tonight.
My gut tells me that this is all much bigger than Penguin and some old knives.
Those of us who run around in the dark will often find ourselves face-to-face with monsters.

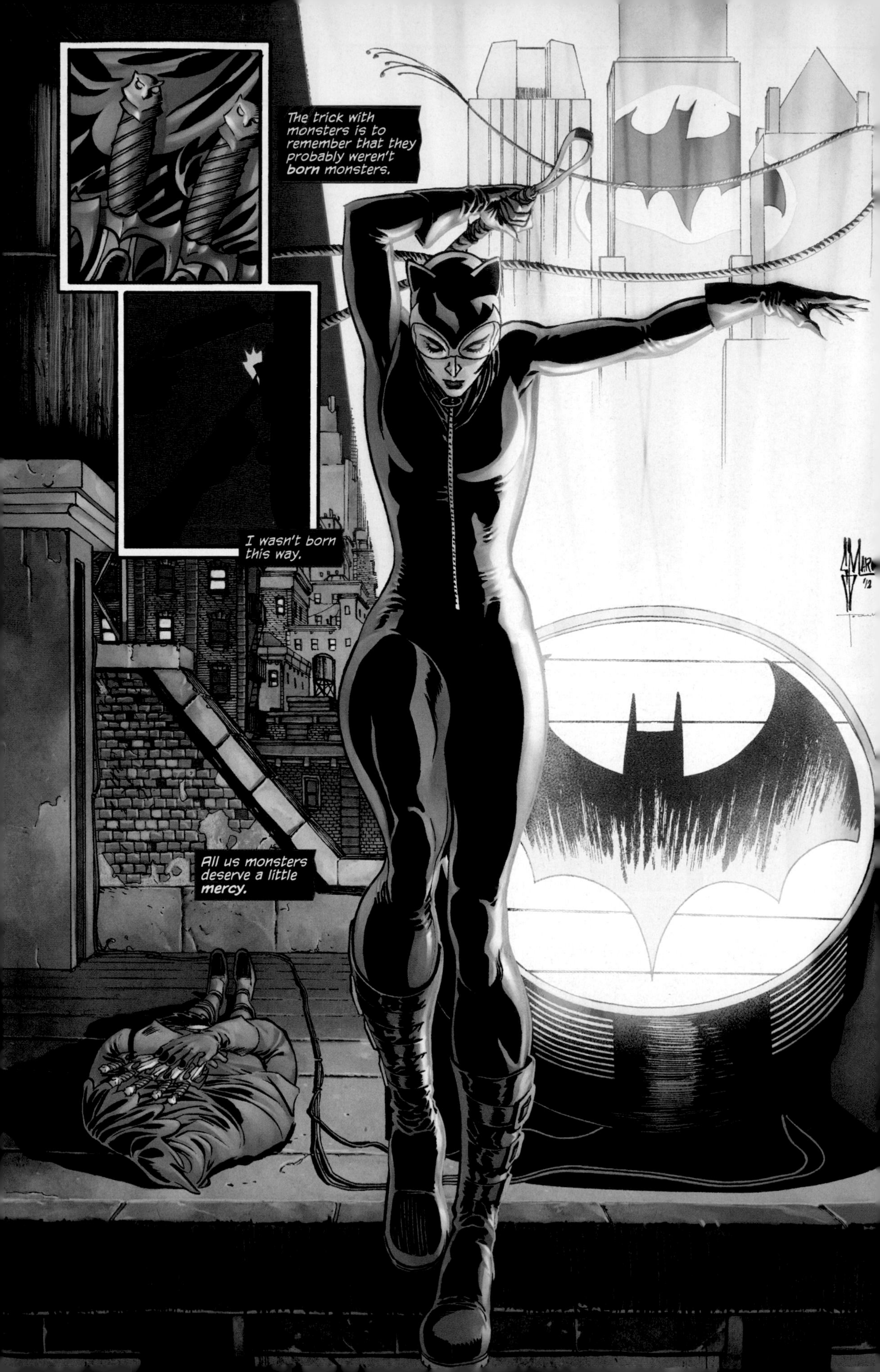
The trick with monsters is to remember that they probably weren't **born** monsters.
I wasn't born this way.
All us monsters deserve a little **mercy.**

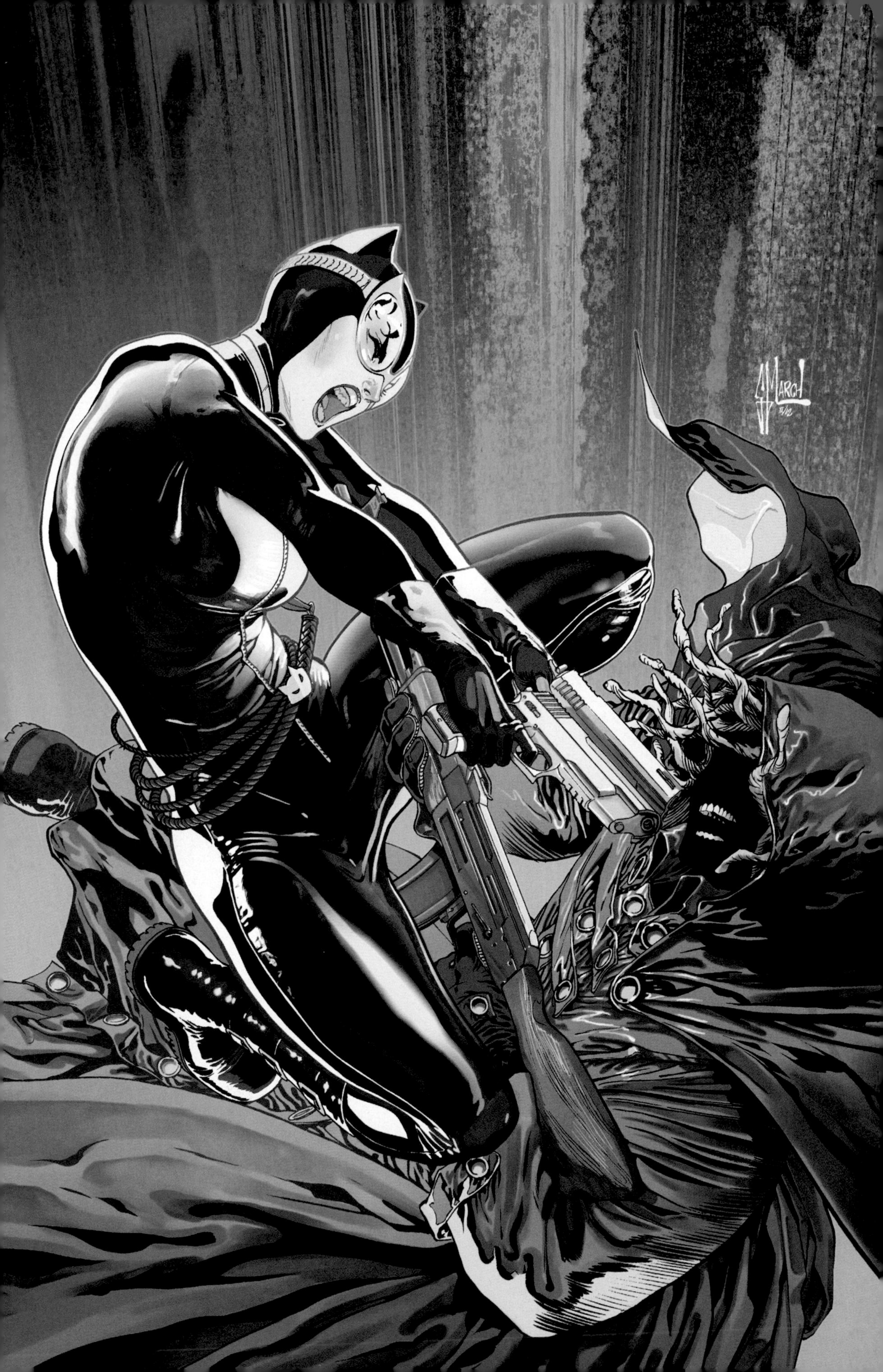

JUDD WINICK writer **GUILLEM MARCH** artist

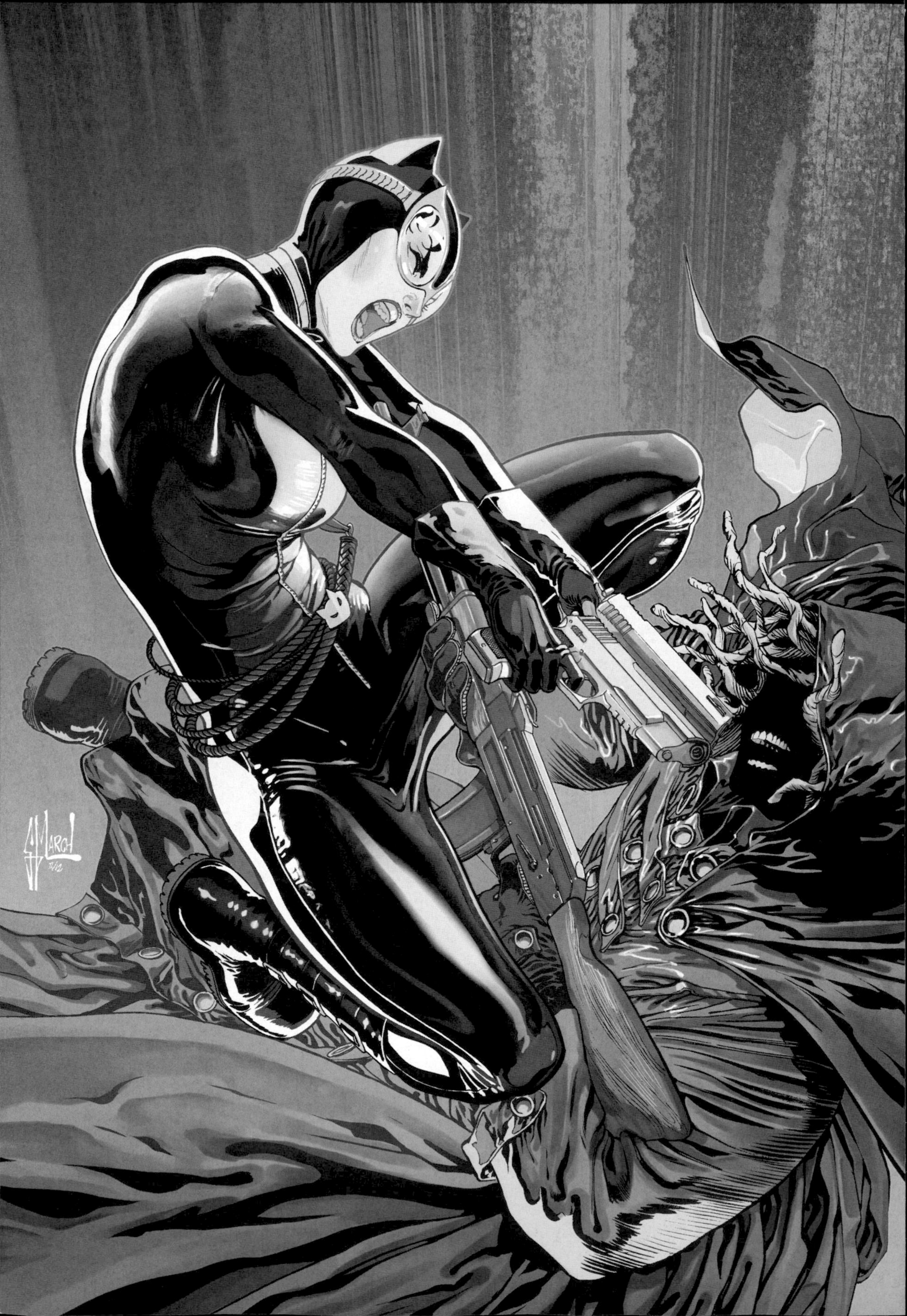

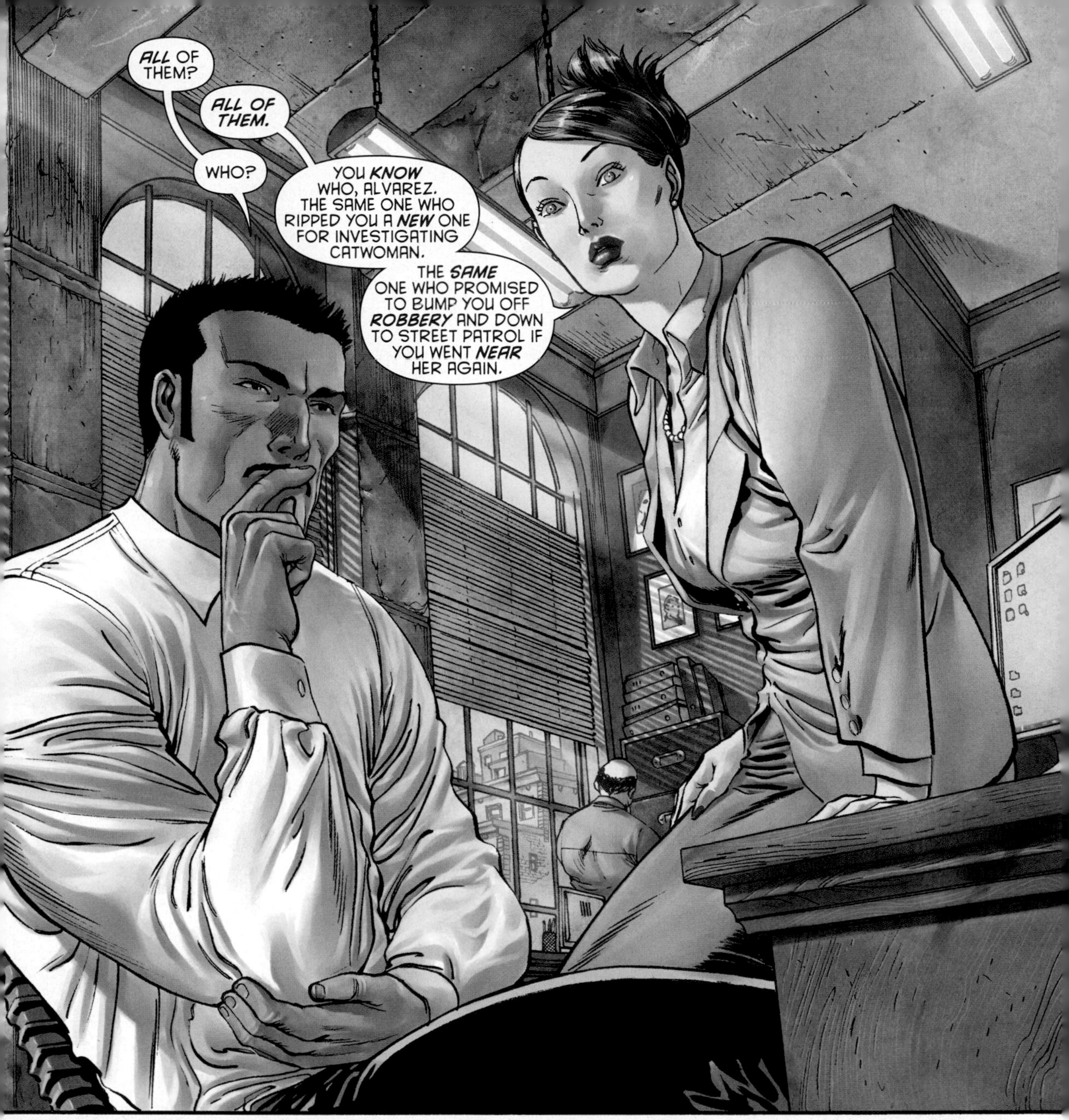
ALL OF THEM?
ALL OF THEM.
WHO?
YOU KNOW WHO, ALVAREZ. THE SAME ONE WHO RIPPED YOU A NEW ONE FOR INVESTIGATING CATWOMAN.
THE SAME ONE WHO PROMISED TO BUMP YOU OFF ROBBERY AND DOWN TO STREET PATROL IF YOU WENT NEAR HER AGAIN.

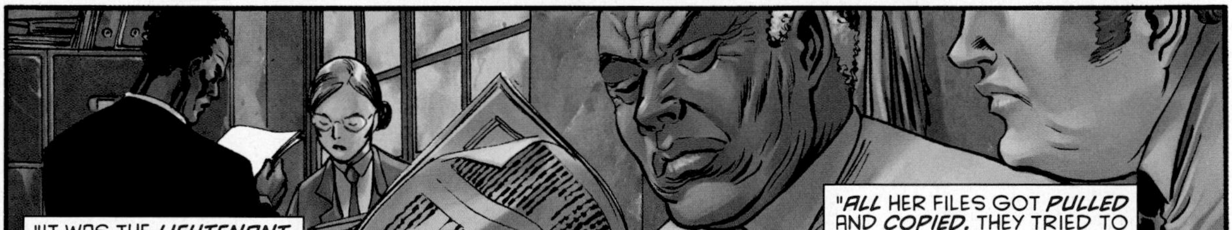
"IT WAS THE LIEUTENANT. AND MULROONEY, DAVIS AND ESTER.
"ALL HER FILES GOT PULLED AND COPIED. THEY TRIED TO DO IT OFF THE BOOKS, BUT I SPOTTED IT."

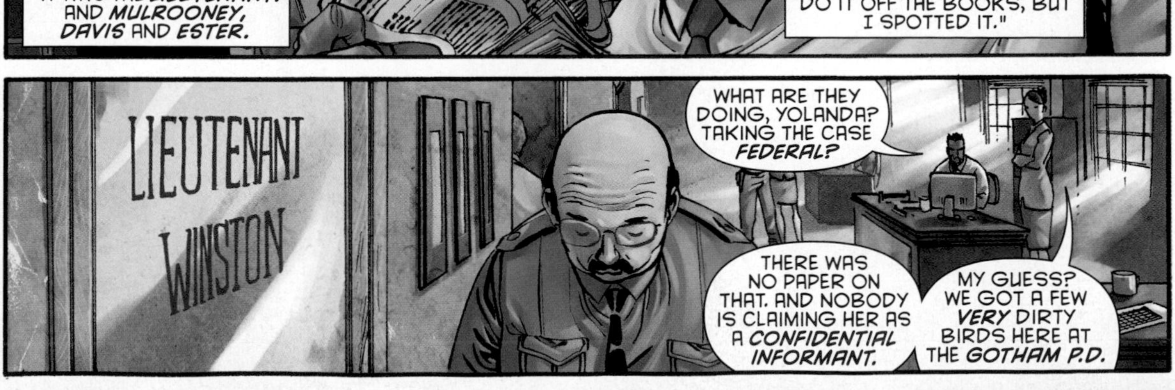
LIEUTENANT WINSTON
WHAT ARE THEY DOING, YOLANDA? TAKING THE CASE FEDERAL?
THERE WAS NO PAPER ON THAT. AND NOBODY IS CLAIMING HER AS A CONFIDENTIAL INFORMANT.
MY GUESS? WE GOT A FEW VERY DIRTY BIRDS HERE AT THE GOTHAM P.D.

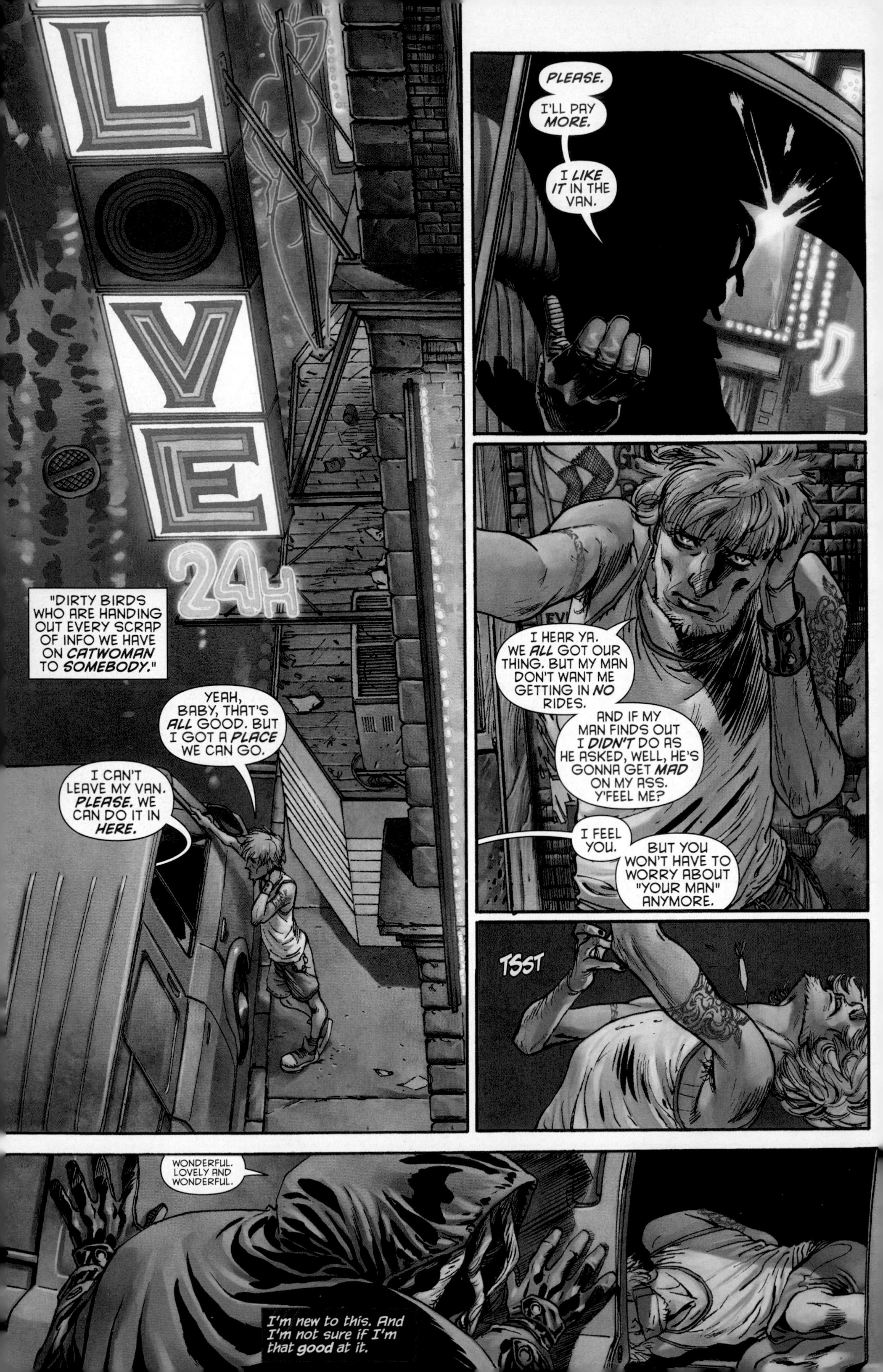
"DIRTY BIRDS WHO ARE HANDING OUT EVERY SCRAP OF INFO WE HAVE ON CATWOMAN TO SOMEBODY."
YEAH, BABY, THAT'S ALL GOOD. BUT I GOT A PLACE WE CAN GO.
I CAN'T LEAVE MY VAN. PLEASE. WE CAN DO IT IN HERE.
PLEASE.
I'LL PAY MORE.
I LIKE IT IN THE VAN.
I HEAR YA. WE ALL GOT OUR THING. BUT MY MAN DON'T WANT ME GETTING IN NO RIDES.
AND IF MY MAN FINDS OUT I DIDN'T DO AS HE ASKED, WELL, HE'S GONNA GET MAD ON MY ASS. Y'FEEL ME?
I FEEL YOU.
BUT YOU WON'T HAVE TO WORRY ABOUT "YOUR MAN" ANYMORE.
TSST
WONDERFUL. LOVELY AND WONDERFUL.
I'm new to this. And I'm not sure if I'm that good at it.

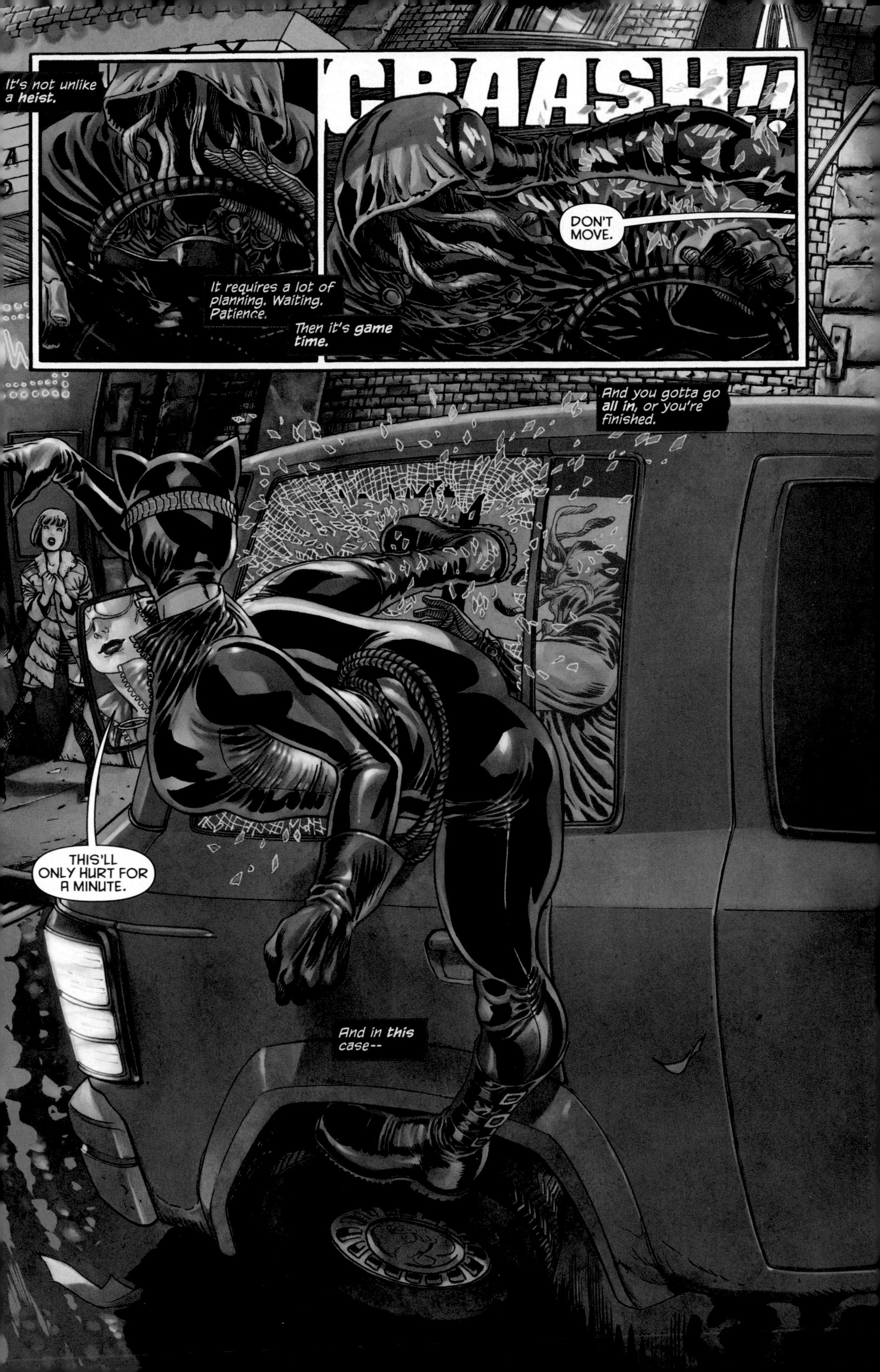
It's not unlike a heist.
CRAASH!!
DON'T MOVE.
It requires a lot of planning. Waiting. Patience.
Then it's game time.
And you gotta go all in, or you're finished.
THIS'LL ONLY HURT FOR A MINUTE.
And in this case--

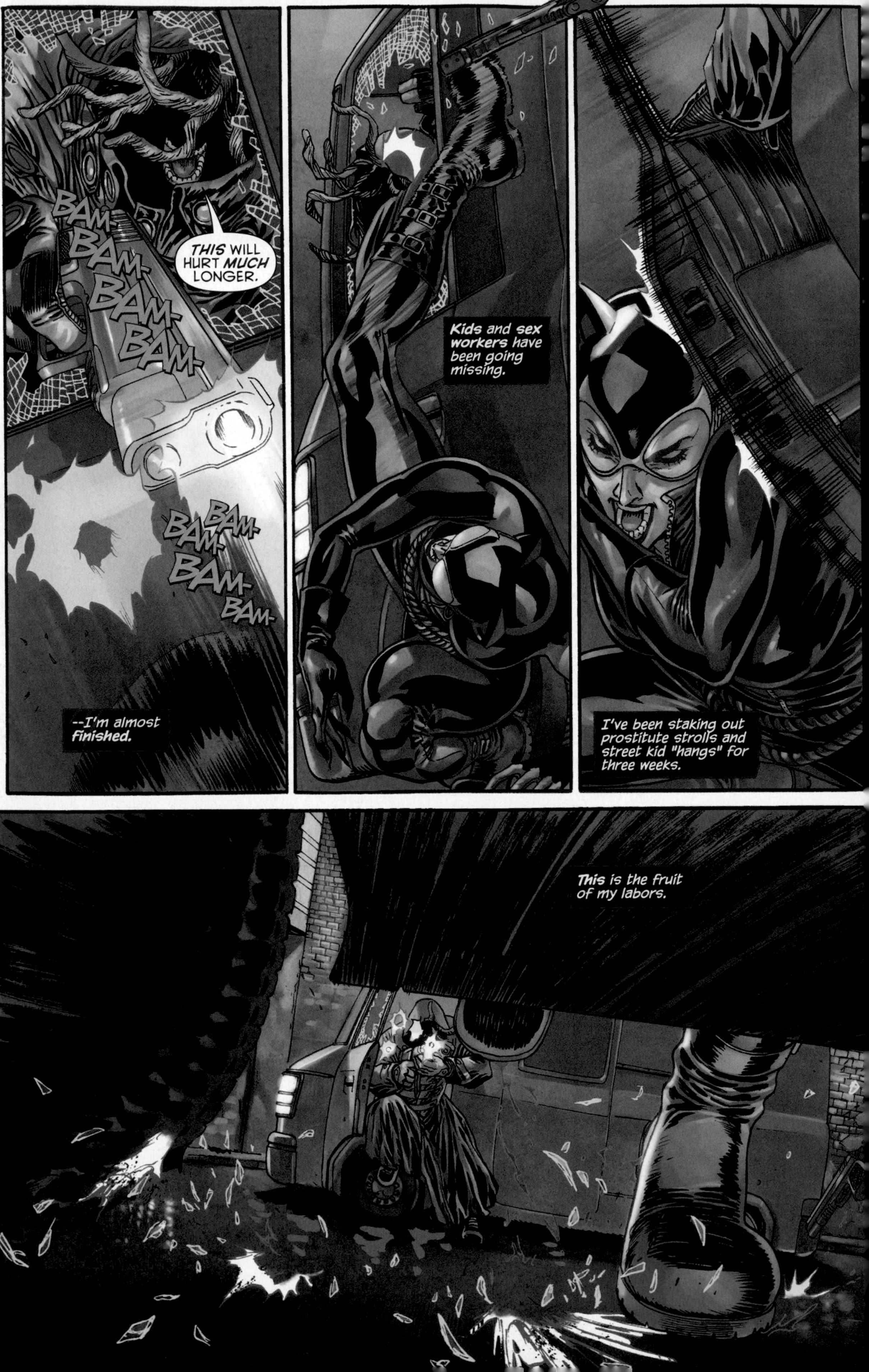
BAM-
BAM-
BAM-
BAM-
THIS WILL HURT MUCH LONGER.
BAM-
BAM-
BAM-
BAM-
--I'm almost finished.
Kids and sex workers have been going missing.
I've been staking out prostitute strolls and street kid "hangs" for three weeks.
This is the fruit of my labors.

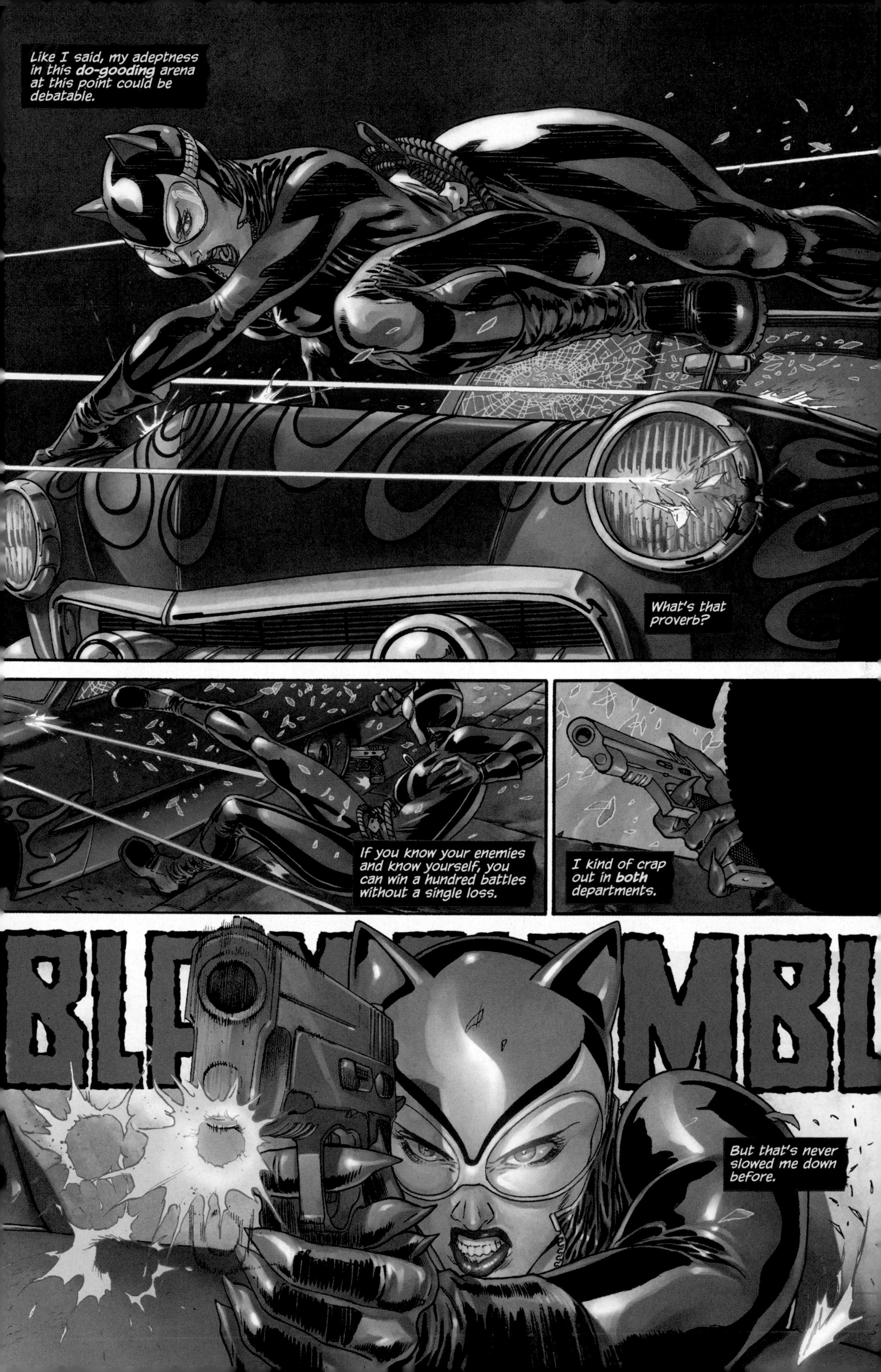
Like I said, my adeptness in this **do-gooding** arena at this point could be debatable.
What's that proverb?
If you know your enemies and know yourself, you can win a hundred battles without a single loss.
I kind of crap out in **both** departments.
But that's never slowed me down before.

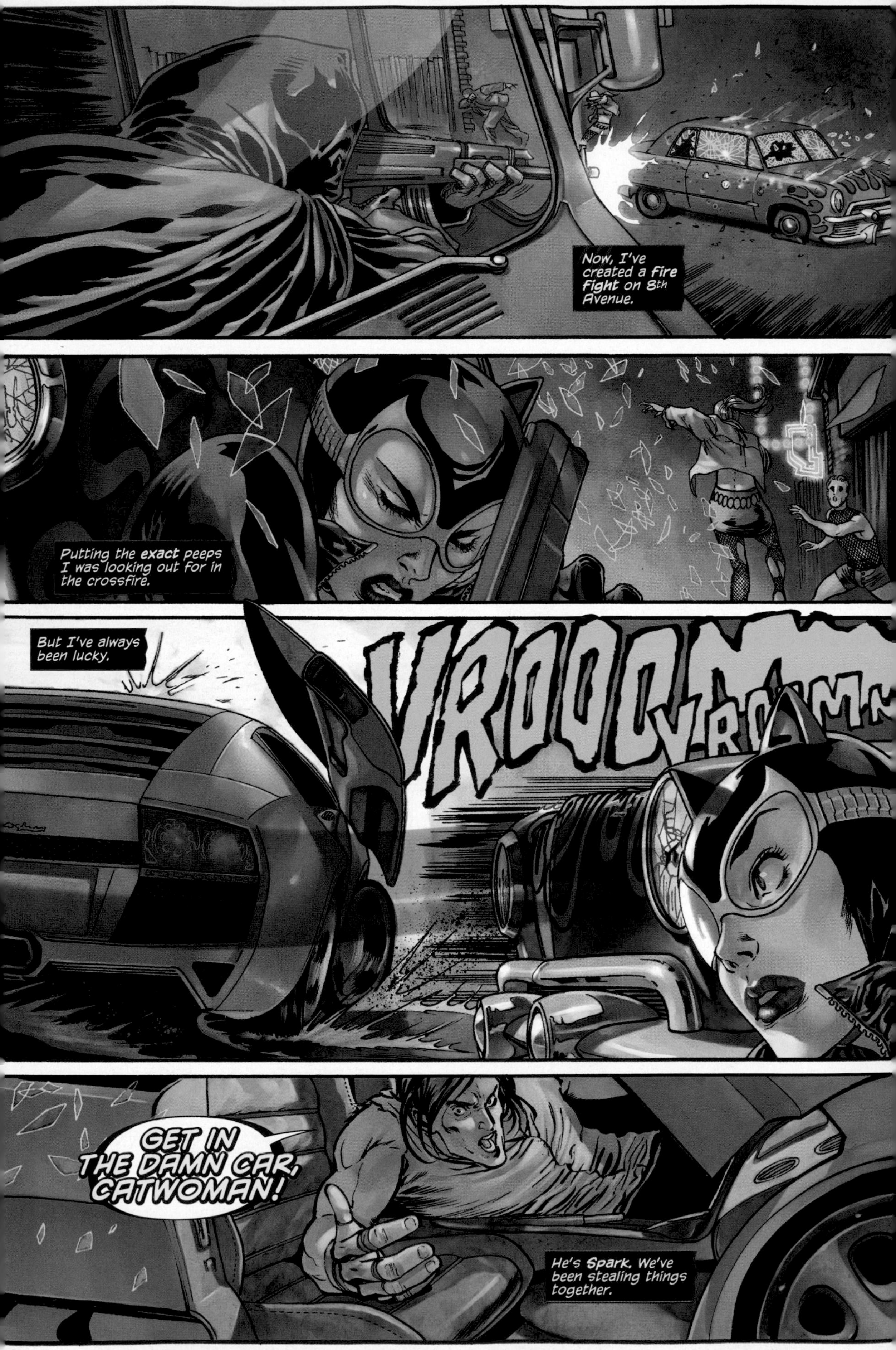
Now, I've created a fire fight on 8th Avenue.
Putting the exact peeps I was looking out for in the crossfire.
But I've always been lucky.
VROOOM
VROOMM
GET IN THE DAMN CAR, CATWOMAN!
He's Spark. We've been stealing things together.

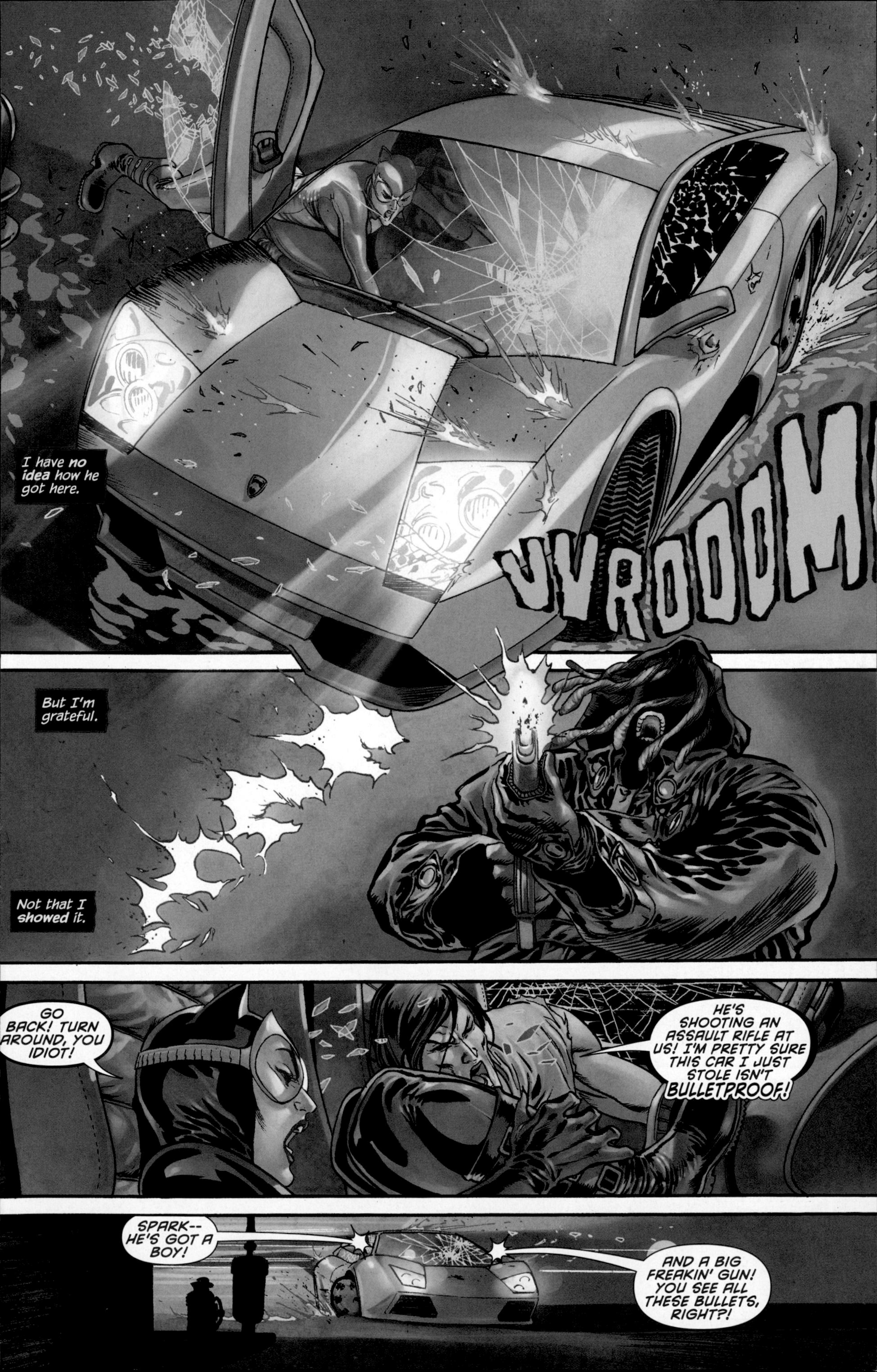
I have no idea how he got here.
VVROOOM
But I'm grateful.
Not that I showed it.
GO BACK! TURN AROUND, YOU IDIOT!
HE'S SHOOTING AN ASSAULT RIFLE AT US! I'M PRETTY SURE THIS CAR I JUST STOLE ISN'T BULLETPROOF!
SPARK-- HE'S GOT A BOY!
AND A BIG FREAKIN' GUN! YOU SEE ALL THESE BULLETS, RIGHT?!

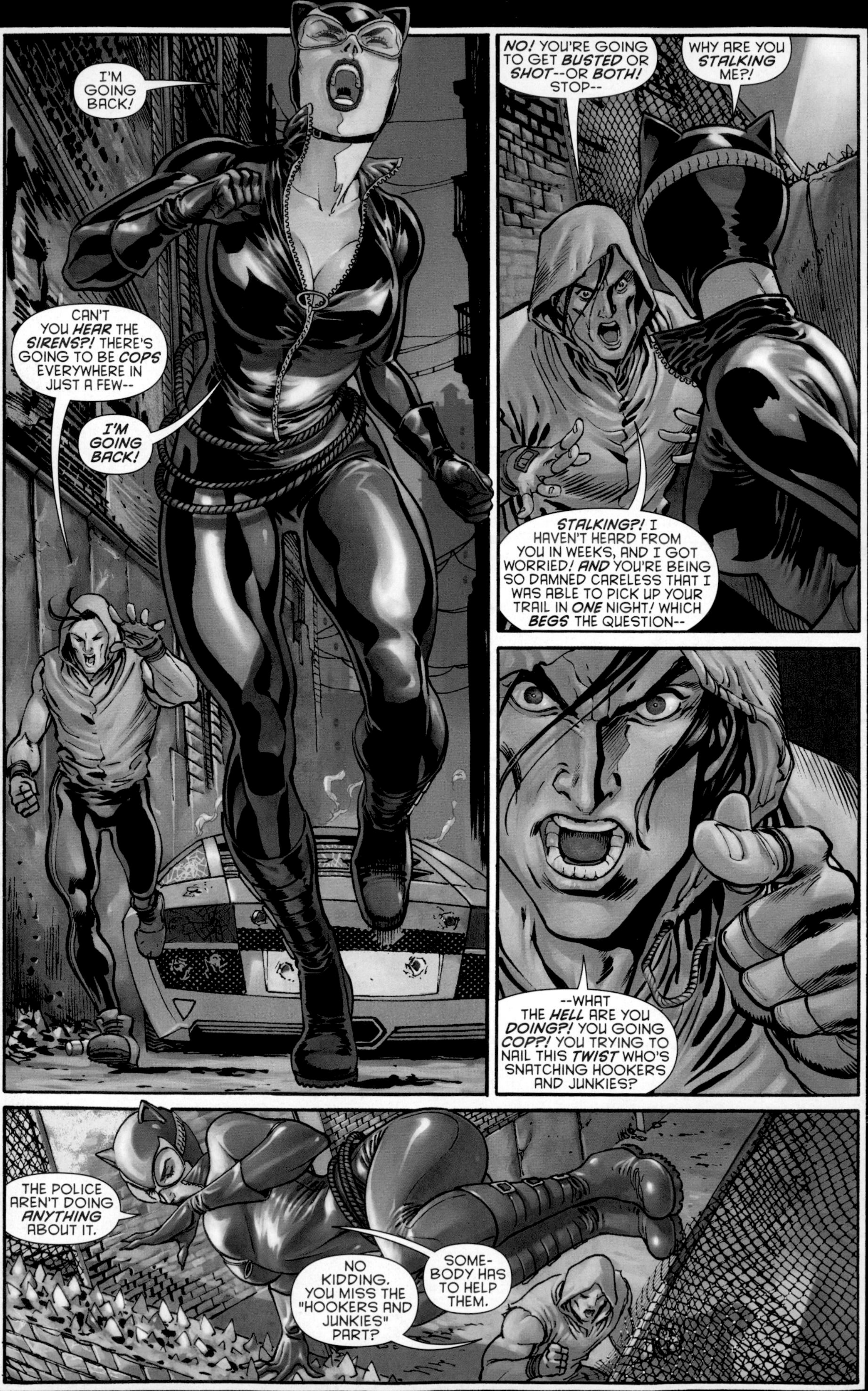
I'M GOING BACK!
CAN'T YOU HEAR THE SIRENS?! THERE'S GOING TO BE COPS EVERYWHERE IN JUST A FEW--
I'M GOING BACK!
NO! YOU'RE GOING TO GET BUSTED OR SHOT--OR BOTH! STOP--
WHY ARE YOU STALKING ME?!
STALKING?! I HAVEN'T HEARD FROM YOU IN WEEKS, AND I GOT WORRIED! AND YOU'RE BEING SO DAMNED CARELESS THAT I WAS ABLE TO PICK UP YOUR TRAIL IN ONE NIGHT! WHICH BEGS THE QUESTION--
--WHAT THE HELL ARE YOU DOING?! YOU GOING COP?! YOU TRYING TO NAIL THIS TWIST WHO'S SNATCHING HOOKERS AND JUNKIES?
THE POLICE AREN'T DOING ANYTHING ABOUT IT.
SOME-BODY HAS TO HELP THEM.
NO KIDDING. YOU MISS THE "HOOKERS AND JUNKIES" PART?

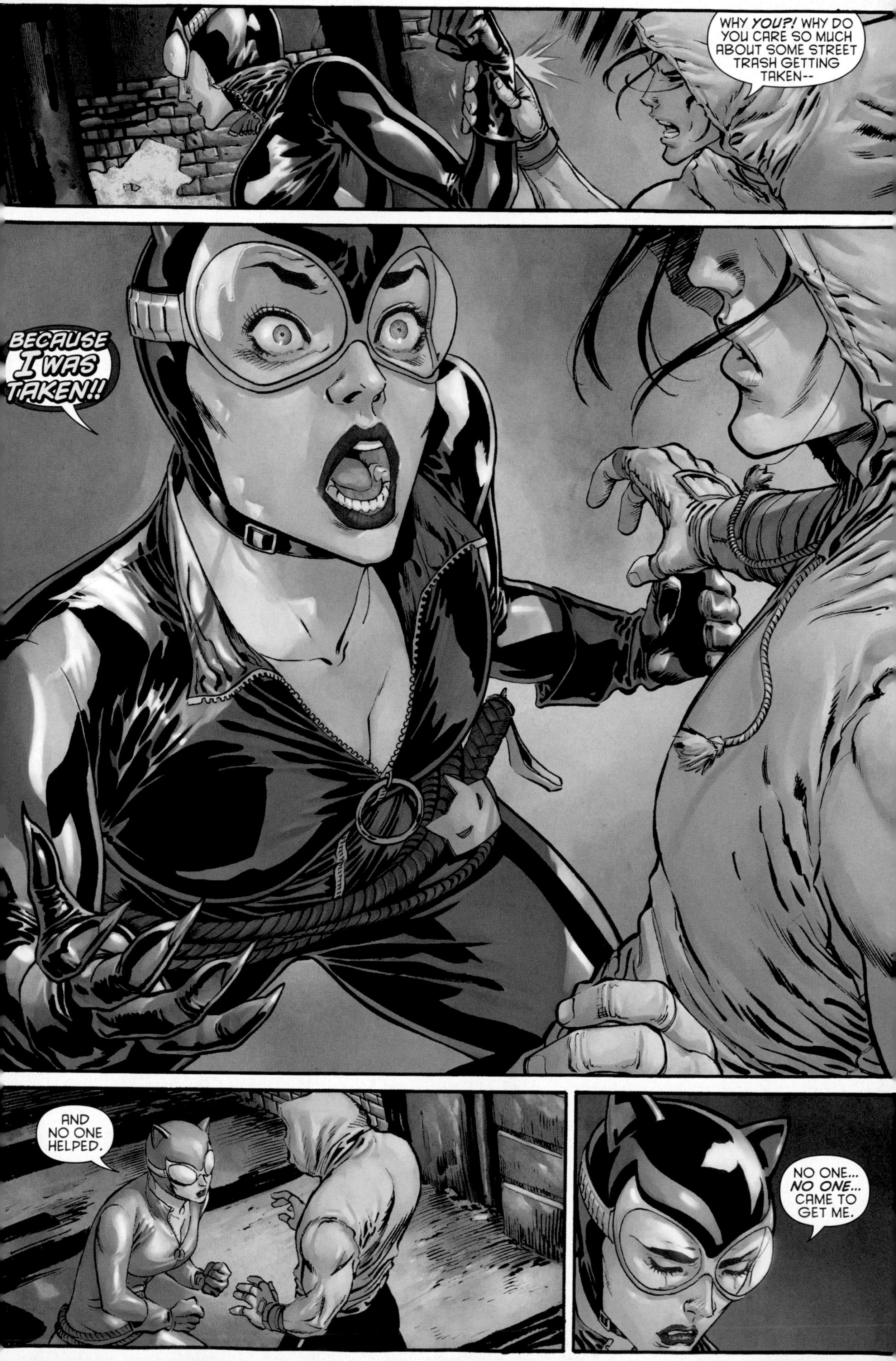
WHY *YOU?!* WHY DO YOU CARE SO MUCH ABOUT SOME STREET TRASH GETTING TAKEN--
BECAUSE I WAS TAKEN!!
AND NO ONE HELPED.
NO ONE... *NO ONE*... CAME TO GET ME.

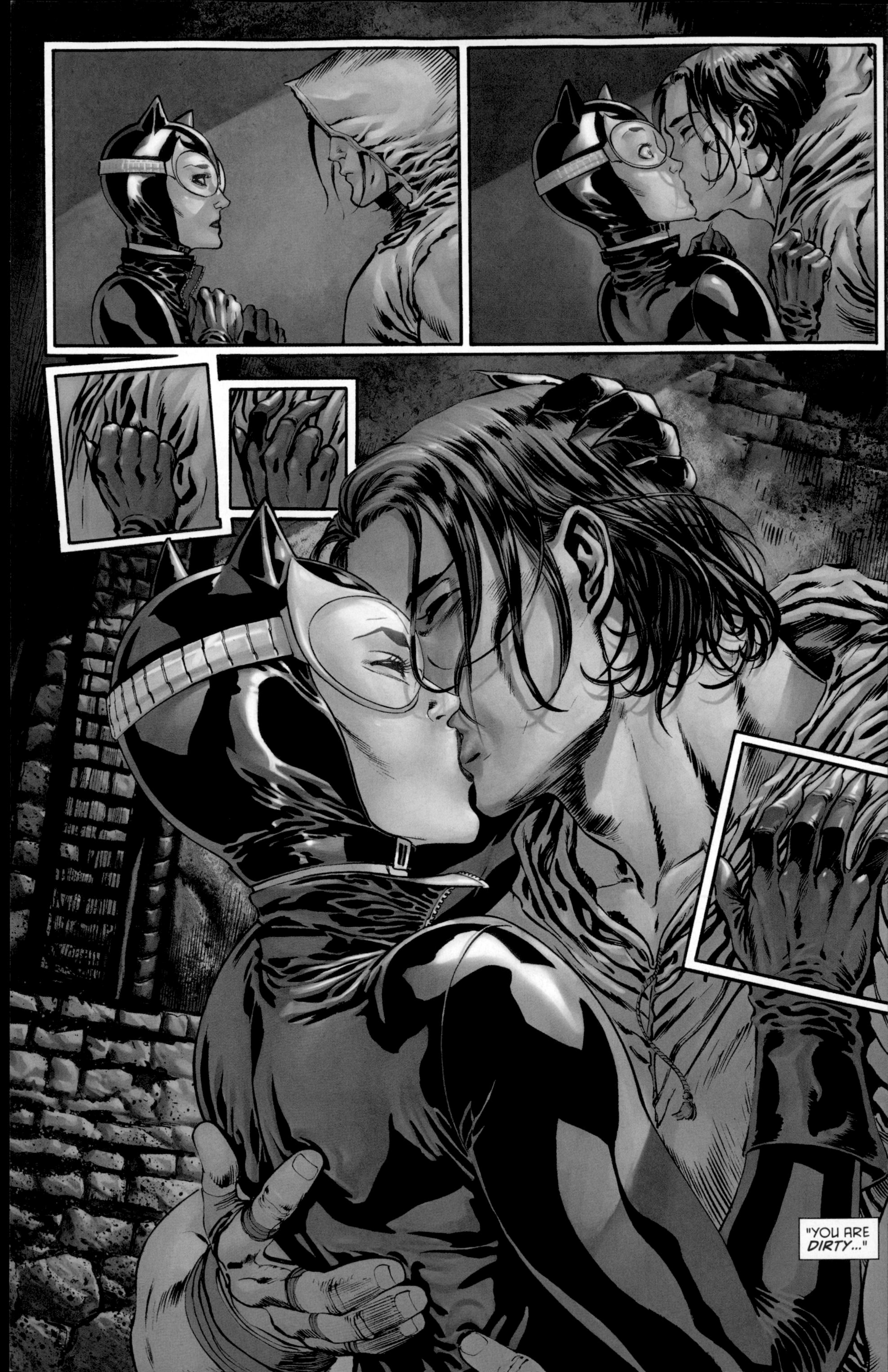

"YOU ARE
DIRTY..."

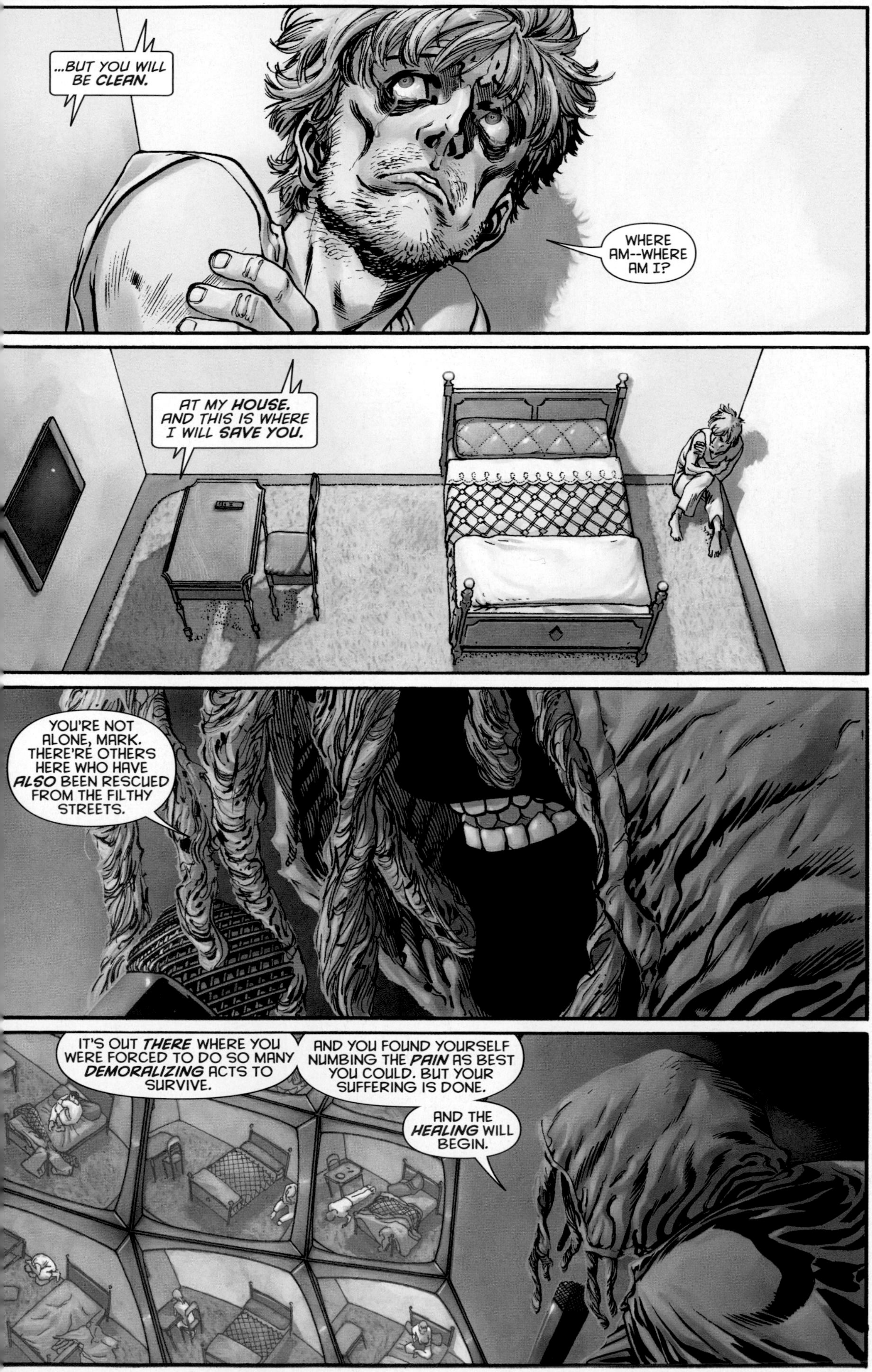
...BUT YOU WILL BE CLEAN.
WHERE AM--WHERE AM I?
AT MY HOUSE. AND THIS IS WHERE I WILL SAVE YOU.
YOU'RE NOT ALONE, MARK. THERE'RE OTHERS HERE WHO HAVE ALSO BEEN RESCUED FROM THE FILTHY STREETS.
IT'S OUT THERE WHERE YOU WERE FORCED TO DO SO MANY DEMORALIZING ACTS TO SURVIVE.
AND YOU FOUND YOURSELF NUMBING THE PAIN AS BEST YOU COULD. BUT YOUR SUFFERING IS DONE.
AND THE HEALING WILL BEGIN.

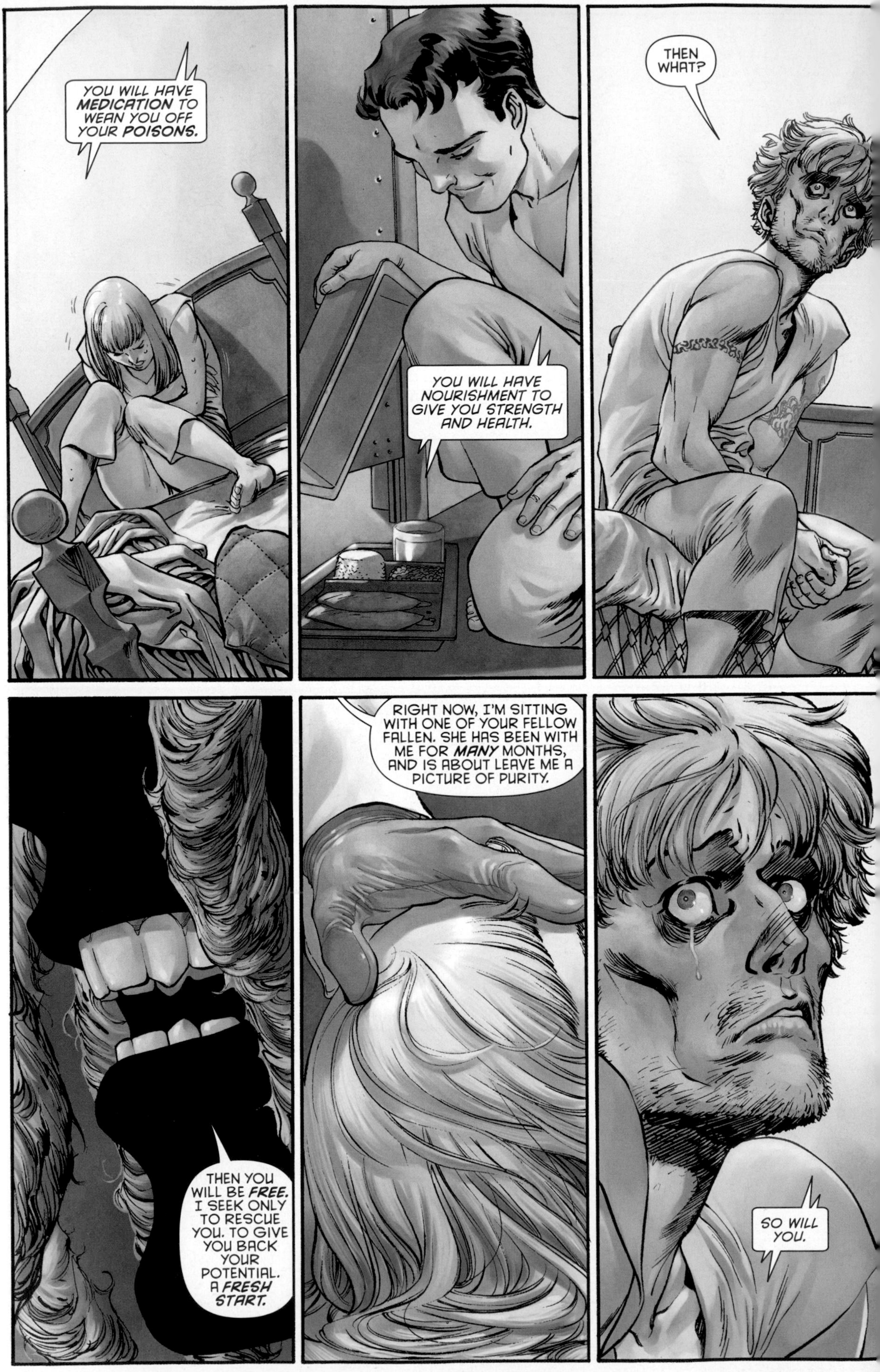
YOU WILL HAVE MEDICATION TO WEAN YOU OFF YOUR POISONS.
YOU WILL HAVE NOURISHMENT TO GIVE YOU STRENGTH AND HEALTH.
THEN WHAT?
THEN YOU WILL BE FREE. I SEEK ONLY TO RESCUE YOU. TO GIVE YOU BACK YOUR POTENTIAL. A FRESH START.
RIGHT NOW, I'M SITTING WITH ONE OF YOUR FELLOW FALLEN. SHE HAS BEEN WITH ME FOR MANY MONTHS, AND IS ABOUT LEAVE ME A PICTURE OF PURITY.
SO WILL YOU.

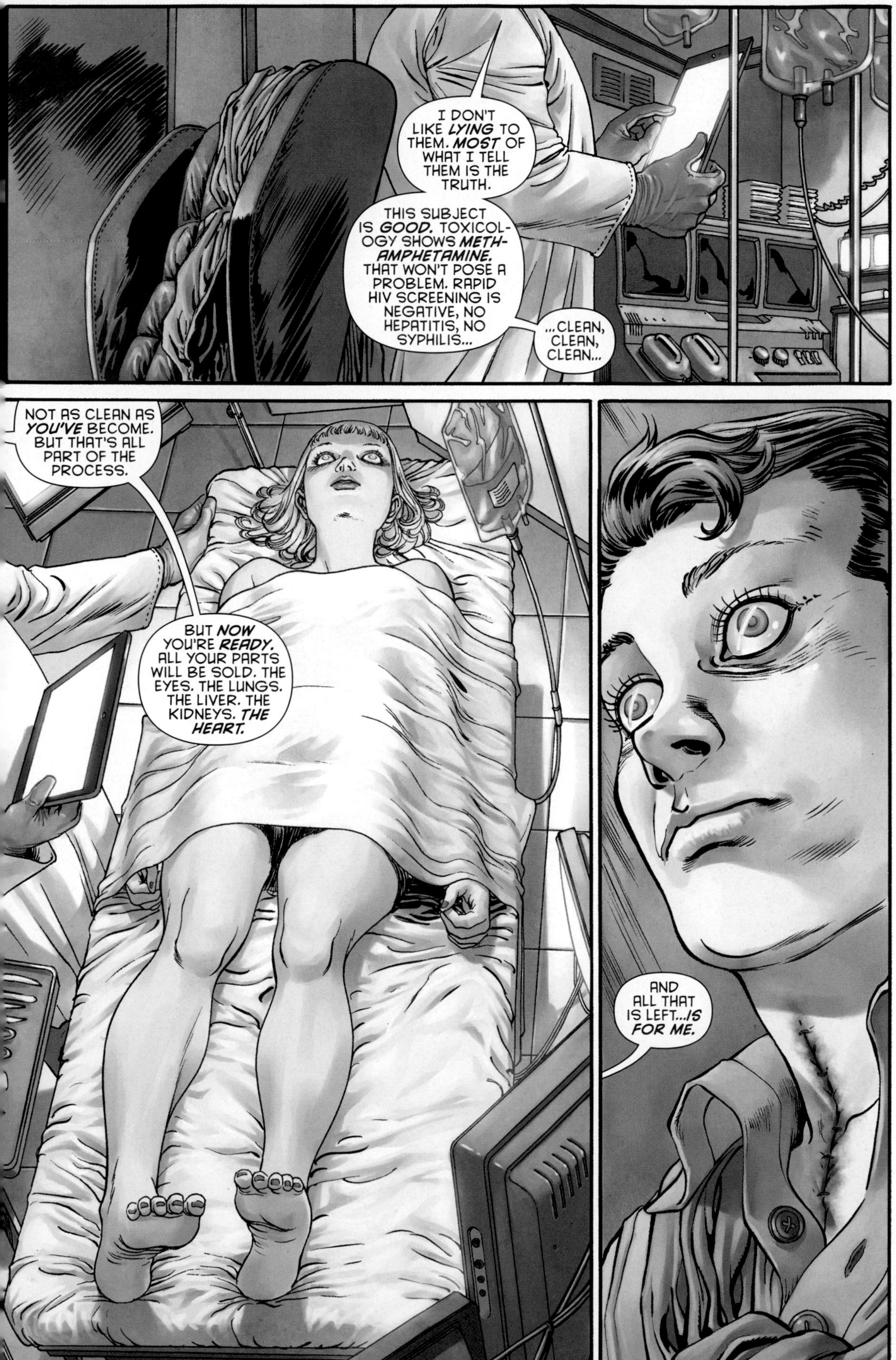
I DON'T LIKE *LYING* TO THEM. *MOST* OF WHAT I TELL THEM IS THE TRUTH.
THIS SUBJECT IS ***GOOD.*** TOXICOLOGY SHOWS ***METH-AMPHETAMINE.*** THAT WON'T POSE A PROBLEM. RAPID HIV SCREENING IS NEGATIVE, NO HEPATITIS, NO SYPHILIS...
...CLEAN, CLEAN, CLEAN...
NOT AS CLEAN AS ***YOU'VE*** BECOME. BUT THAT'S ALL PART OF THE PROCESS.
BUT ***NOW*** YOU'RE ***READY.*** ALL YOUR PARTS WILL BE SOLD. THE EYES. THE LUNGS. THE LIVER. THE KIDNEYS. ***THE HEART.***
AND ALL THAT IS LEFT...***IS FOR ME.***

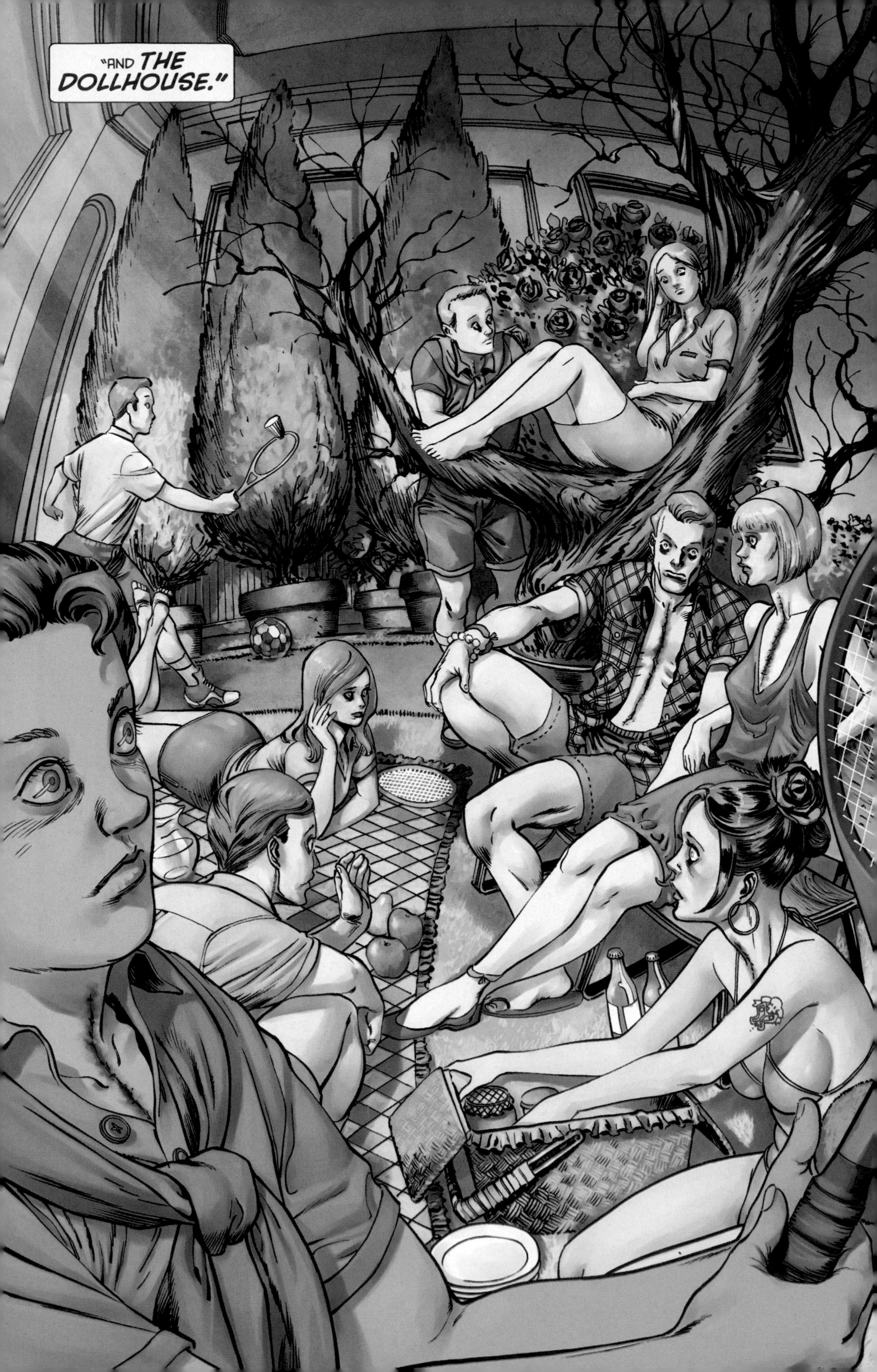
"AND THE DOLLHOUSE."

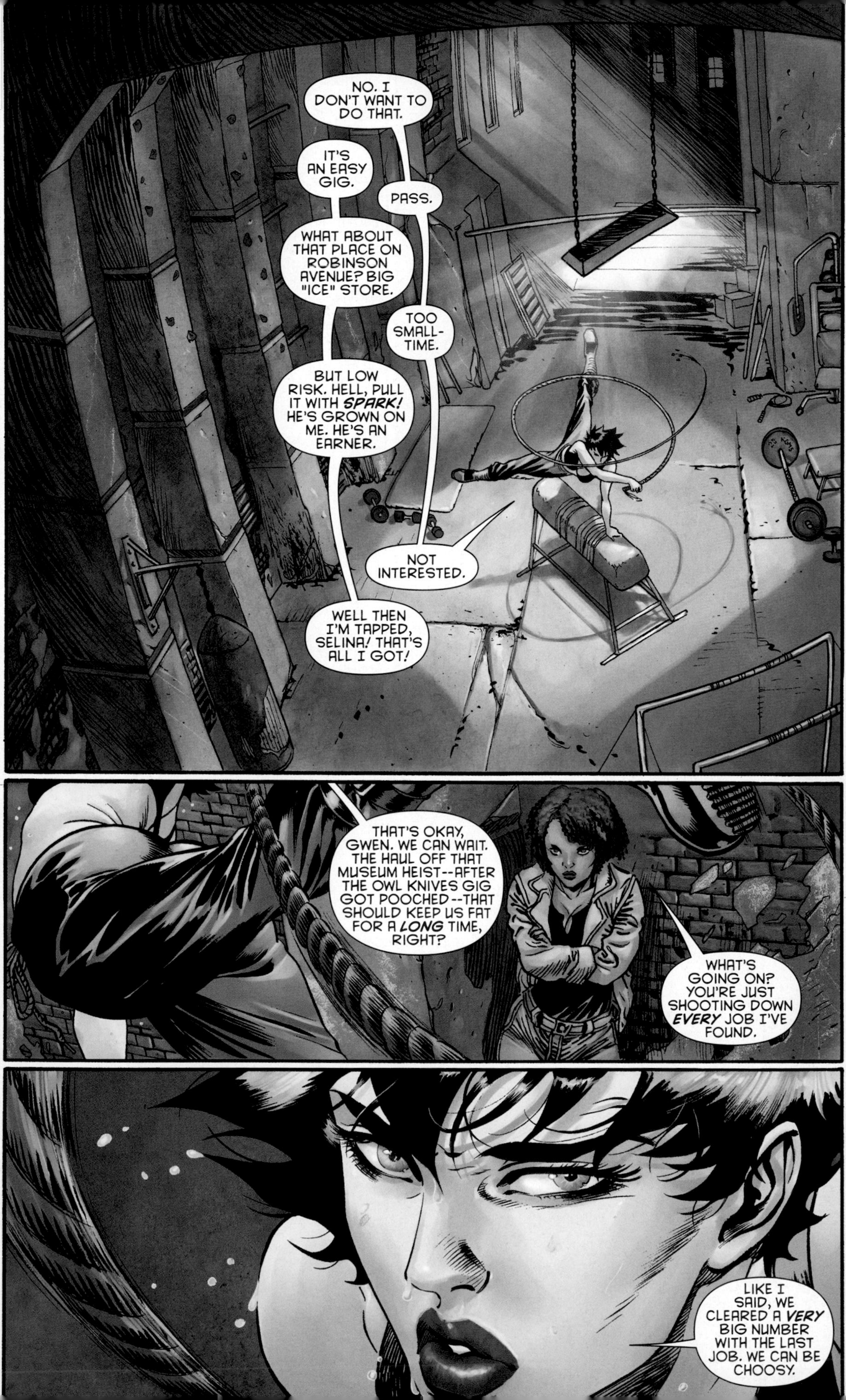

NO. I DON'T WANT TO DO THAT.
IT'S AN EASY GIG.
PASS.
WHAT ABOUT THAT PLACE ON ROBINSON AVENUE? BIG "ICE" STORE.
TOO SMALL-TIME.
BUT LOW RISK. HELL, PULL IT WITH SPARK! HE'S GROWN ON ME. HE'S AN EARNER.
NOT INTERESTED.
WELL THEN I'M TAPPED, SELINA! THAT'S ALL I GOT!
THAT'S OKAY, GWEN. WE CAN WAIT. THE HAUL OFF THAT MUSEUM HEIST--AFTER THE OWL KNIVES GIG GOT POOCHED--THAT SHOULD KEEP US FAT FOR A LONG TIME, RIGHT?
WHAT'S GOING ON? YOU'RE JUST SHOOTING DOWN EVERY JOB I'VE FOUND.
LIKE I SAID, WE CLEARED A VERY BIG NUMBER WITH THE LAST JOB. WE CAN BE CHOOSY.

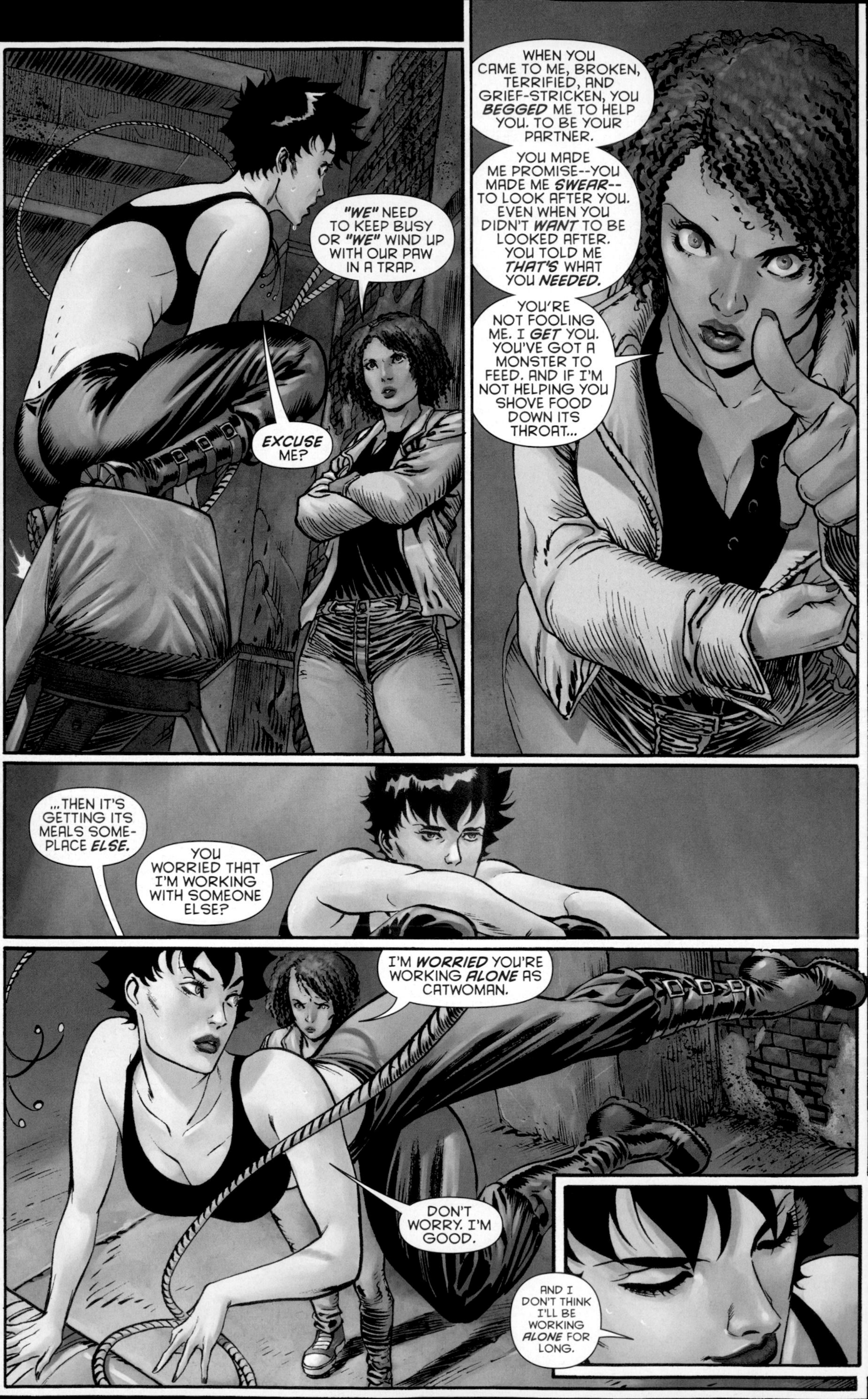
"WE" NEED TO KEEP BUSY OR "WE" WIND UP WITH OUR PAW IN A TRAP.
EXCUSE ME?
WHEN YOU CAME TO ME, BROKEN, TERRIFIED, AND GRIEF-STRICKEN, YOU BEGGED ME TO HELP YOU. TO BE YOUR PARTNER.
YOU MADE ME PROMISE--YOU MADE ME SWEAR--TO LOOK AFTER YOU. EVEN WHEN YOU DIDN'T WANT TO BE LOOKED AFTER. YOU TOLD ME THAT'S WHAT YOU NEEDED.
YOU'RE NOT FOOLING ME. I GET YOU. YOU'VE GOT A MONSTER TO FEED. AND IF I'M NOT HELPING YOU SHOVE FOOD DOWN ITS THROAT...
...THEN IT'S GETTING ITS MEALS SOMEPLACE ELSE.
YOU WORRIED THAT I'M WORKING WITH SOMEONE ELSE?
I'M WORRIED YOU'RE WORKING ALONE AS CATWOMAN.
DON'T WORRY. I'M GOOD.
AND I DON'T THINK I'LL BE WORKING ALONE FOR LONG.

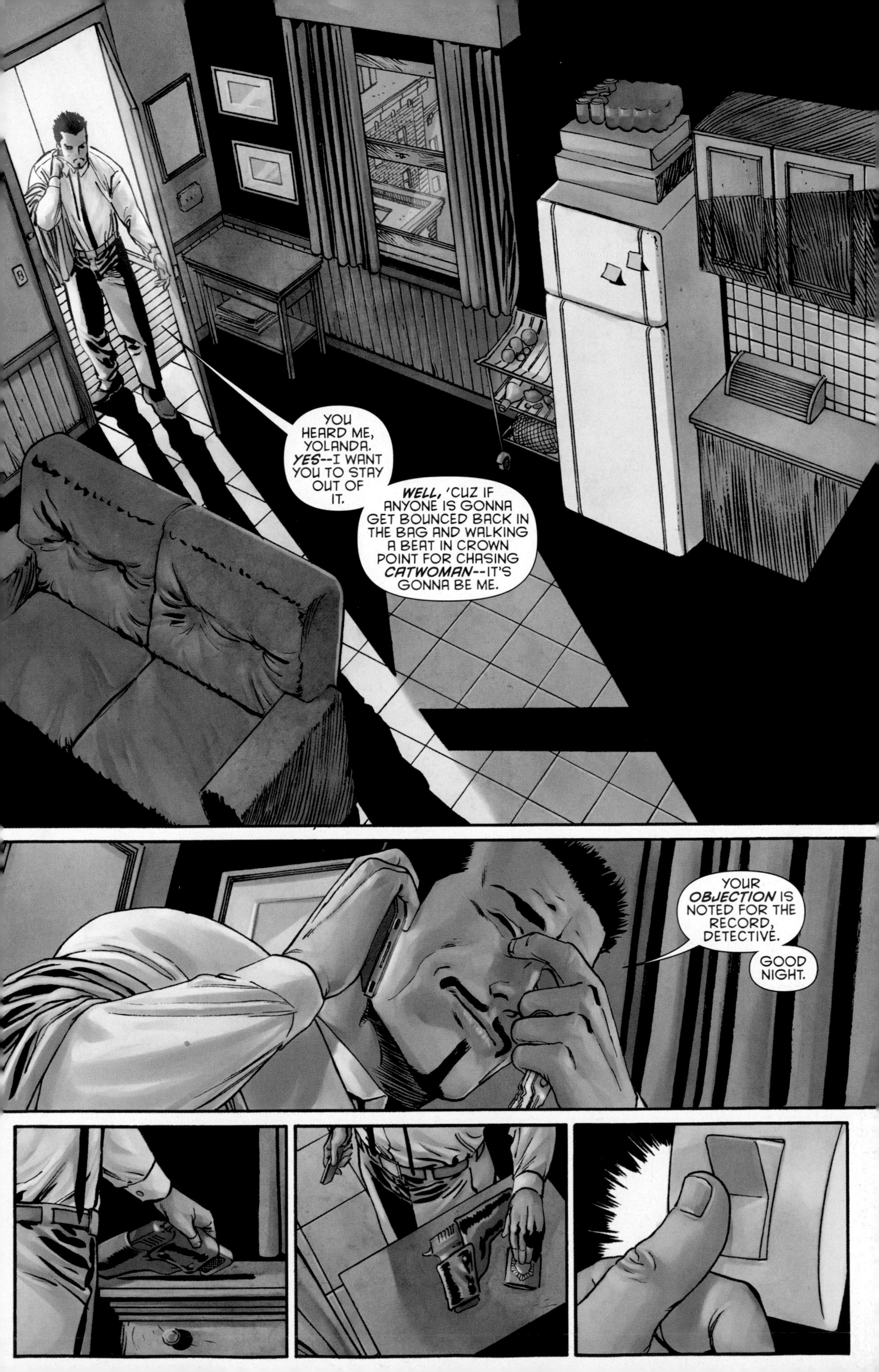
YOU HEARD ME, YOLANDA. YES--I WANT YOU TO STAY OUT OF IT.
WELL, 'CUZ IF ANYONE IS GONNA GET BOUNCED BACK IN THE BAG AND WALKING A BEAT IN CROWN POINT FOR CHASING CATWOMAN--IT'S GONNA BE ME.
YOUR OBJECTION IS NOTED FOR THE RECORD, DETECTIVE.
GOOD NIGHT.

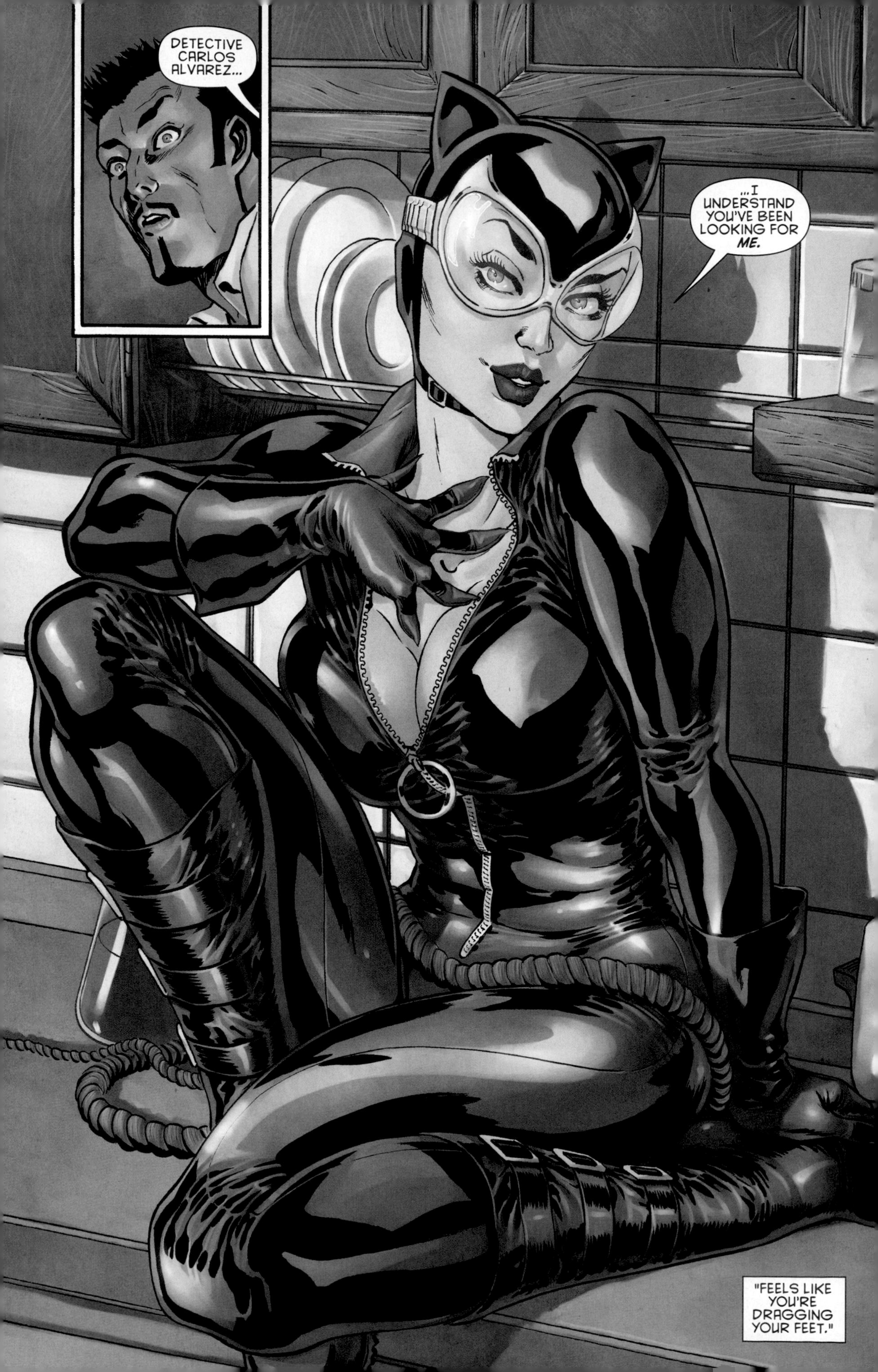
DETECTIVE CARLOS ALVAREZ...
...I UNDERSTAND YOU'VE BEEN LOOKING FOR ME.
"FEELS LIKE YOU'RE DRAGGING YOUR FEET."

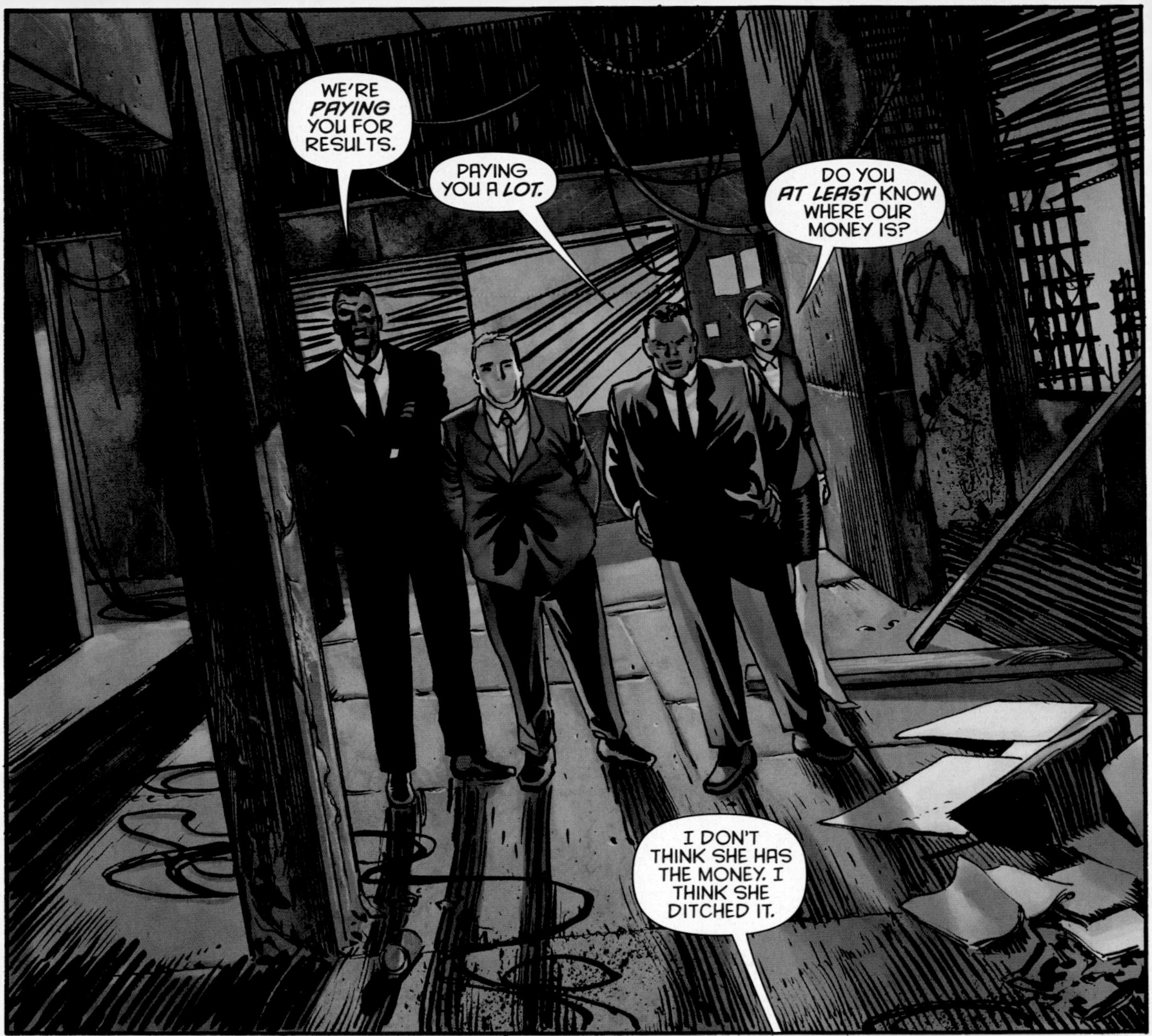
WE'RE *PAYING* YOU FOR RESULTS.
PAYING YOU A *LOT.*
DO YOU *AT LEAST* KNOW WHERE OUR MONEY IS?
I DON'T THINK SHE HAS THE MONEY. I THINK SHE DITCHED IT.

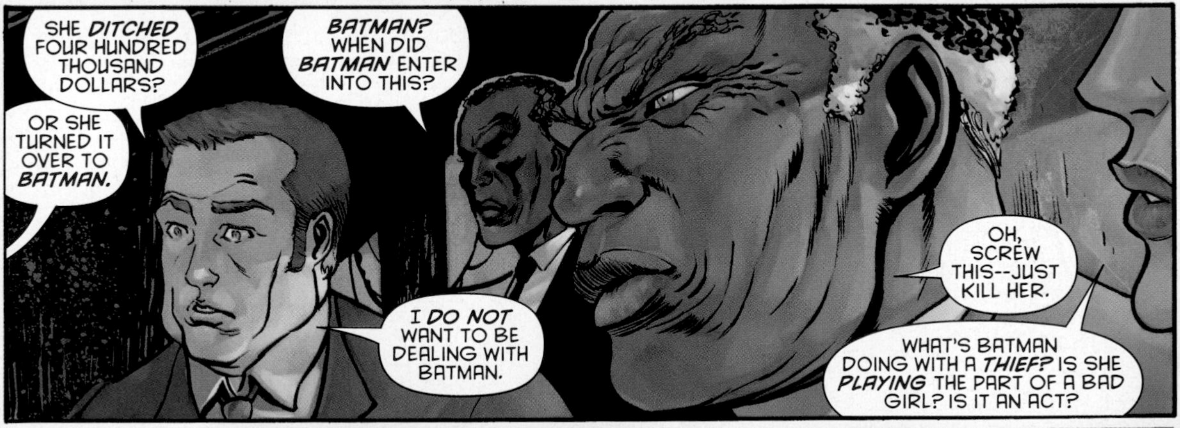
SHE *DITCHED* FOUR HUNDRED THOUSAND DOLLARS?
OR SHE TURNED IT OVER TO *BATMAN.*
BATMAN? WHEN DID *BATMAN* ENTER INTO THIS?
I *DO NOT* WANT TO BE DEALING WITH BATMAN.
OH, SCREW THIS--JUST KILL HER.
WHAT'S BATMAN DOING WITH A *THIEF?* IS SHE *PLAYING* THE PART OF A BAD GIRL? IS IT AN ACT?

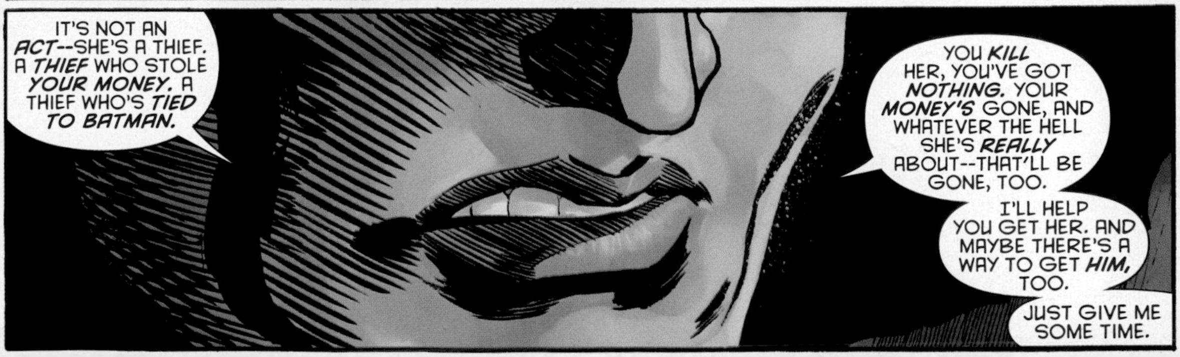
IT'S NOT AN *ACT*--SHE'S A THIEF. A *THIEF* WHO STOLE *YOUR MONEY.* A THIEF WHO'S *TIED TO BATMAN.*
YOU *KILL* HER, YOU'VE GOT *NOTHING.* YOUR *MONEY'S* GONE, AND WHATEVER THE HELL SHE'S *REALLY* ABOUT--THAT'LL BE GONE, TOO.
I'LL HELP YOU GET HER. AND MAYBE THERE'S A WAY TO GET *HIM,* TOO.
JUST GIVE ME SOME TIME.

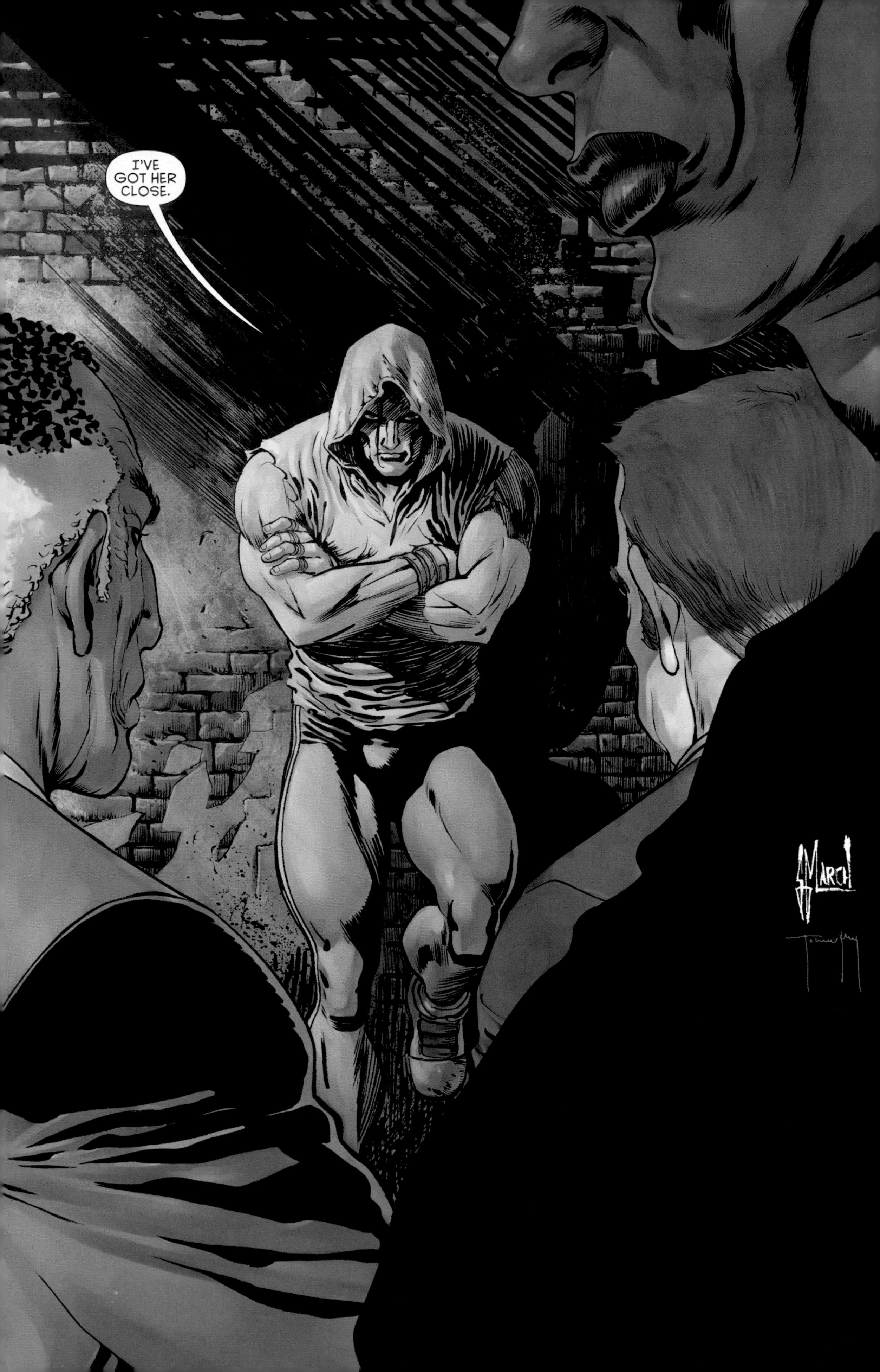
I'VE GOT HER CLOSE.

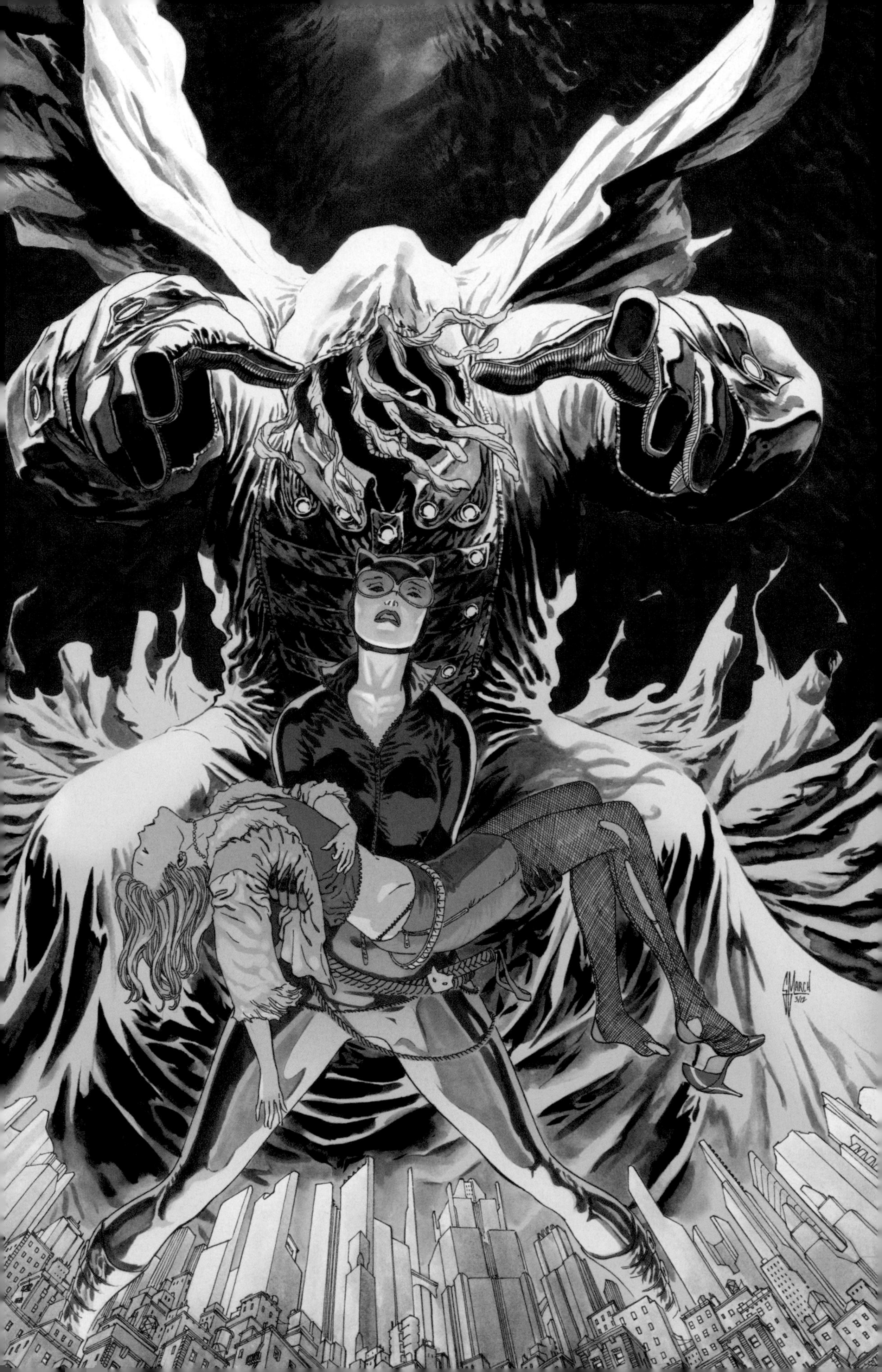
MARCH
3/12

JUDD WINICK writer **ADRIANA MELLO** penciller **JÚLIO FERREIRA** inker

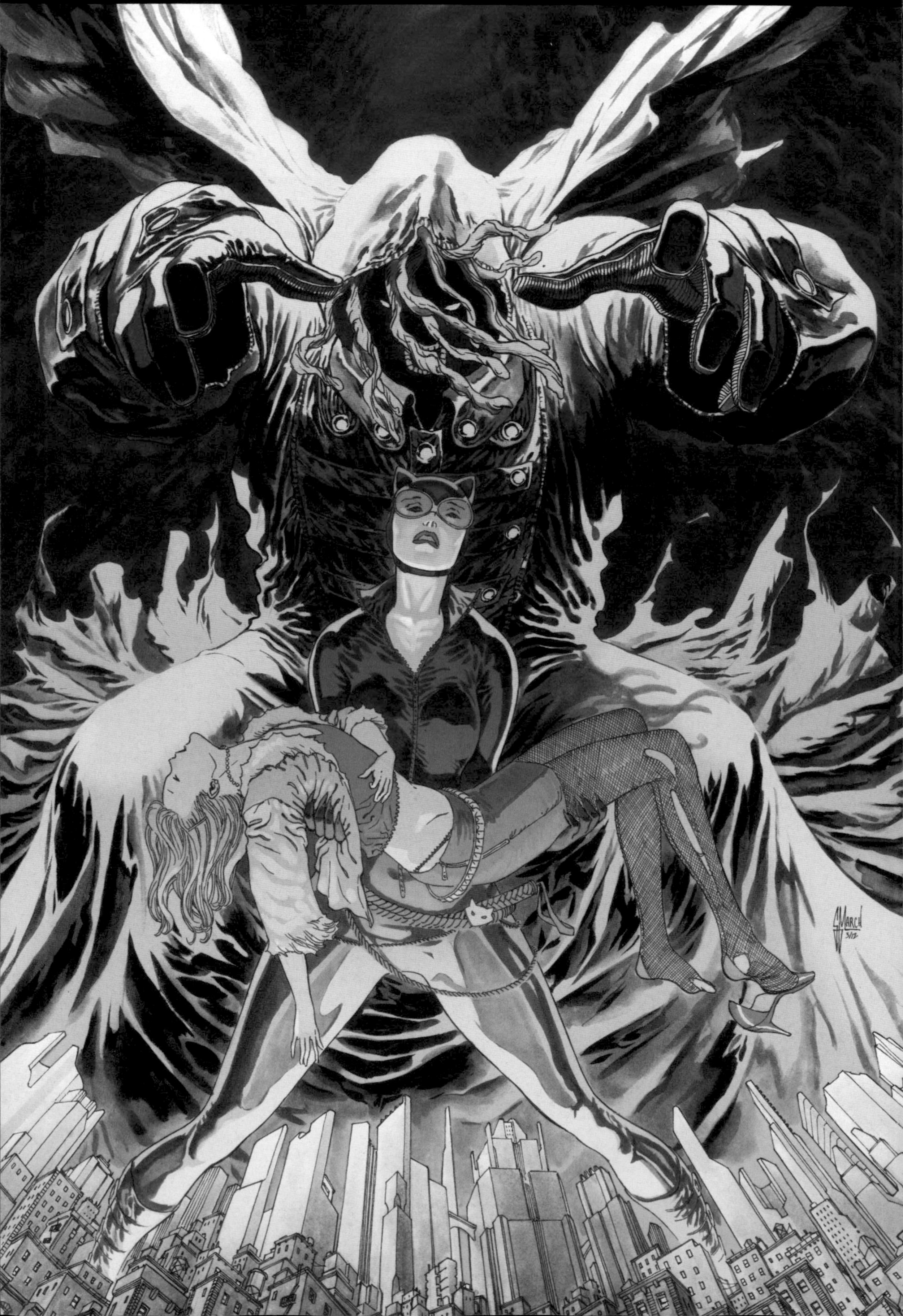

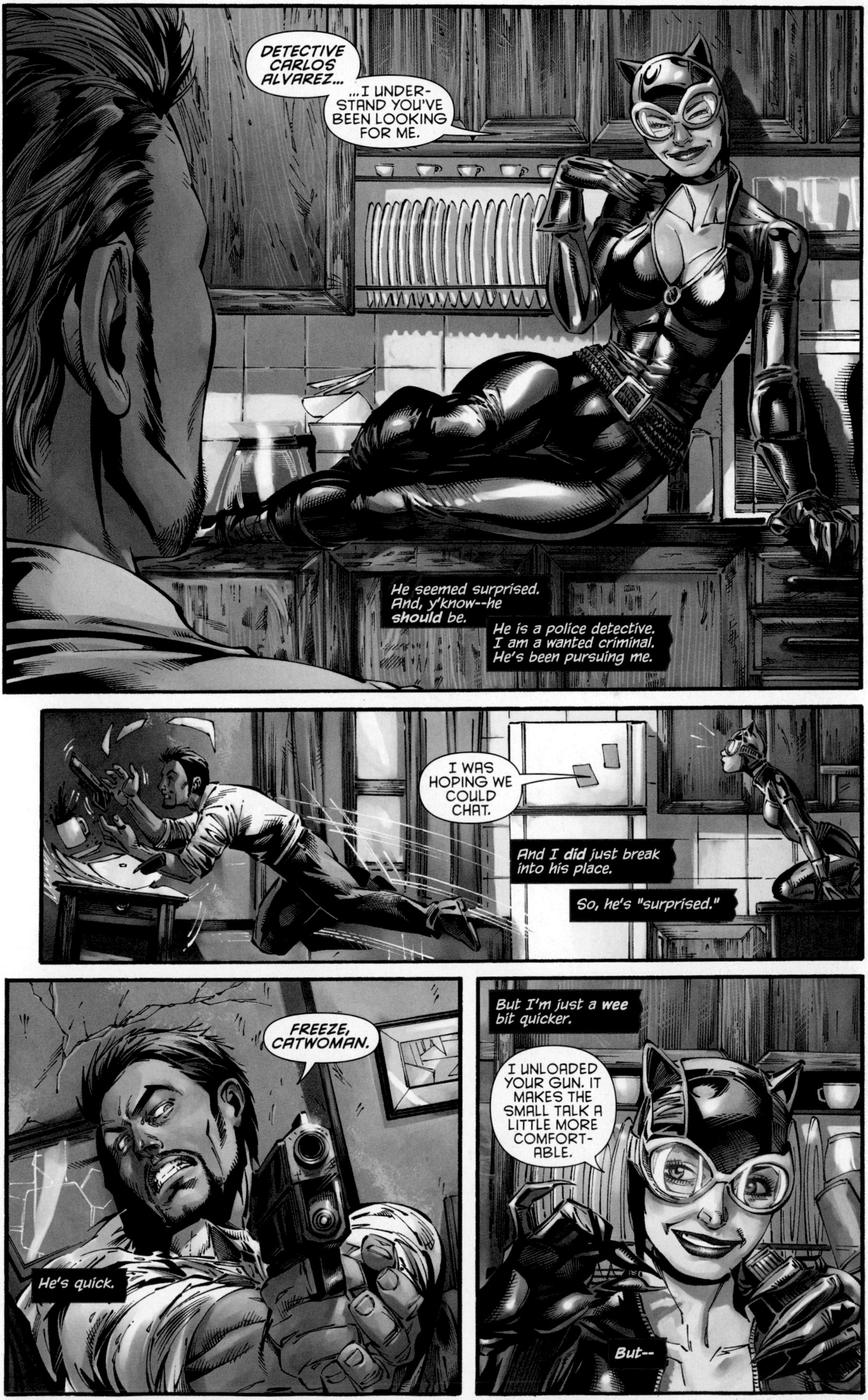
DETECTIVE CARLOS ALVAREZ...
...I UNDERSTAND YOU'VE BEEN LOOKING FOR ME.
He seemed surprised. And, y'know--he should be.
He is a police detective. I am a wanted criminal. He's been pursuing me.
I WAS HOPING WE COULD CHAT.
And I did just break into his place.
So, he's "surprised."
FREEZE, CATWOMAN.
He's quick.
But I'm just a wee bit quicker.
I UNLOADED YOUR GUN. IT MAKES THE SMALL TALK A LITTLE MORE COMFORTABLE.
But--

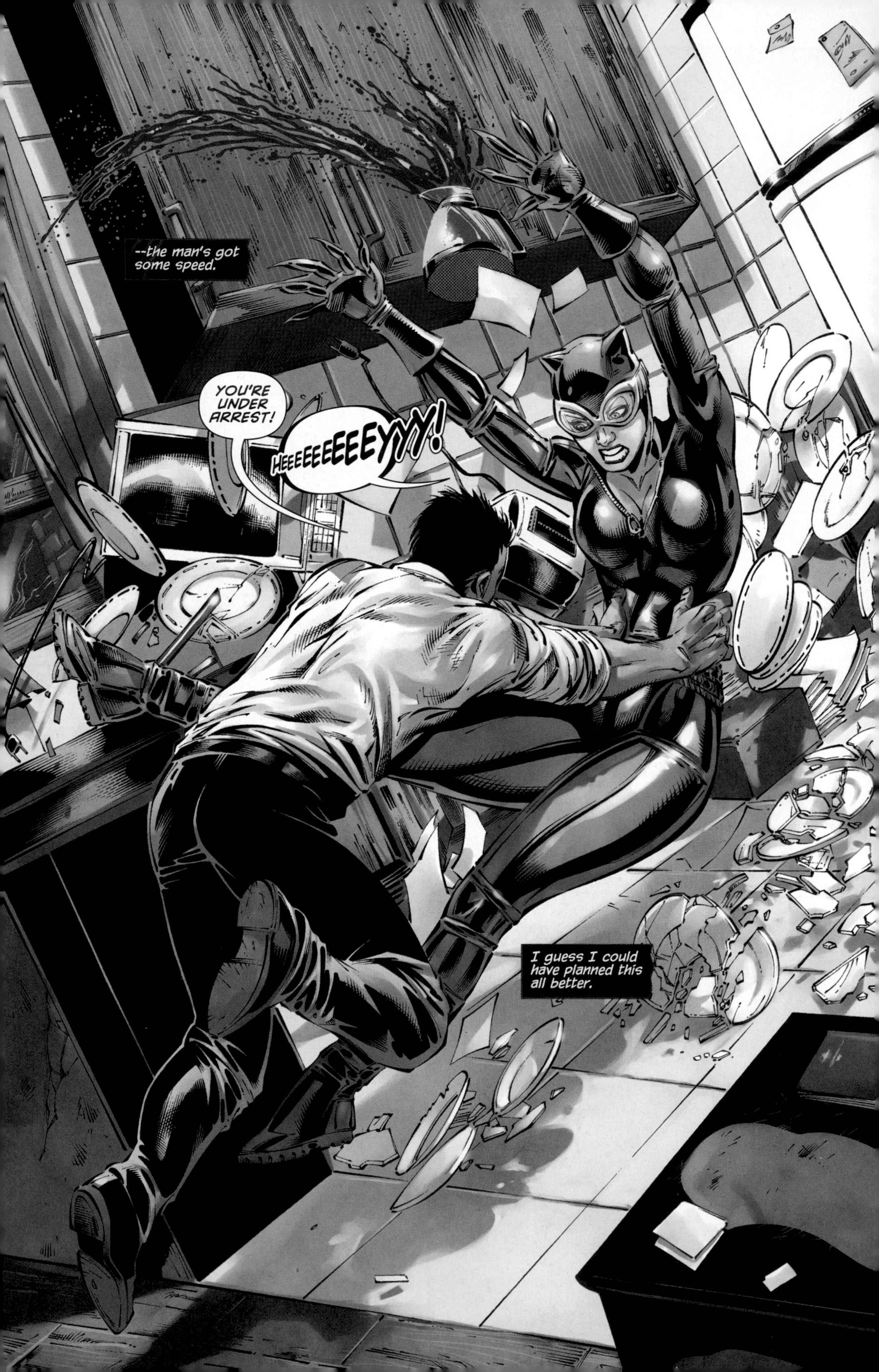
--the man's got some speed.
YOU'RE UNDER ARREST!
HEEEEEEEEEYYYY!
I guess I could have planned this all better.

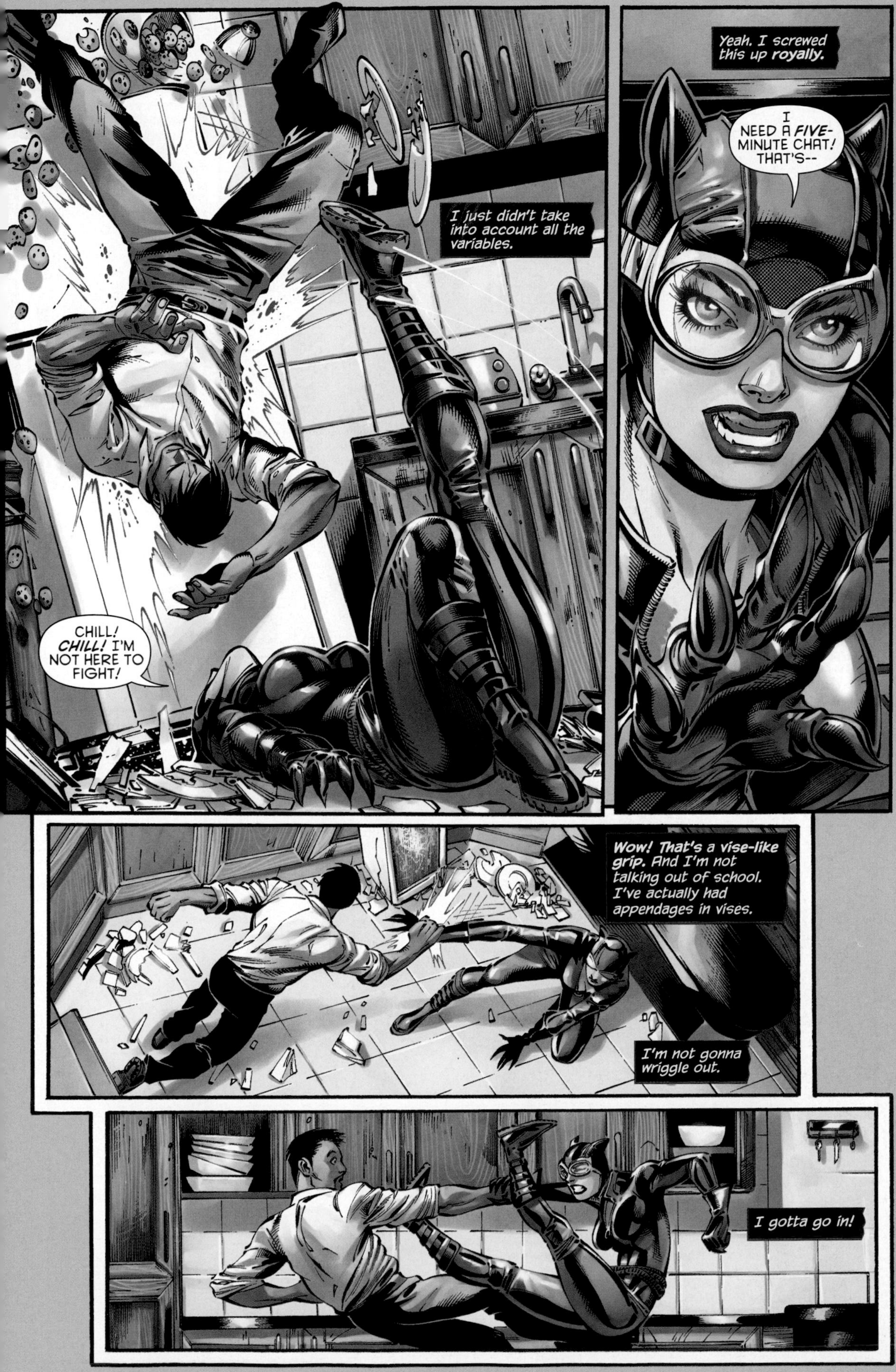
I just didn't take into account all the variables.
CHILL! CHILL! I'M NOT HERE TO FIGHT!
Yeah. I screwed this up royally.
I NEED A FIVE-MINUTE CHAT! THAT'S--
Wow! That's a vise-like grip. And I'm not talking out of school. I've actually had appendages in vises.
I'm not gonna wriggle out.
I gotta go in!

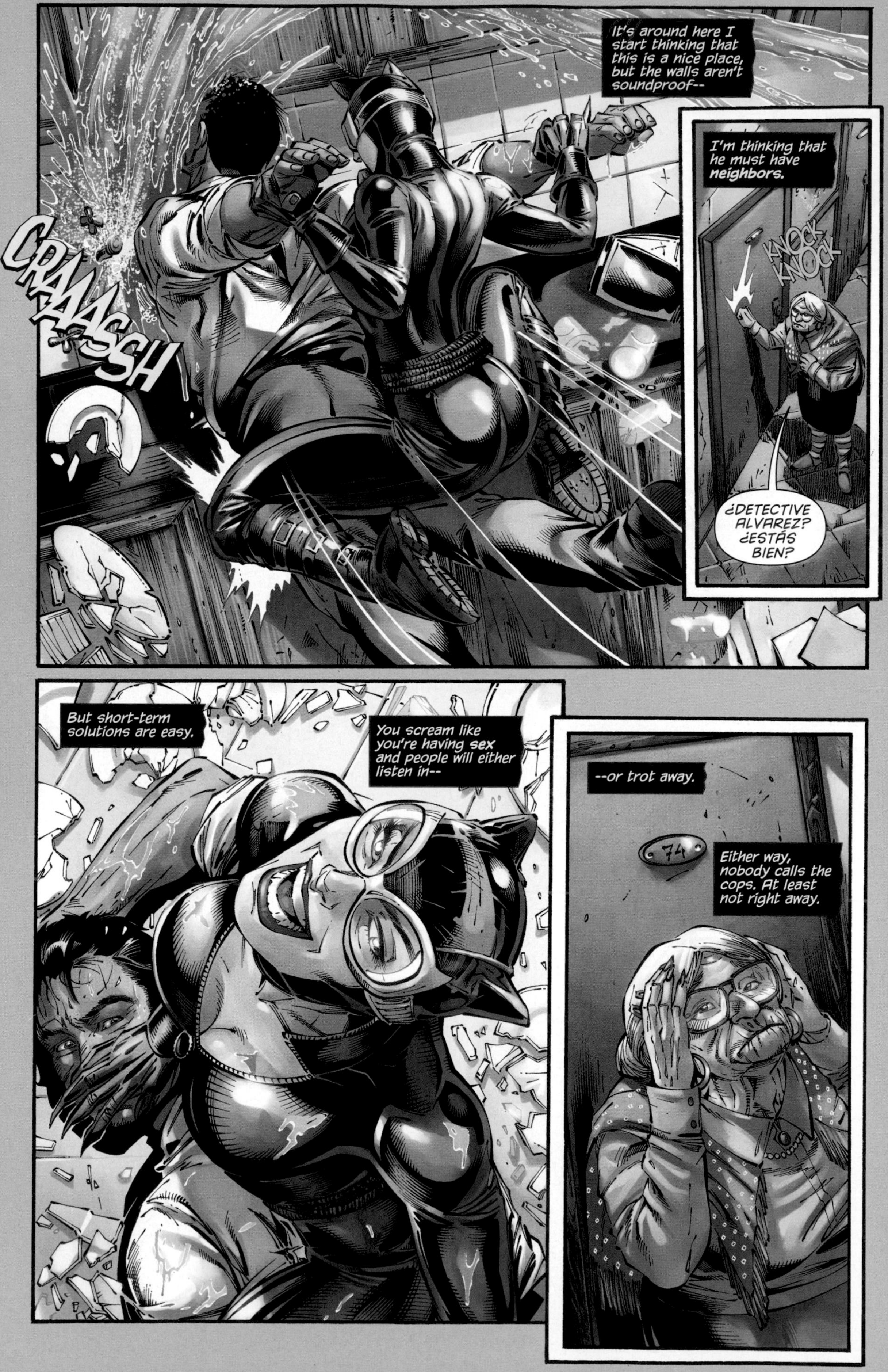

It's around here I start thinking that this is a nice place, but the walls aren't soundproof--
CRAAASSH
I'm thinking that he must have neighbors.
KNOCK KNOCK
¿DETECTIVE ALVAREZ? ¿ESTÁS BIEN?
But short-term solutions are easy.
You scream like you're having sex and people will either listen in--
--or trot away.
74
Either way, nobody calls the cops. At least not right away.

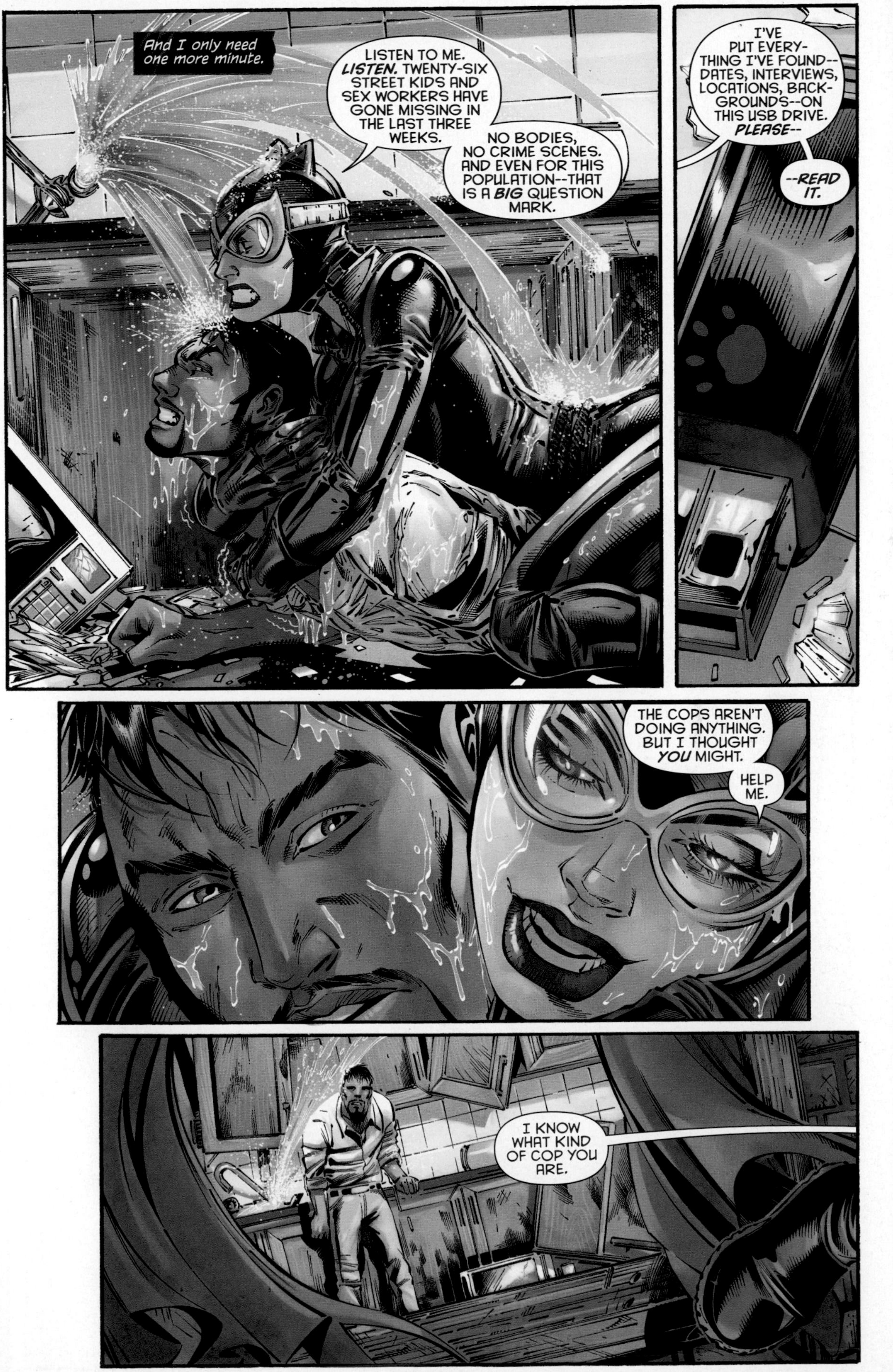
And I only need one more minute.
LISTEN TO ME. LISTEN. TWENTY-SIX STREET KIDS AND SEX WORKERS HAVE GONE MISSING IN THE LAST THREE WEEKS.
NO BODIES, NO CRIME SCENES. AND EVEN FOR THIS POPULATION--THAT IS A BIG QUESTION MARK.
I'VE PUT EVERYTHING I'VE FOUND--DATES, INTERVIEWS, LOCATIONS, BACKGROUNDS--ON THIS USB DRIVE. PLEASE--
--READ IT.
THE COPS AREN'T DOING ANYTHING. BUT I THOUGHT YOU MIGHT.
HELP ME.
I KNOW WHAT KIND OF COP YOU ARE.

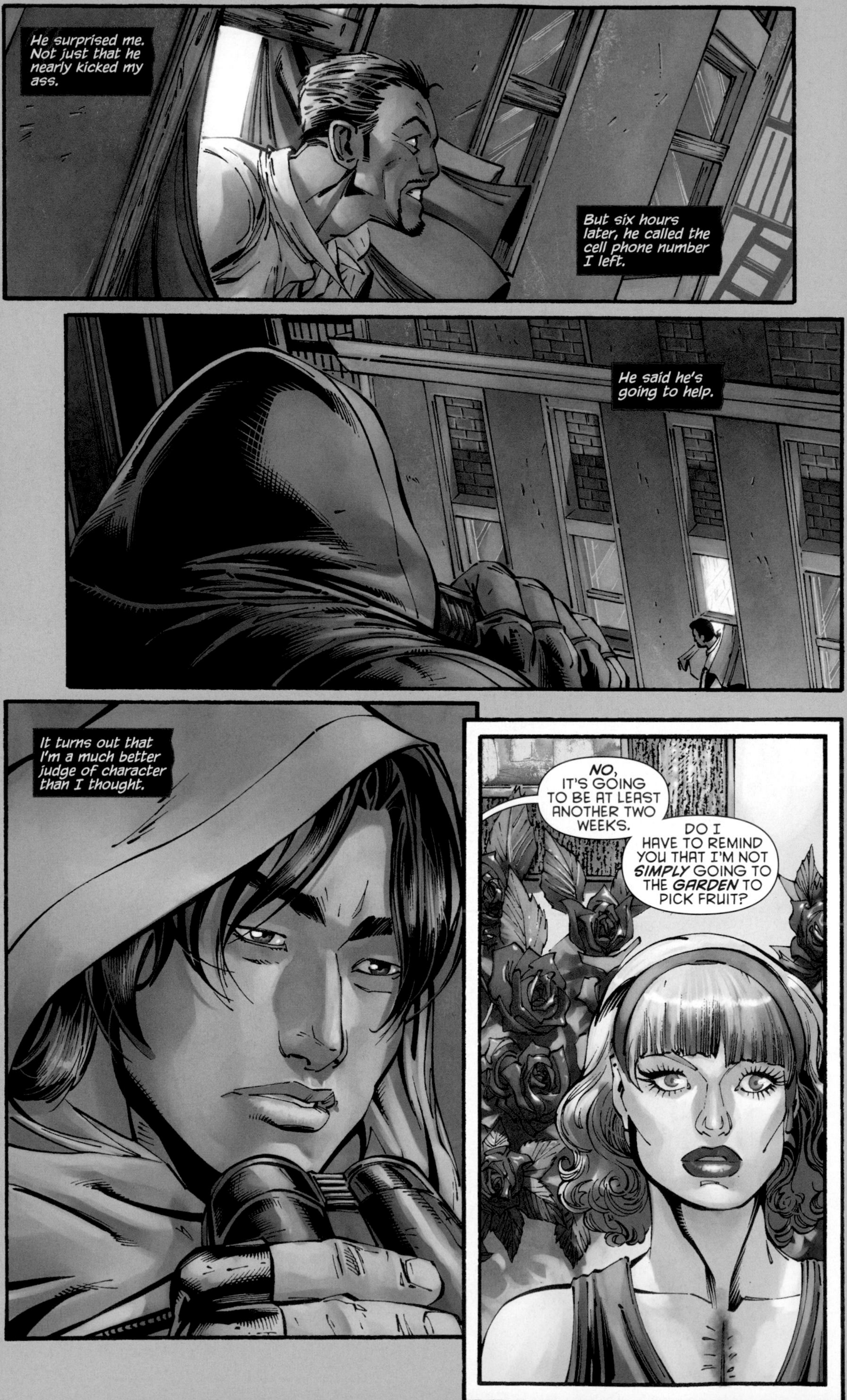

He surprised me. Not just that he nearly kicked my ass.
But six hours later, he called the cell phone number I left.
He said he's going to help.
It turns out that I'm a much better judge of character than I thought.
NO, IT'S GOING TO BE AT LEAST ANOTHER TWO WEEKS.
DO I HAVE TO REMIND YOU THAT I'M NOT SIMPLY GOING TO THE GARDEN TO PICK FRUIT?

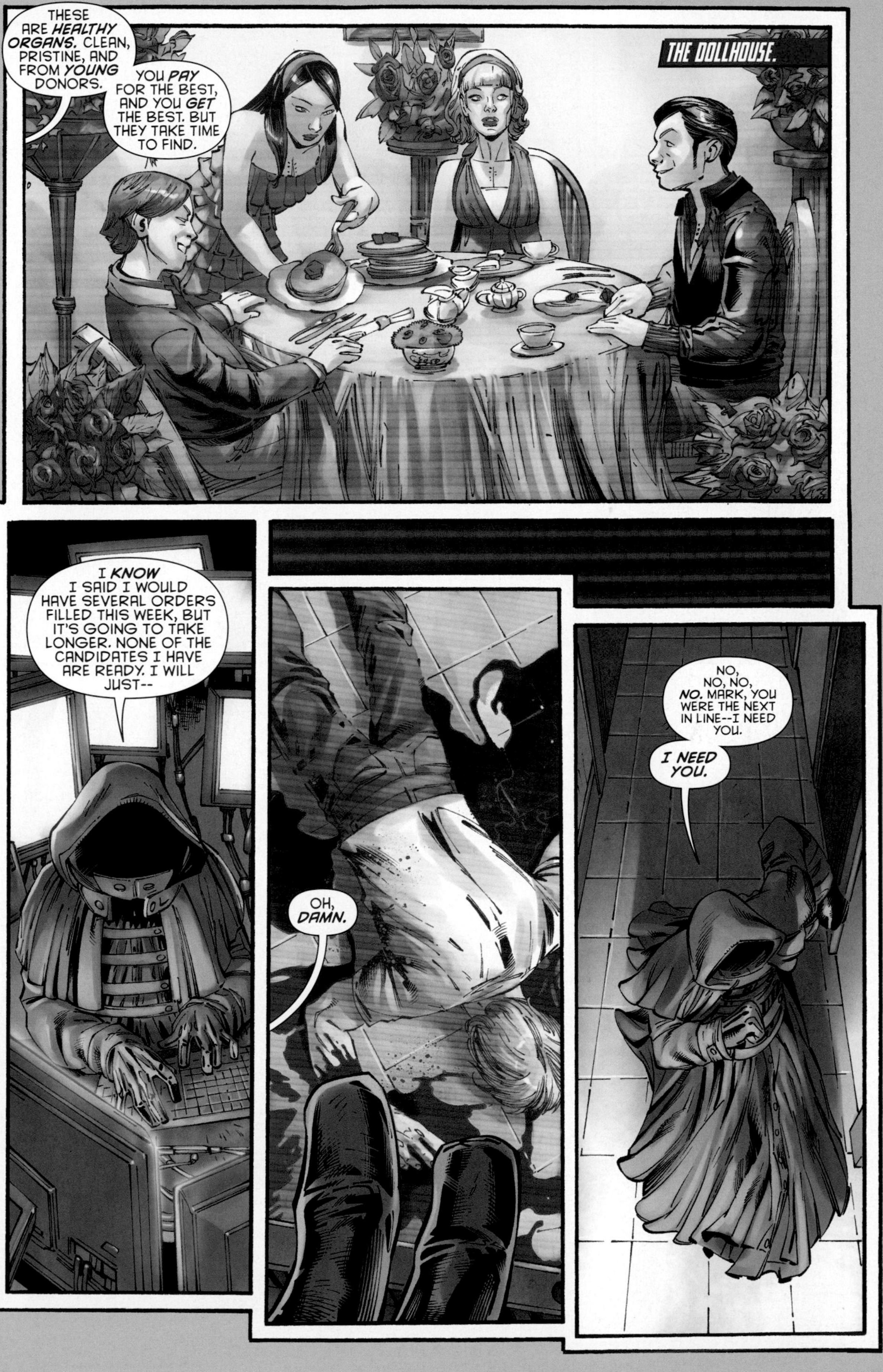
THE DOLLHOUSE.
THESE ARE HEALTHY ORGANS. CLEAN, PRISTINE, AND FROM YOUNG DONORS.
YOU PAY FOR THE BEST, AND YOU GET THE BEST. BUT THEY TAKE TIME TO FIND.
I KNOW I SAID I WOULD HAVE SEVERAL ORDERS FILLED THIS WEEK, BUT IT'S GOING TO TAKE LONGER. NONE OF THE CANDIDATES I HAVE ARE READY. I WILL JUST--
OH, DAMN.
NO, NO, NO, NO. MARK, YOU WERE THE NEXT IN LINE--I NEED YOU.
I NEED YOU.

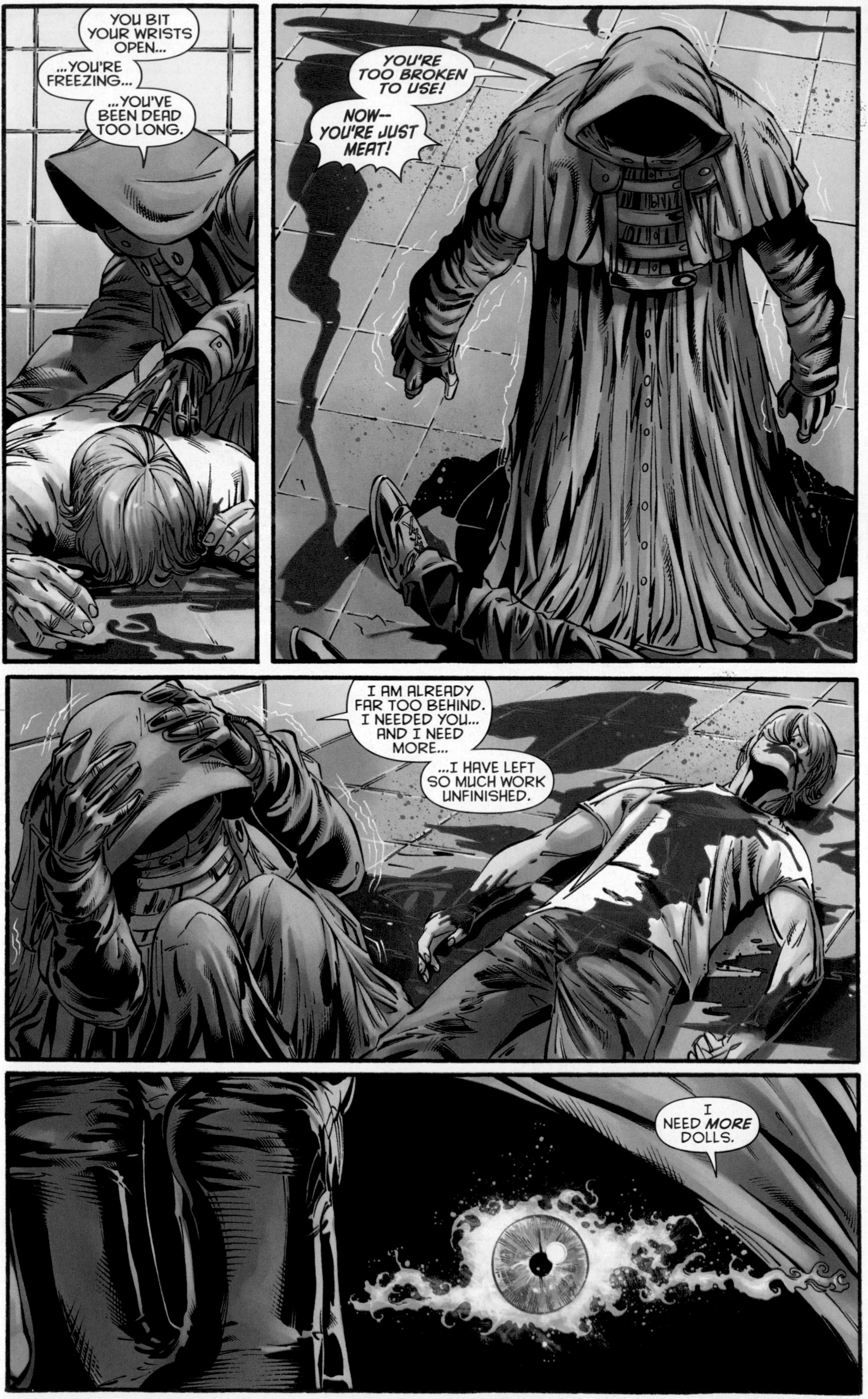
YOU BIT YOUR WRISTS OPEN...
...YOU'RE FREEZING...
...YOU'VE BEEN DEAD TOO LONG.
YOU'RE TOO BROKEN TO USE!
NOW-- YOU'RE JUST MEAT!
I AM ALREADY FAR TOO BEHIND. I NEEDED YOU... AND I NEED MORE...
...I HAVE LEFT SO MUCH WORK UNFINISHED.
I NEED MORE DOLLS.

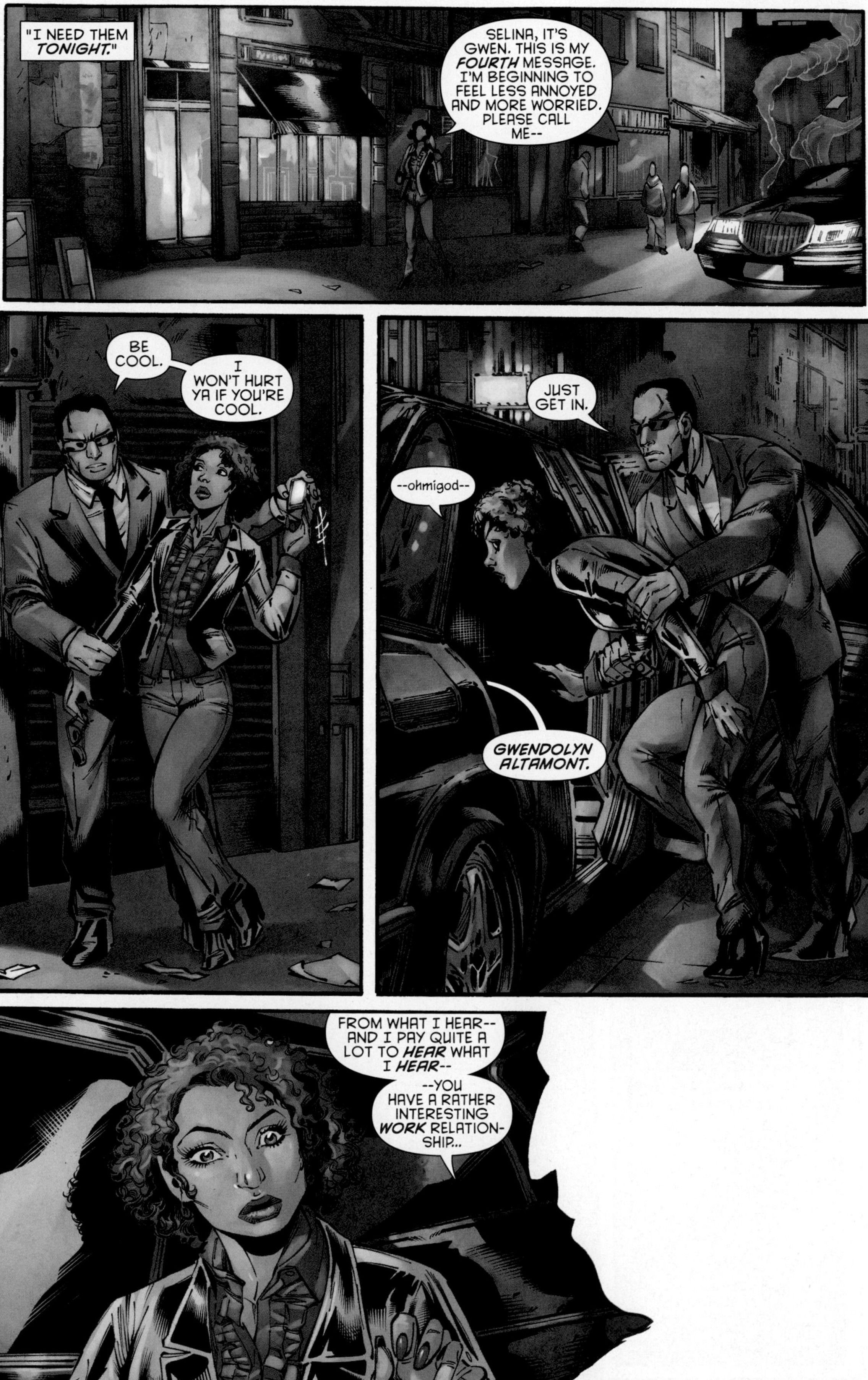
"I NEED THEM TONIGHT."
SELINA, IT'S GWEN. THIS IS MY FOURTH MESSAGE. I'M BEGINNING TO FEEL LESS ANNOYED AND MORE WORRIED. PLEASE CALL ME--
BE COOL.
I WON'T HURT YA IF YOU'RE COOL.
JUST GET IN.
--ohmigod--
GWENDOLYN ALTAMONT.
FROM WHAT I HEAR-- AND I PAY QUITE A LOT TO HEAR WHAT I HEAR--
--YOU HAVE A RATHER INTERESTING WORK RELATION-SHIP...

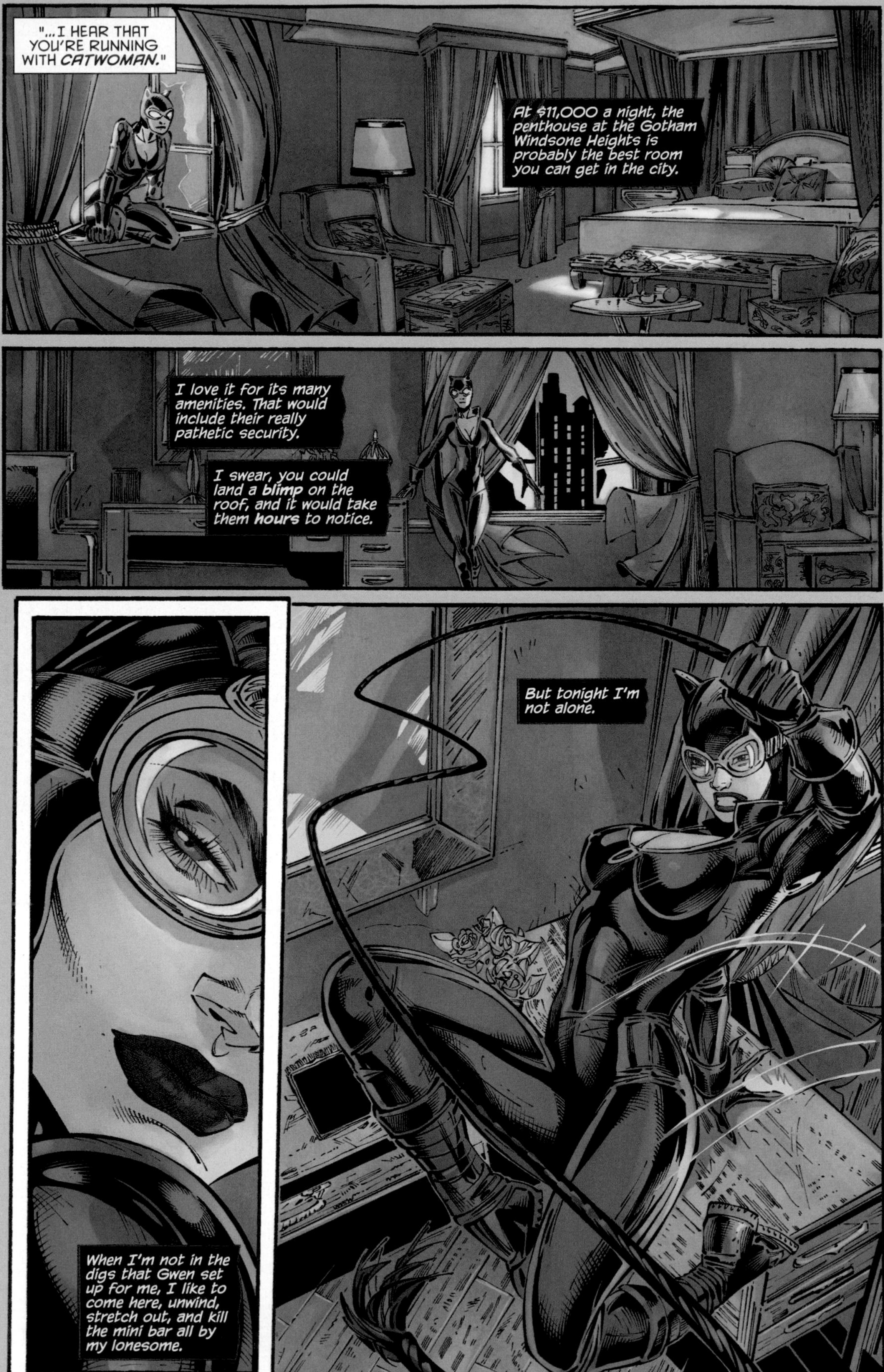
"...I HEAR THAT YOU'RE RUNNING WITH CATWOMAN."
At $11,000 a night, the penthouse at the Gotham Windsone Heights is probably the best room you can get in the city.
I love it for its many amenities. That would include their really pathetic security.
I swear, you could land a blimp on the roof, and it would take them hours to notice.
When I'm not in the digs that Gwen set up for me, I like to come here, unwind, stretch out, and kill the mini bar all by my lonesome.
But tonight I'm not alone.

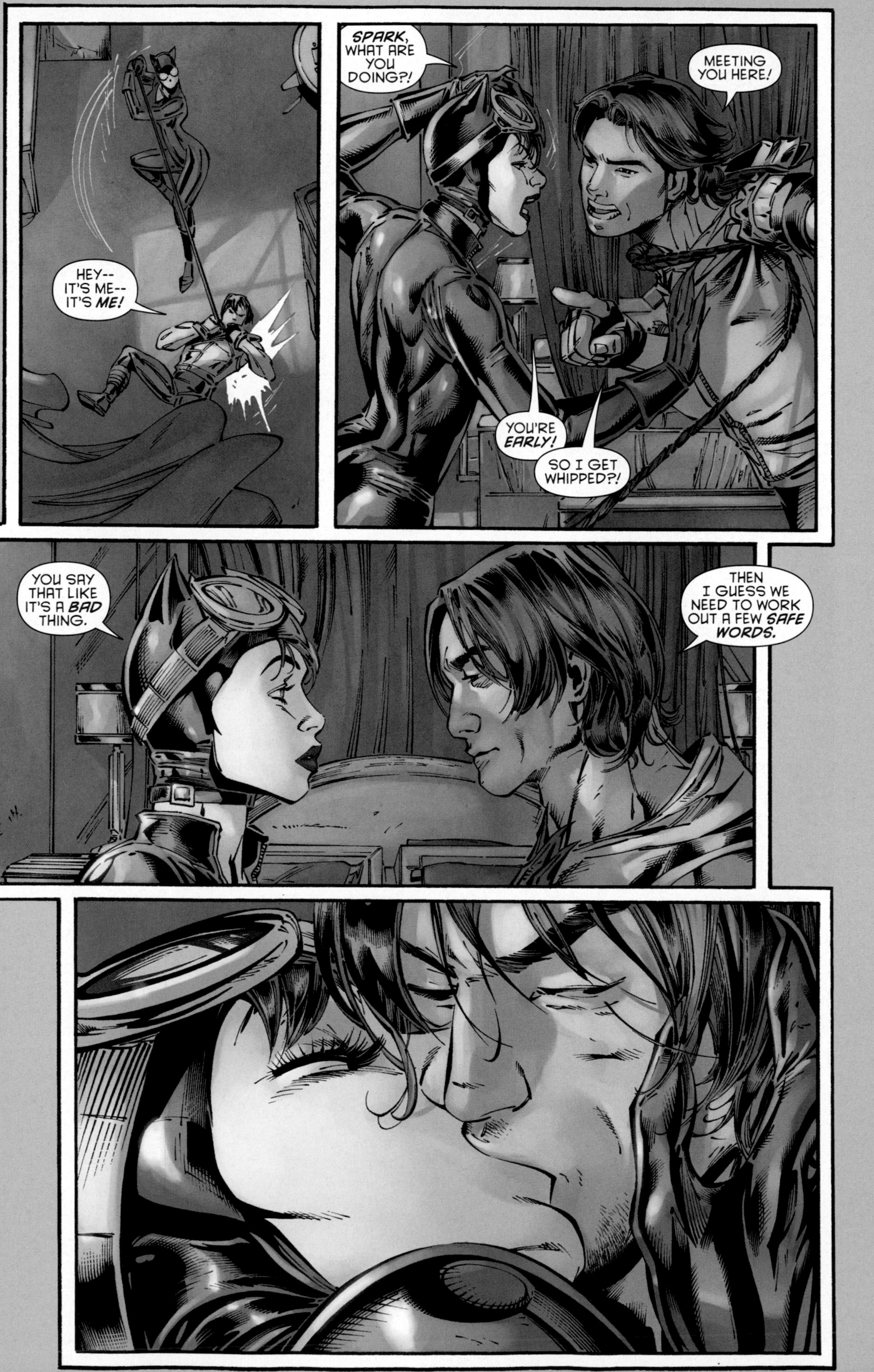
HEY-- IT'S ME-- IT'S ME!
SPARK, WHAT ARE YOU DOING?!
MEETING YOU HERE!
YOU'RE EARLY!
SO I GET WHIPPED?!
YOU SAY THAT LIKE IT'S A BAD THING.
THEN I GUESS WE NEED TO WORK OUT A FEW SAFE WORDS.

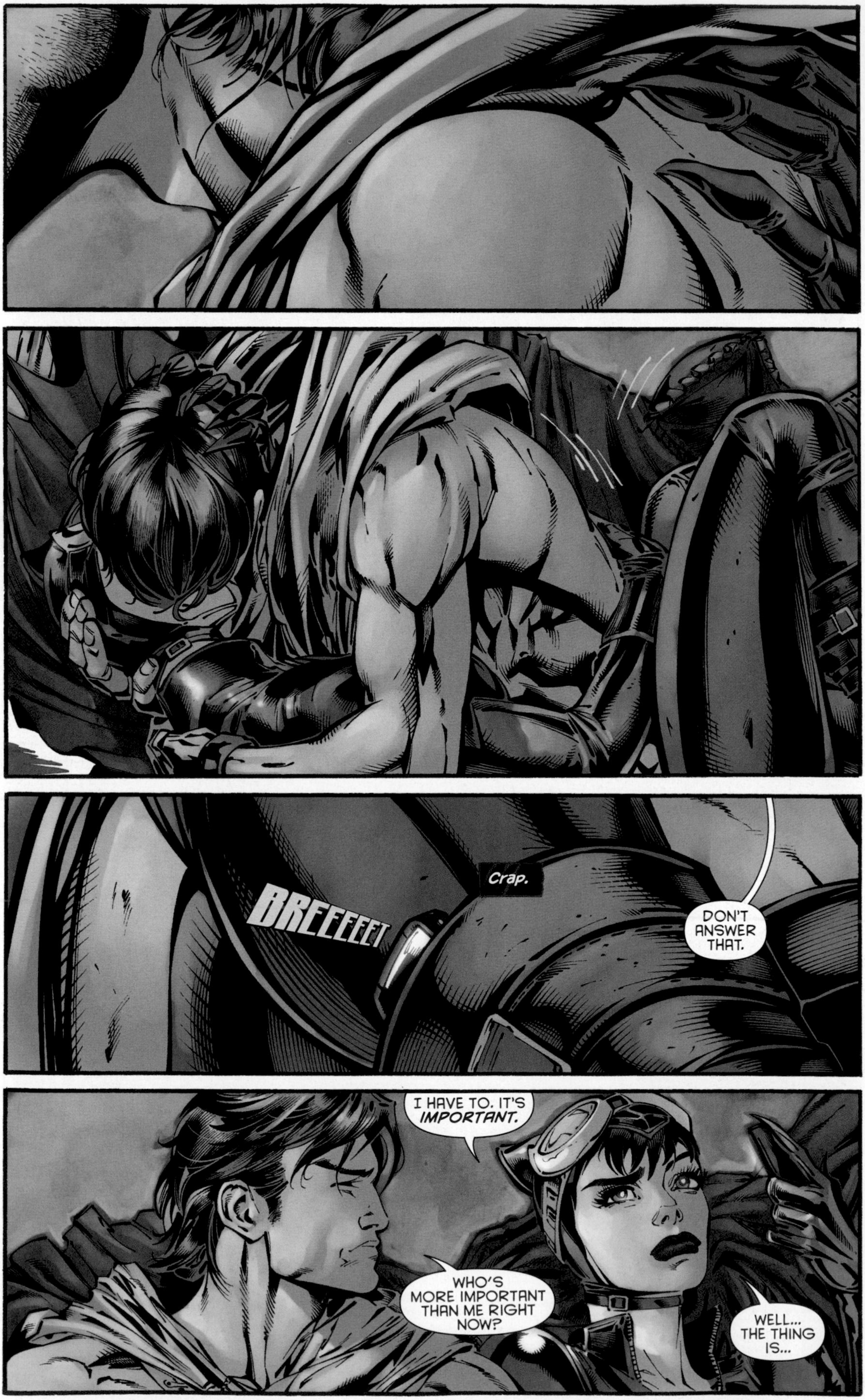
BREEEEEET
Crap.
DON'T ANSWER THAT.
I HAVE TO. IT'S *IMPORTANT.*
WHO'S MORE IMPORTANT THAN ME RIGHT NOW?
WELL... THE THING IS...

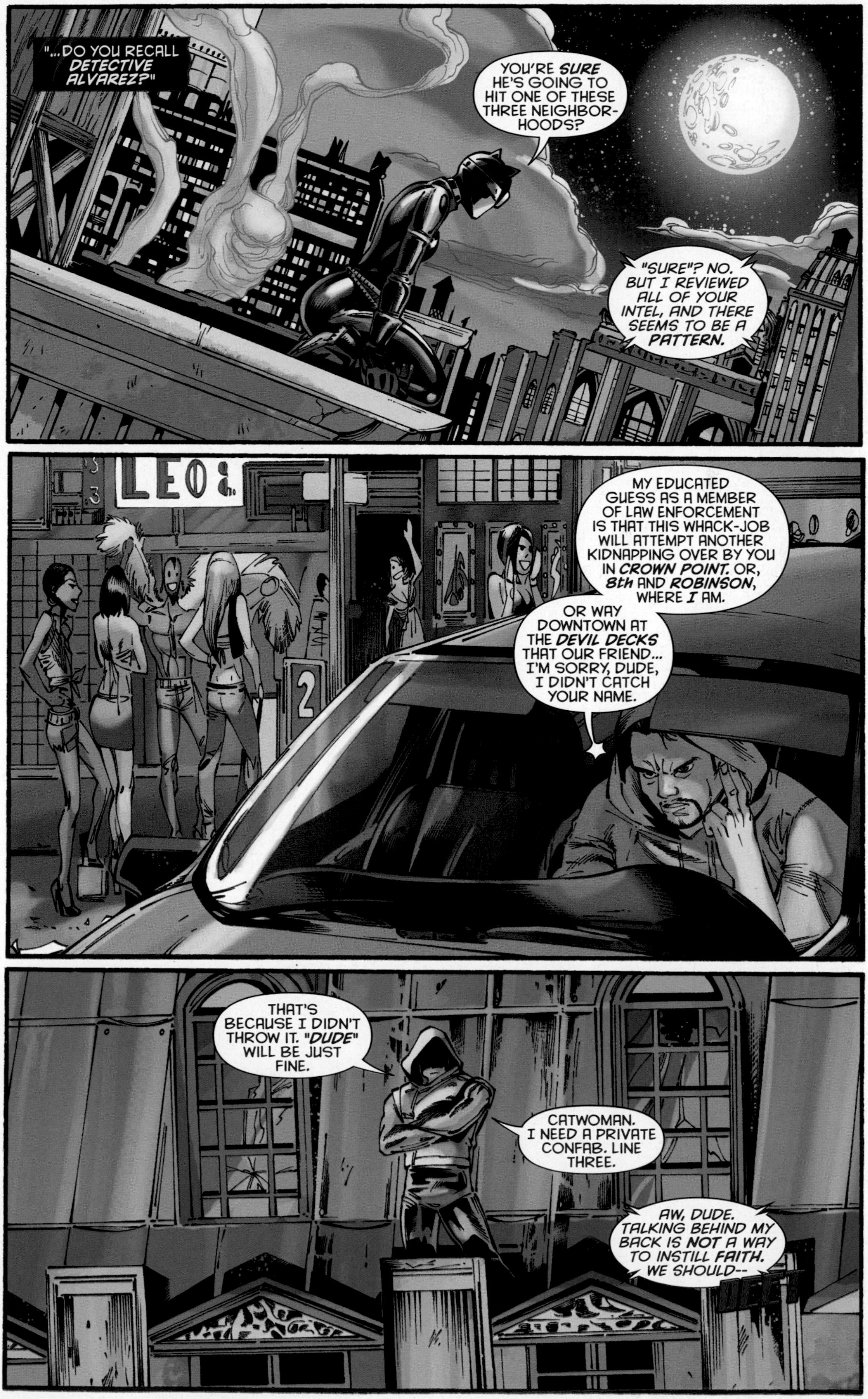
"...DO YOU RECALL DETECTIVE ALVAREZ?"
YOU'RE SURE HE'S GOING TO HIT ONE OF THESE THREE NEIGHBORHOODS?
"SURE"? NO. BUT I REVIEWED ALL OF YOUR INTEL, AND THERE SEEMS TO BE A PATTERN.
LEO
MY EDUCATED GUESS AS A MEMBER OF LAW ENFORCEMENT IS THAT THIS WHACK-JOB WILL ATTEMPT ANOTHER KIDNAPPING OVER BY YOU IN CROWN POINT. OR, 8th AND ROBINSON, WHERE I AM.
OR WAY DOWNTOWN AT THE DEVIL DECKS THAT OUR FRIEND... I'M SORRY, DUDE, I DIDN'T CATCH YOUR NAME.
THAT'S BECAUSE I DIDN'T THROW IT. "DUDE" WILL BE JUST FINE.
CATWOMAN. I NEED A PRIVATE CONFAB. LINE THREE.
AW, DUDE. TALKING BEHIND MY BACK IS NOT A WAY TO INSTILL FAITH. WE SHOULD--

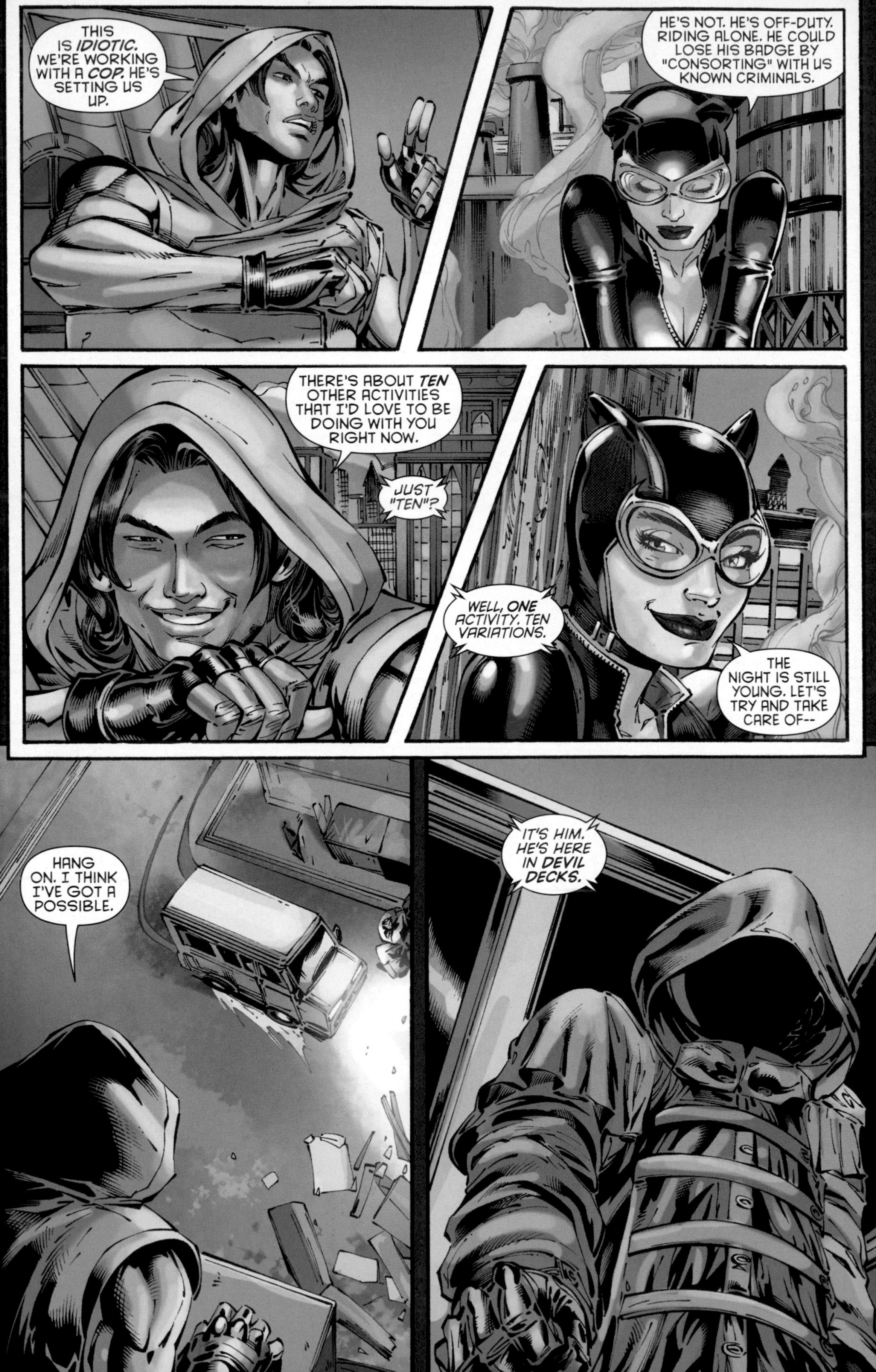
THIS IS *IDIOTIC.* WE'RE WORKING WITH A *COP.* HE'S SETTING US UP.
HE'S NOT. HE'S OFF-DUTY. RIDING ALONE. HE COULD LOSE HIS BADGE BY "CONSORTING" WITH US KNOWN CRIMINALS.
THERE'S ABOUT *TEN* OTHER ACTIVITIES THAT I'D LOVE TO BE DOING WITH YOU RIGHT NOW.
JUST "TEN"?
WELL, *ONE* ACTIVITY. TEN VARIATIONS.
THE NIGHT IS STILL YOUNG. LET'S TRY AND TAKE CARE OF--
HANG ON. I THINK I'VE GOT A POSSIBLE.
IT'S HIM. HE'S HERE IN *DEVIL DECKS.*

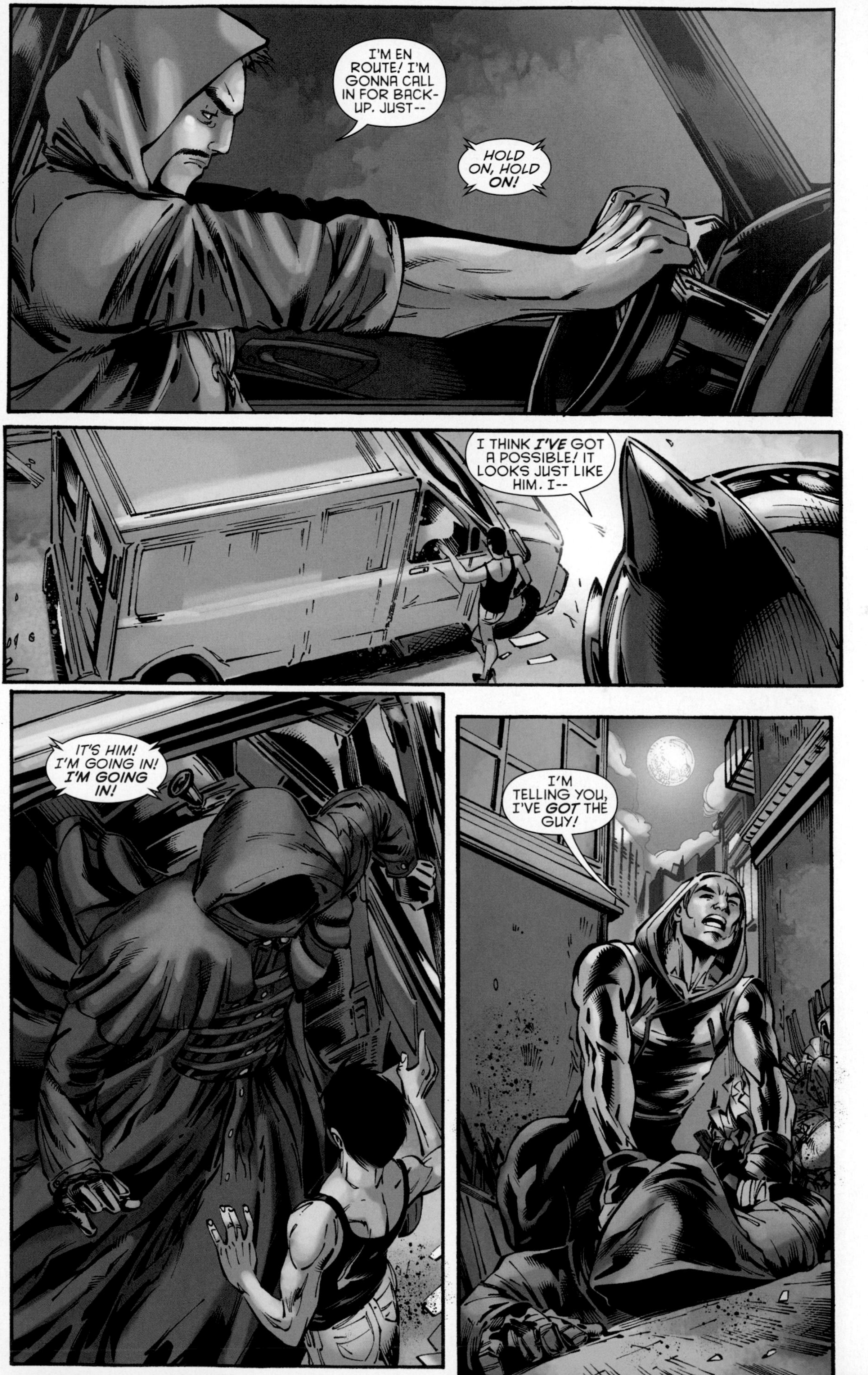
I'M EN ROUTE! I'M GONNA CALL IN FOR BACK-UP. JUST--
HOLD ON, HOLD ON!
I THINK I'VE GOT A POSSIBLE! IT LOOKS JUST LIKE HIM. I--
IT'S HIM! I'M GOING IN! I'M GOING IN!
I'M TELLING YOU, I'VE GOT THE GUY!

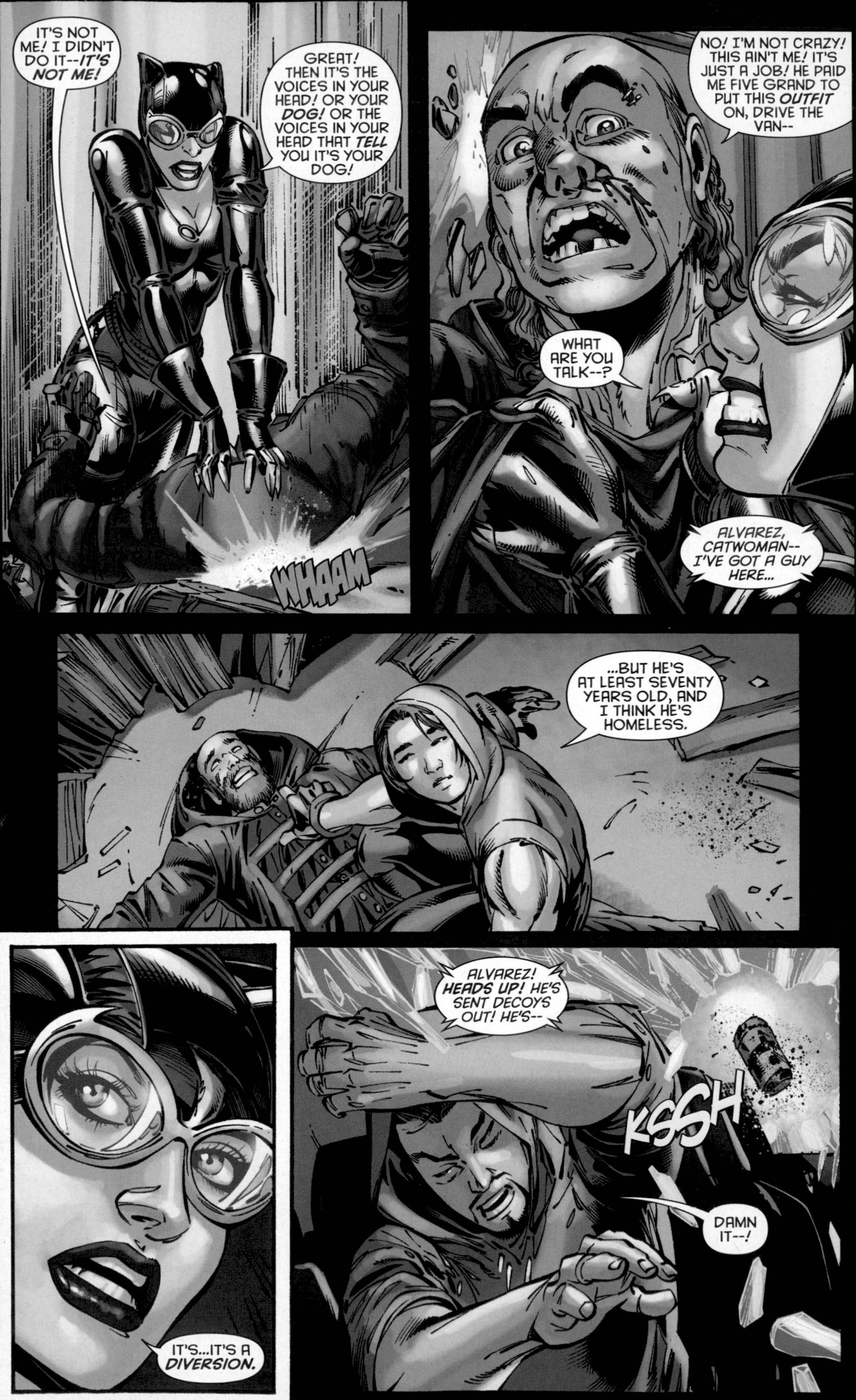
IT'S NOT ME! I DIDN'T DO IT--*IT'S NOT ME!*
GREAT! THEN IT'S THE VOICES IN YOUR HEAD! OR YOUR *DOG!* OR THE VOICES IN YOUR HEAD THAT *TELL* YOU IT'S YOUR DOG!
WHAAM
NO! I'M NOT CRAZY! THIS AIN'T ME! IT'S JUST A JOB! HE PAID ME FIVE GRAND TO PUT THIS *OUTFIT* ON, DRIVE THE VAN--
WHAT ARE YOU TALK--?
ALVAREZ, CATWOMAN-- I'VE GOT A GUY HERE...
...BUT HE'S AT LEAST SEVENTY YEARS OLD, AND I THINK HE'S HOMELESS.
IT'S...IT'S A *DIVERSION.*
ALVAREZ! *HEADS UP!* HE'S SENT DECOYS OUT! HE'S--
KSSH
DAMN IT--!

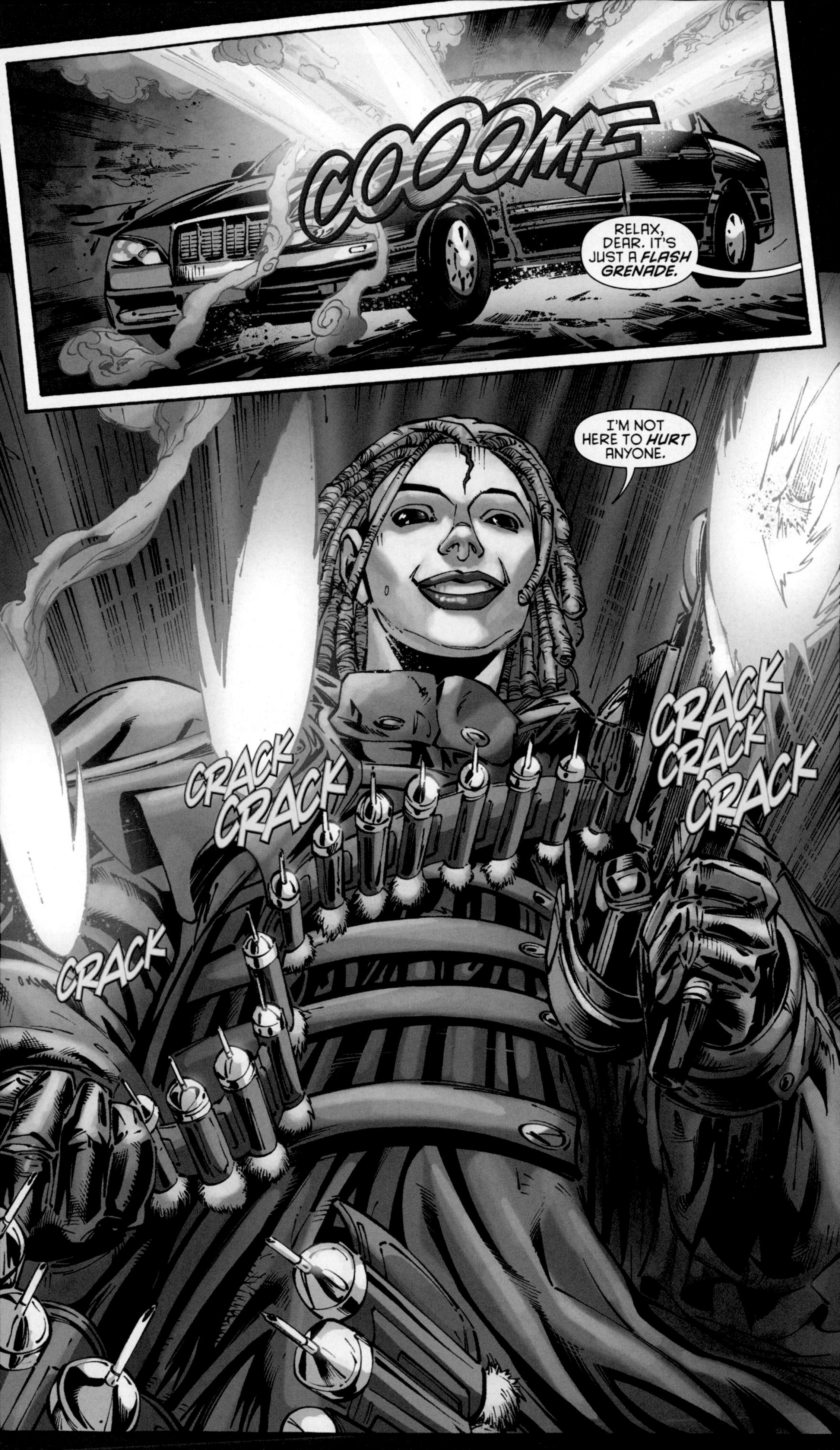
COOOMF
RELAX, DEAR. IT'S JUST A *FLASH GRENADE.*
I'M NOT HERE TO *HURT* ANYONE.
CRACK CRACK
CRACK CRACK CRACK
CRACK

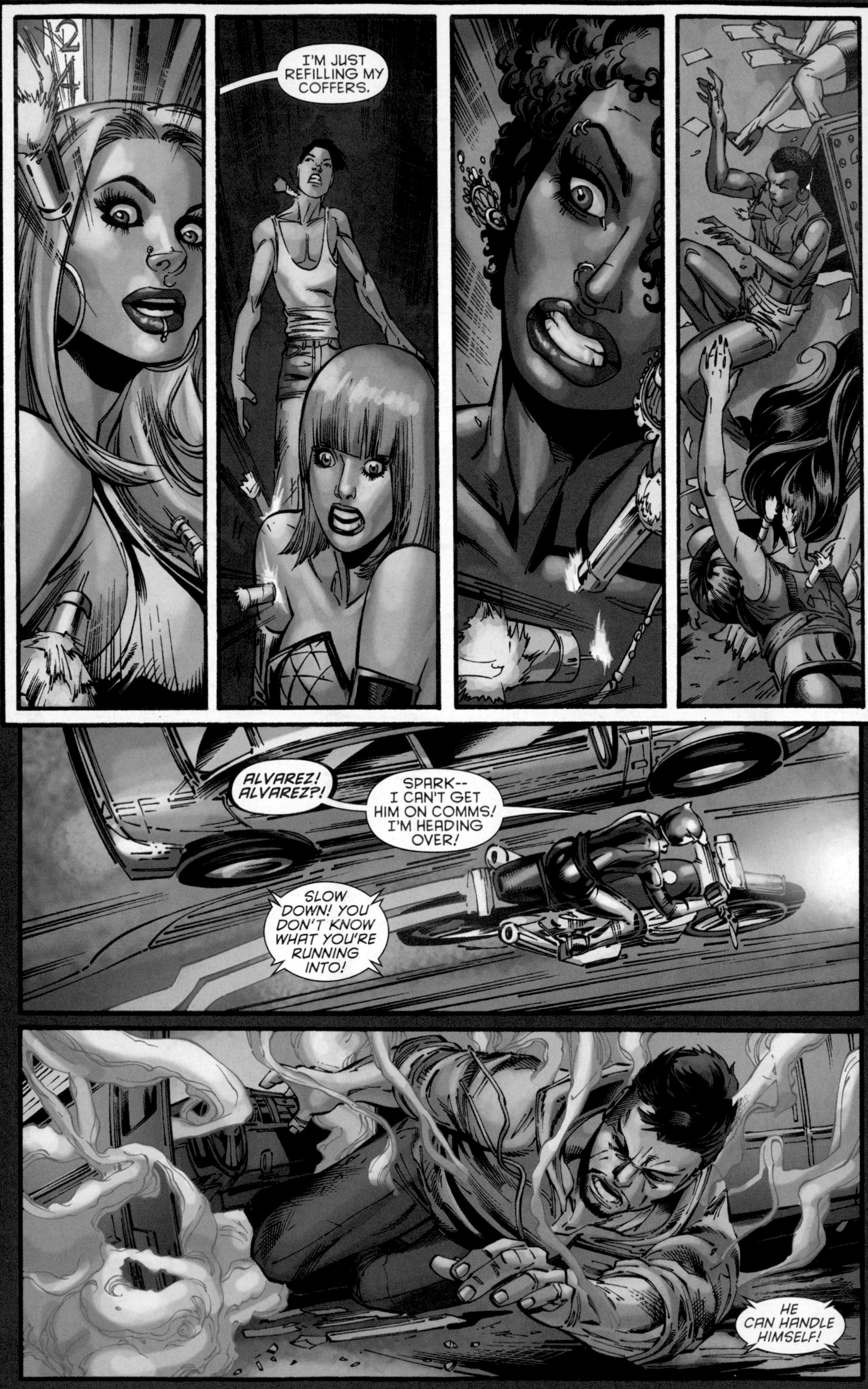
I'M JUST REFILLING MY COFFERS.
ALVAREZ! ALVAREZ?!
SPARK-- I CAN'T GET HIM ON COMMS! I'M HEADING OVER!
SLOW DOWN! YOU DON'T KNOW WHAT YOU'RE RUNNING INTO!
HE CAN HANDLE HIMSELF!

NOT AS MANY AS I'D LIKE...BUT IT'S ALL I CAN CARRY. IT WILL HAVE TO DO.

I'M ON MY WAY, CATWOMAN! WAIT FOR ME!

IT'S NOT SAFE FACING HIM ALONE! I'LL BE THERE IN JUST--

THERE'S NO TIME! I'M THREE BLOCKS AWAY! MEET ME THERE! HURRY!

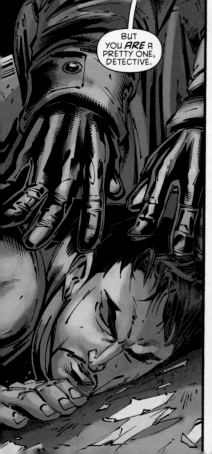

BUT YOU *ARE* A PRETTY ONE, DETECTIVE.

GOD.

I guess I could have planned this all better.

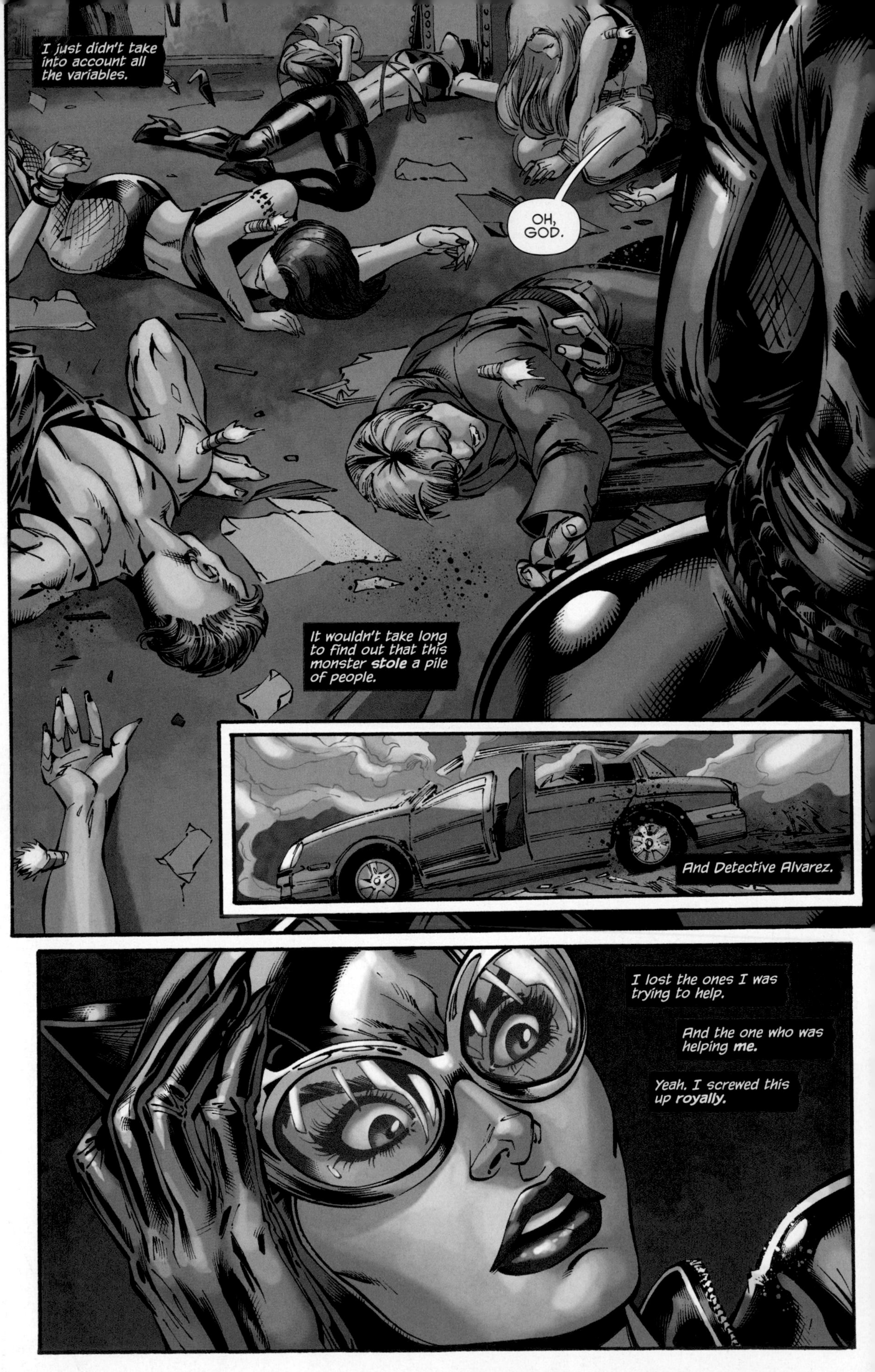

I just didn't take into account all the variables.
OH, GOD.
It wouldn't take long to find out that this monster **stole** a pile of people.
And Detective Alvarez.
I lost the ones I was trying to help.
And the one who was helping **me**.
Yeah. I screwed this up **royally**.

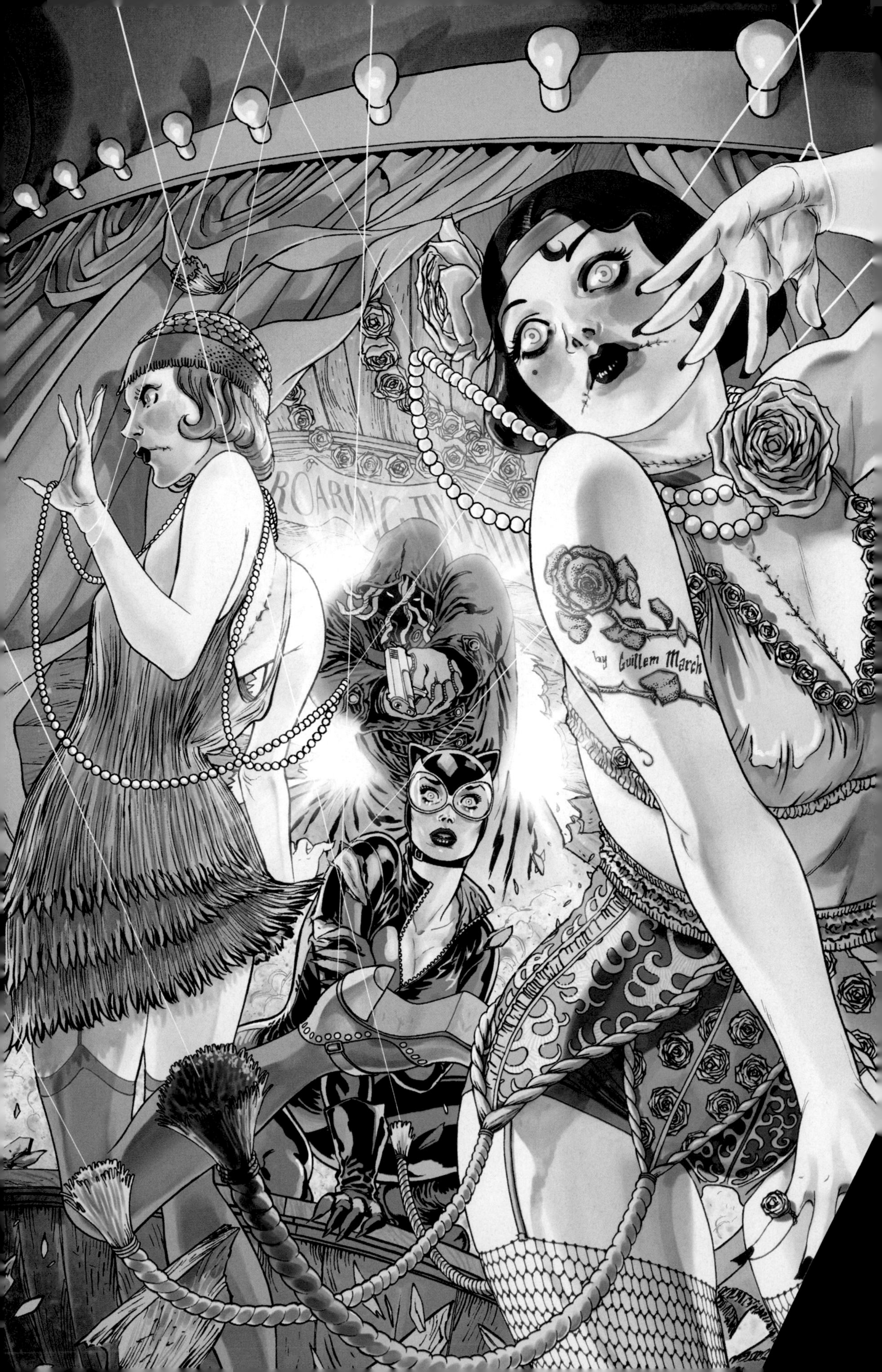
ROARING
by Guillem March

JUDD WINICK writer **ADRIANA MELO** penciller **JULIO FERREIRA** inker

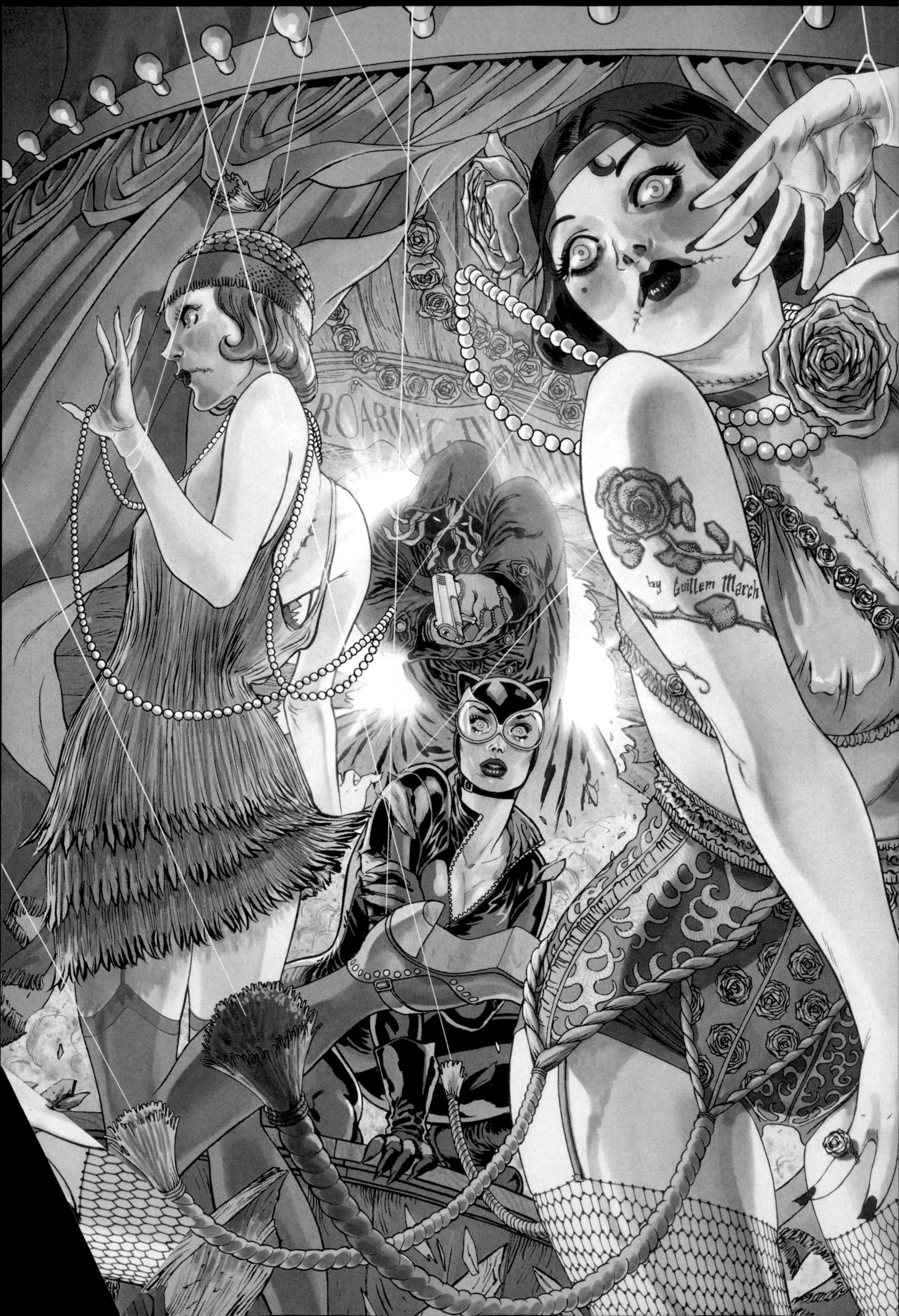
by Guillem March

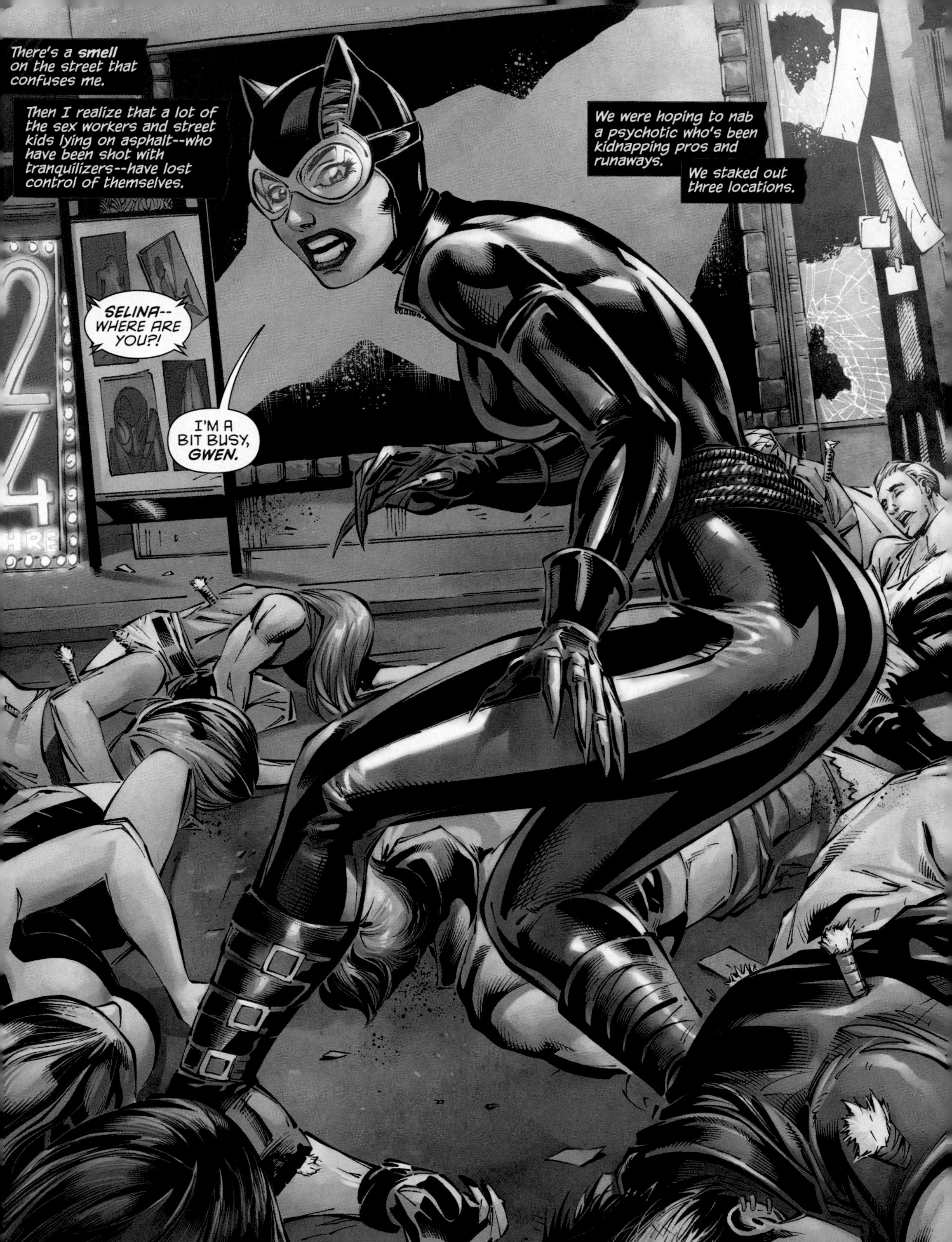
There's a smell on the street that confuses me.
Then I realize that a lot of the sex workers and street kids lying on asphalt--who have been shot with tranquilizers--have lost control of themselves.
We were hoping to nab a psychotic who's been kidnapping pros and runaways.
We staked out three locations.
SELINA-- WHERE ARE YOU?!
I'M A BIT BUSY, GWEN.

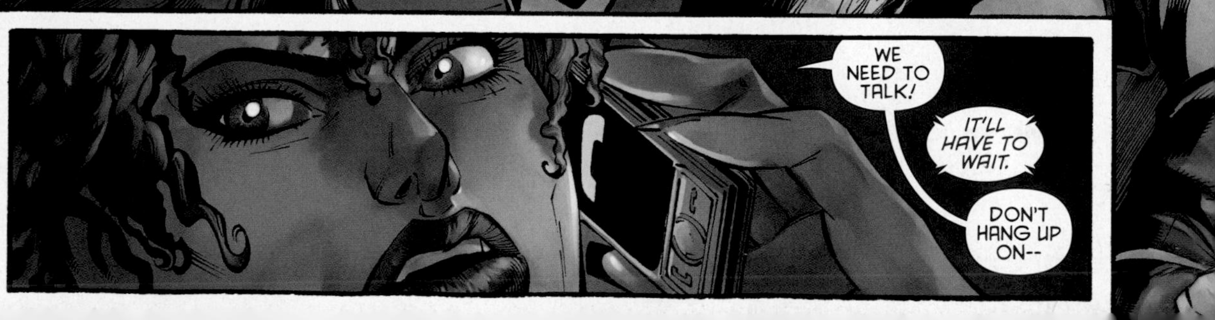
WE NEED TO TALK!
IT'LL HAVE TO WAIT.
DON'T HANG UP ON--

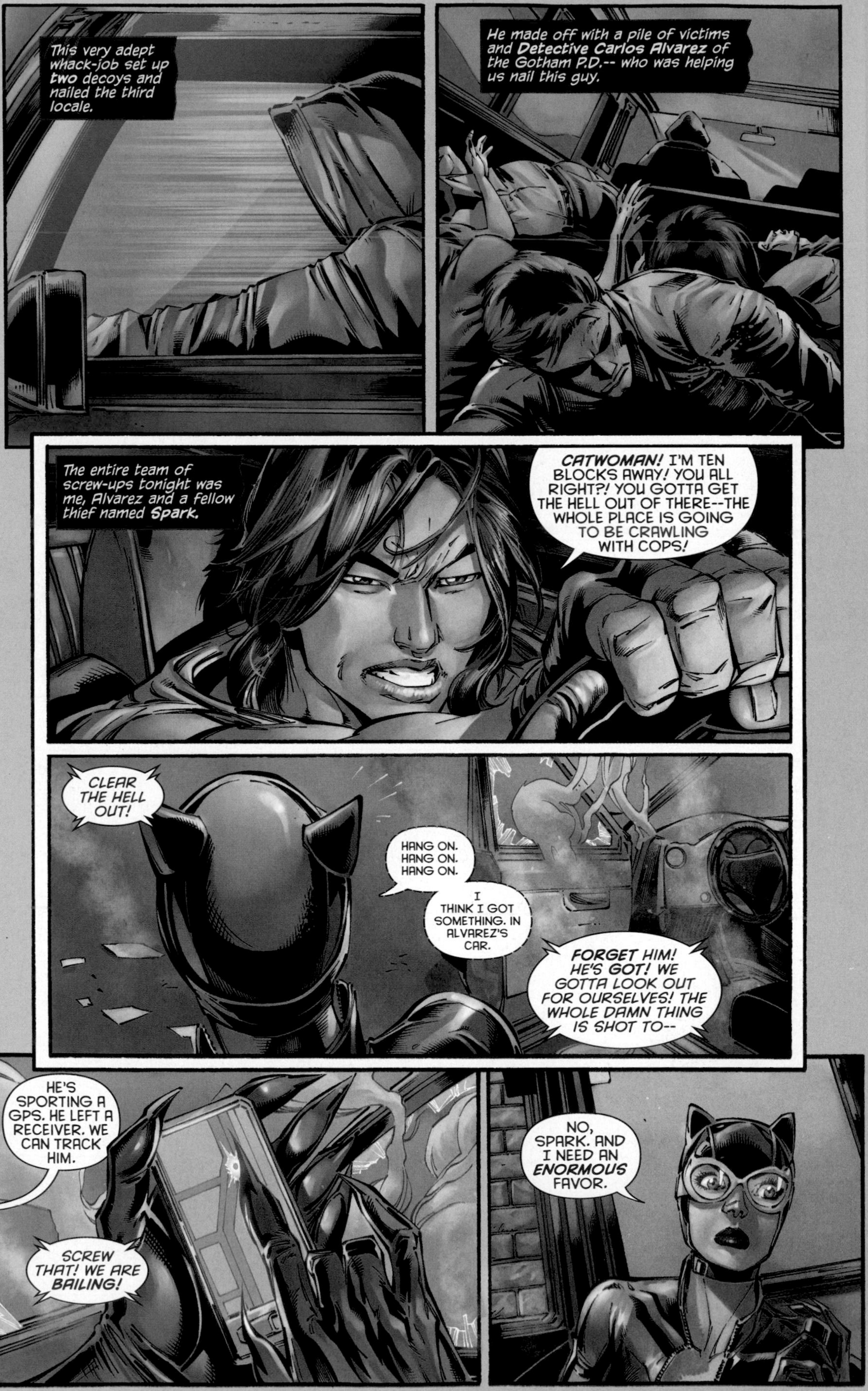

This very adept whack-job set up **two** decoys and nailed the third locale.
He made off with a pile of victims and **Detective Carlos Alvarez** of the Gotham P.D.-- who was helping us nail this guy.
The entire team of screw-ups tonight was me, Alvarez and a fellow thief named **Spark.**
CATWOMAN! I'M TEN BLOCKS AWAY! YOU ALL RIGHT?! YOU GOTTA GET THE HELL OUT OF THERE--THE WHOLE PLACE IS GOING TO BE CRAWLING WITH COPS!
CLEAR THE HELL OUT!
HANG ON. HANG ON. HANG ON.
I THINK I GOT SOMETHING. IN ALVAREZ'S CAR.
FORGET HIM! HE'S **GOT!** WE GOTTA LOOK OUT FOR OURSELVES! THE WHOLE DAMN THING IS SHOT TO--
HE'S SPORTING A GPS. HE LEFT A RECEIVER. WE CAN TRACK HIM.
SCREW THAT! WE ARE **BAILING!**
NO, SPARK. AND I NEED AN **ENORMOUS** FAVOR.

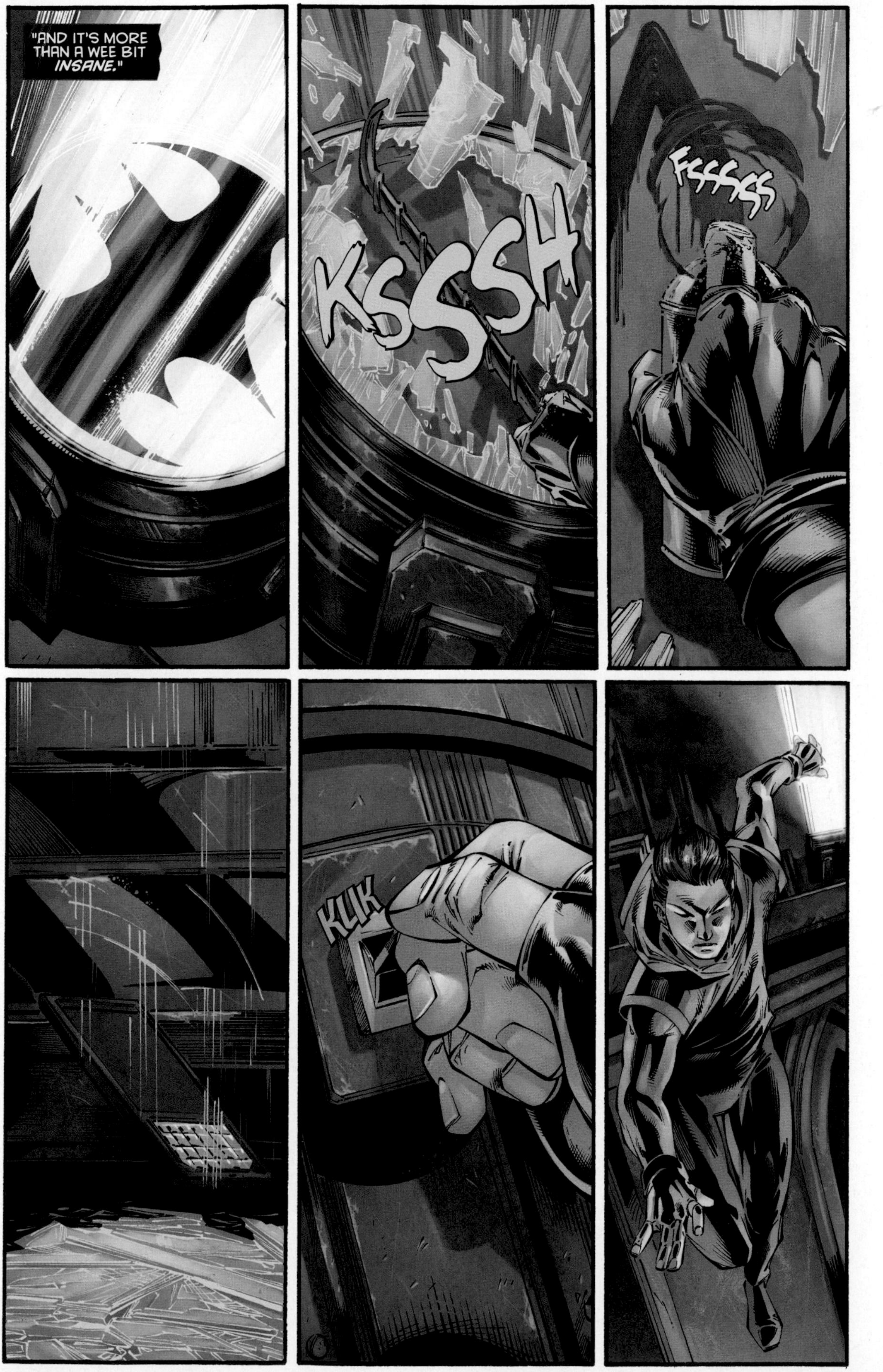
"AND IT'S MORE THAN A WEE BIT *INSANE.*"
KSSSH
FSSSSS
KLIK

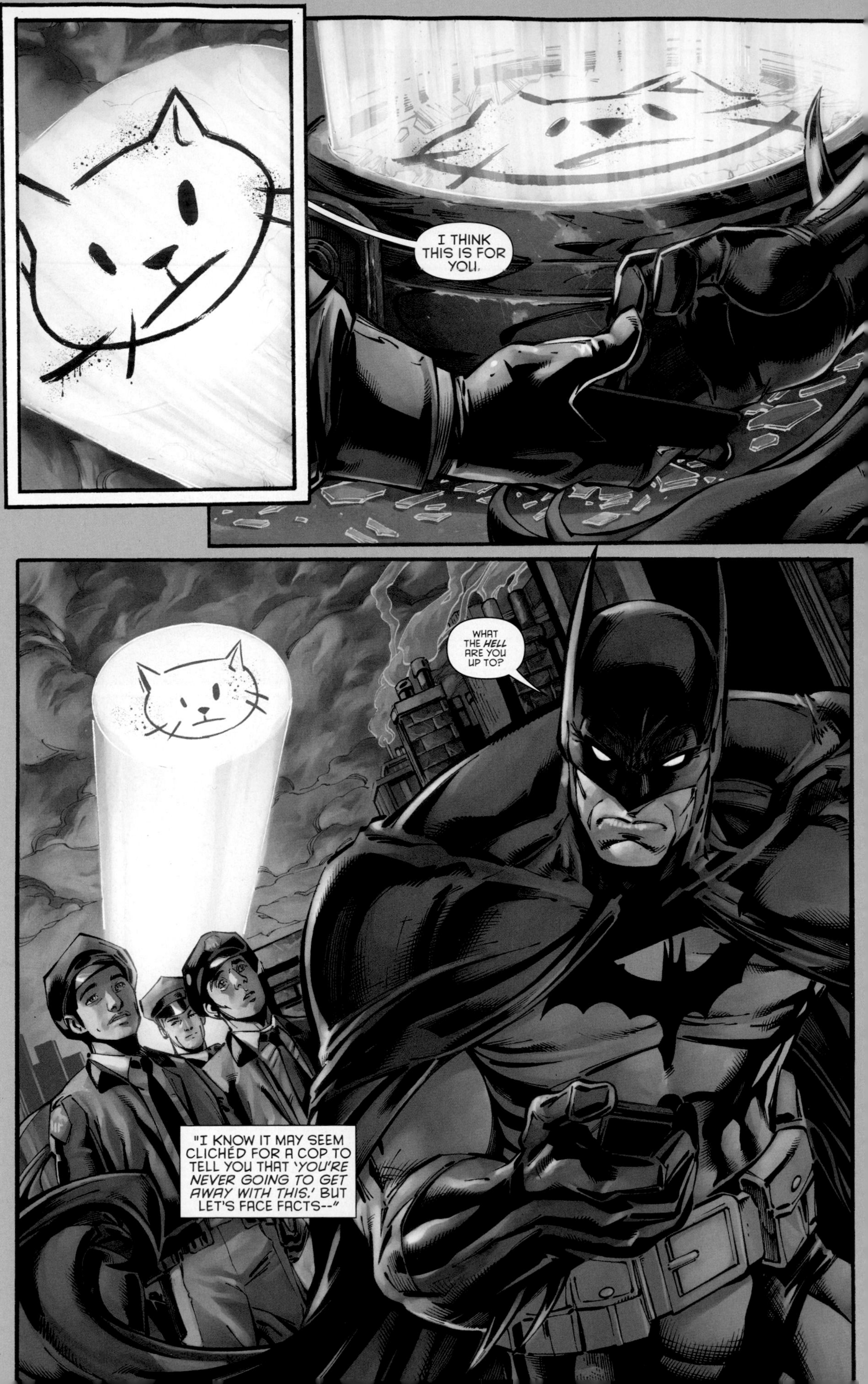
I THINK THIS IS FOR YOU.
WHAT THE *HELL* ARE YOU UP TO?
"I KNOW IT MAY SEEM CLICHÉD FOR A COP TO TELL YOU THAT '*YOU'RE NEVER GOING TO GET AWAY WITH THIS.*' BUT LET'S FACE FACTS--"

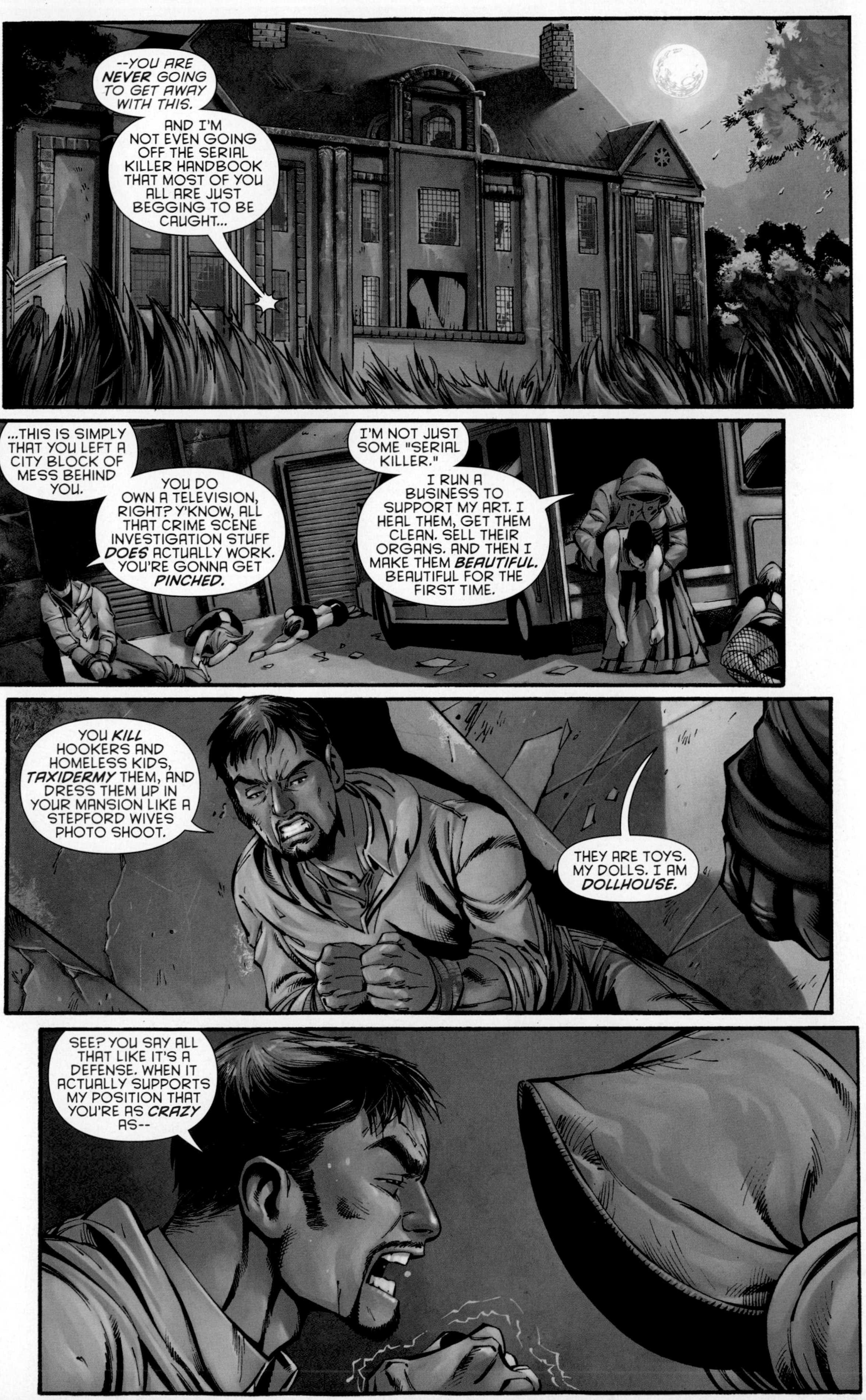
--YOU ARE NEVER GOING TO GET AWAY WITH THIS.
AND I'M NOT EVEN GOING OFF THE SERIAL KILLER HANDBOOK THAT MOST OF YOU ALL ARE JUST BEGGING TO BE CAUGHT...
...THIS IS SIMPLY THAT YOU LEFT A CITY BLOCK OF MESS BEHIND YOU.
YOU DO OWN A TELEVISION, RIGHT? Y'KNOW, ALL THAT CRIME SCENE INVESTIGATION STUFF DOES ACTUALLY WORK. YOU'RE GONNA GET PINCHED.
I'M NOT JUST SOME "SERIAL KILLER."
I RUN A BUSINESS TO SUPPORT MY ART. I HEAL THEM, GET THEM CLEAN. SELL THEIR ORGANS. AND THEN I MAKE THEM BEAUTIFUL. BEAUTIFUL FOR THE FIRST TIME.
YOU KILL HOOKERS AND HOMELESS KIDS, TAXIDERMY THEM, AND DRESS THEM UP IN YOUR MANSION LIKE A STEPFORD WIVES PHOTO SHOOT.
THEY ARE TOYS. MY DOLLS. I AM DOLLHOUSE.
SEE? YOU SAY ALL THAT LIKE IT'S A DEFENSE. WHEN IT ACTUALLY SUPPORTS MY POSITION THAT YOU'RE AS CRAZY AS--

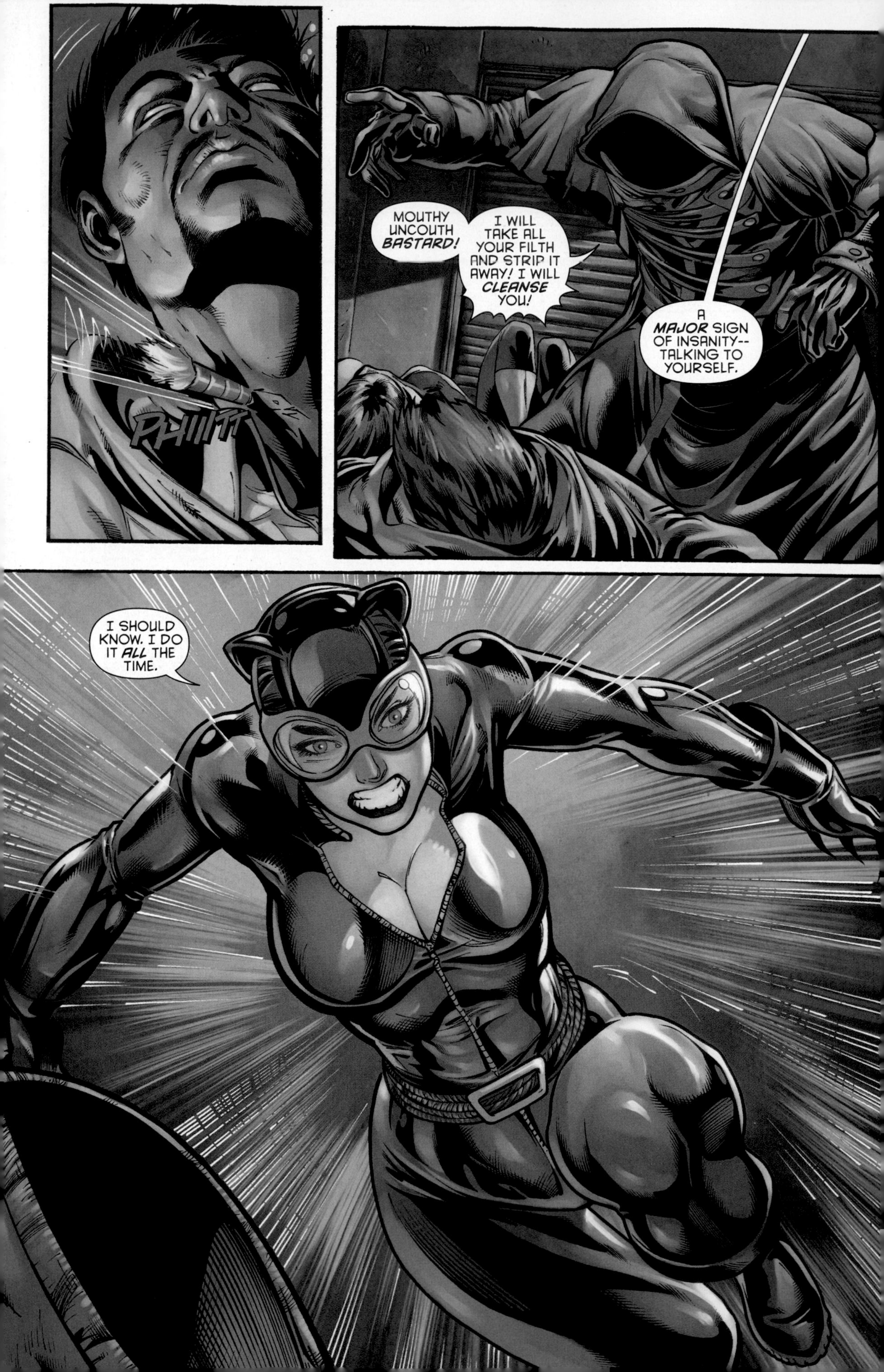
PHHTT
MOUTHY UNCOUTH BASTARD!
I WILL TAKE ALL YOUR FILTH AND STRIP IT AWAY! I WILL CLEANSE YOU!
A MAJOR SIGN OF INSANITY-- TALKING TO YOURSELF.
I SHOULD KNOW. I DO IT ALL THE TIME.

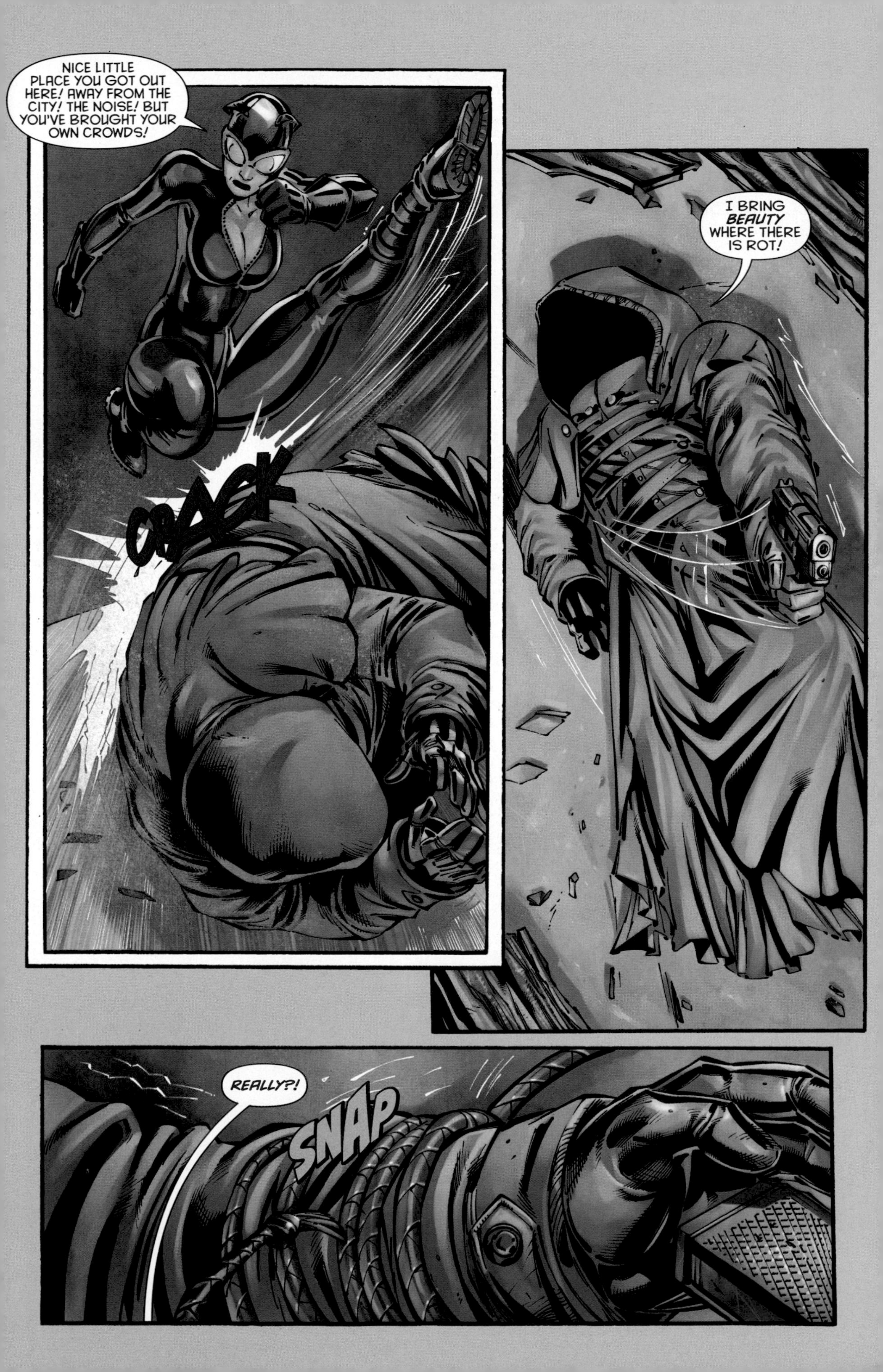
NICE LITTLE PLACE YOU GOT OUT HERE! AWAY FROM THE CITY! THE NOISE! BUT YOU'VE BROUGHT YOUR OWN CROWDS!
CRACK
I BRING BEAUTY WHERE THERE IS ROT!
REALLY?!
SNAP

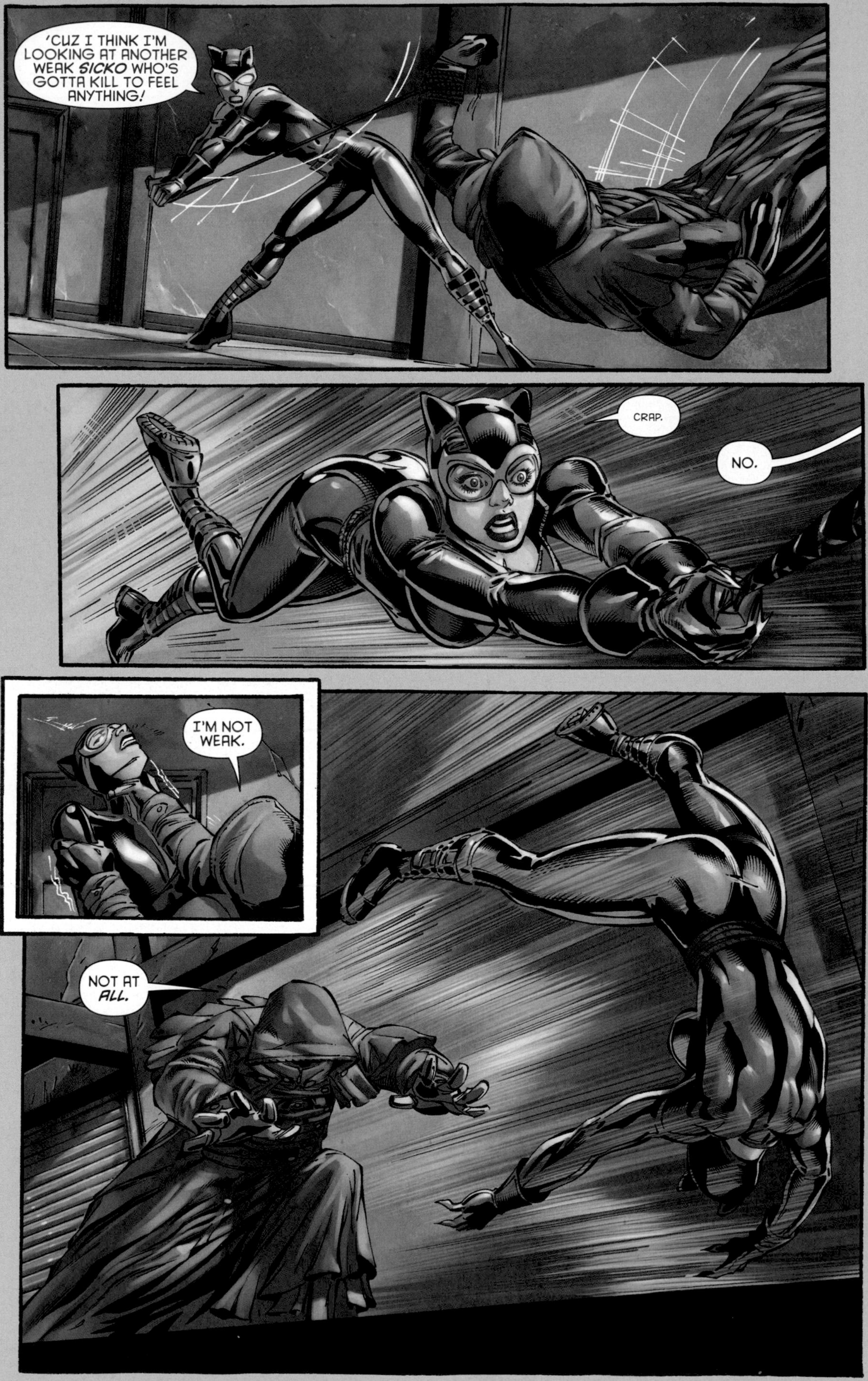
'CUZ I THINK I'M LOOKING AT ANOTHER WEAK *SICKO* WHO'S GOTTA KILL TO FEEL ANYTHING!
CRAP.
NO.
I'M NOT WEAK.
NOT AT *ALL.*

TUNK

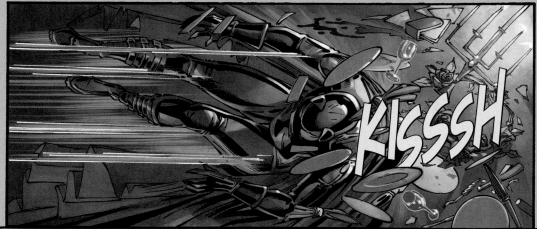

KISSSH

THE HELL... WHAT THE *HELL* IS THIS?

WHAT ARE YOU *DOING* TO THESE PEOPLE?

I AM CARRYING ON WHAT HAS BEEN DONE FOR GENERATIONS.

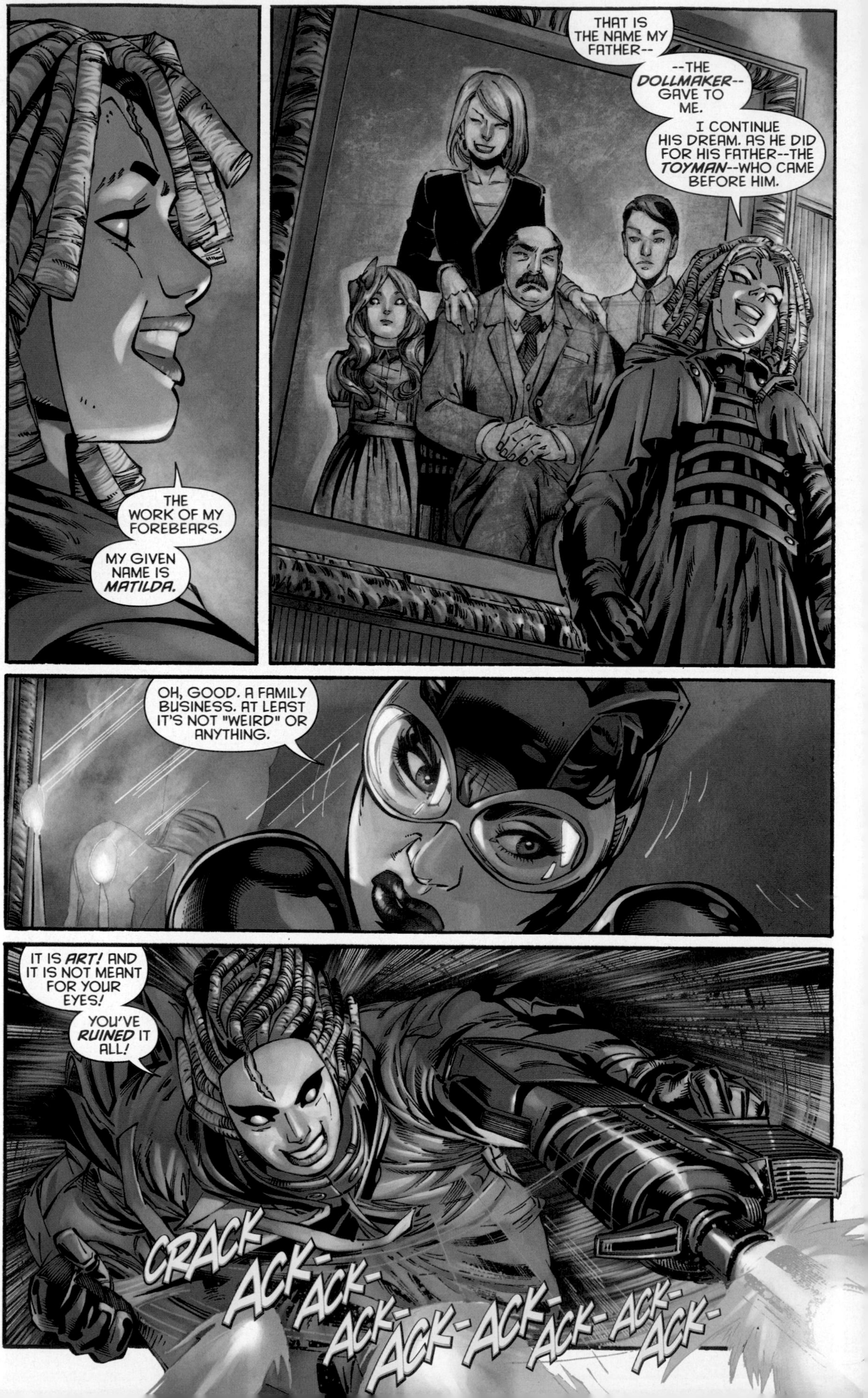
THE WORK OF MY FOREBEARS.
MY GIVEN NAME IS *MATILDA.*
THAT IS THE NAME MY FATHER--
--THE *DOLLMAKER*-- GAVE TO ME.
I CONTINUE HIS DREAM. AS HE DID FOR HIS FATHER--THE *TOYMAN*--WHO CAME BEFORE HIM.
OH, GOOD. A FAMILY BUSINESS. AT LEAST IT'S NOT "WEIRD" OR ANYTHING.
IT IS *ART!* AND IT IS NOT MEANT FOR YOUR EYES!
YOU'VE *RUINED* IT ALL!
CRACK-ACK-ACK-ACK-ACK-ACK-ACK-ACK-ACK-

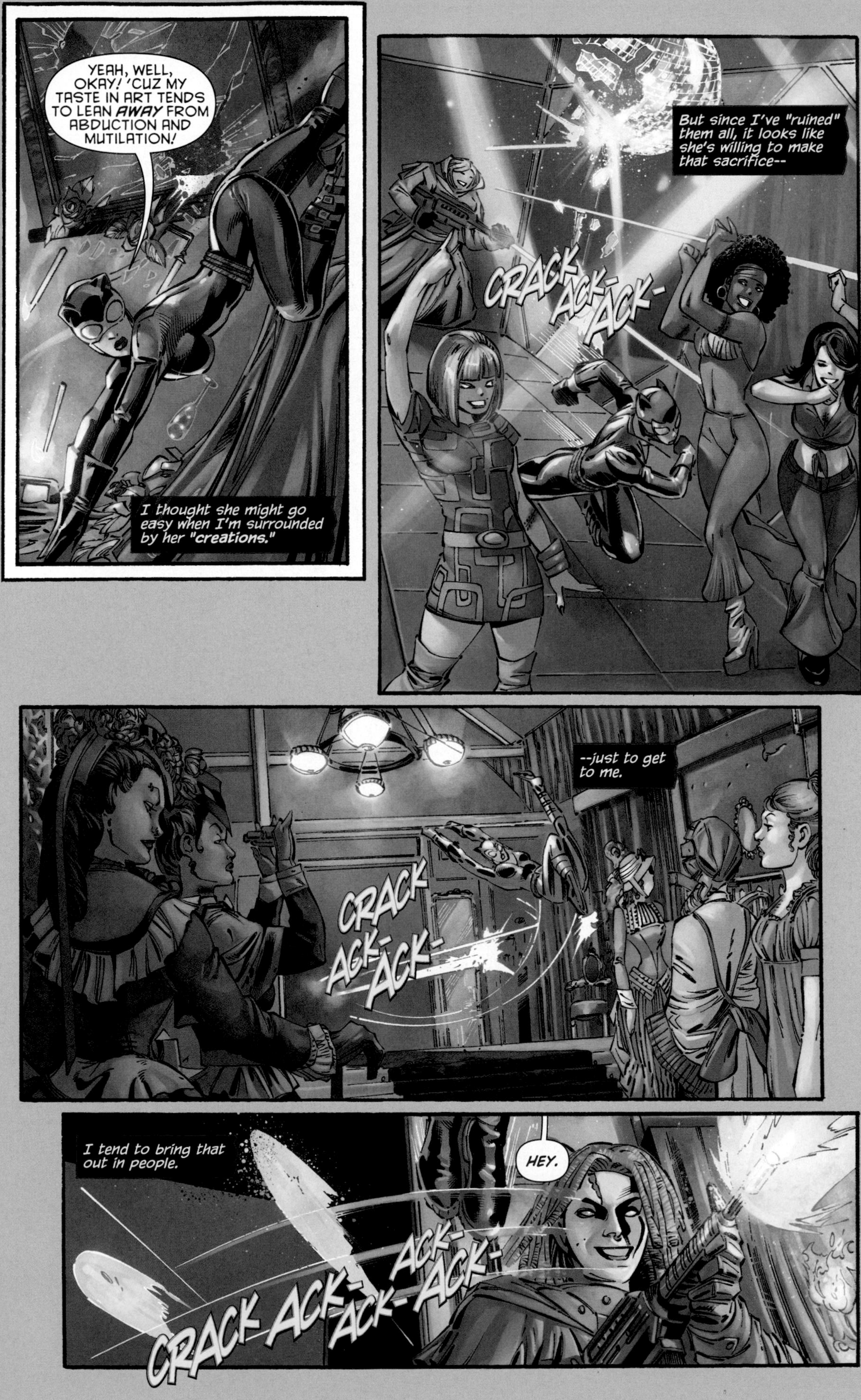
YEAH, WELL, OKAY! 'CUZ MY TASTE IN ART TENDS TO LEAN AWAY FROM ABDUCTION AND MUTILATION!
I thought she might go easy when I'm surrounded by her "creations."
But since I've "ruined" them all, it looks like she's willing to make that sacrifice--
CRACK ACK-ACK-
--just to get to me.
CRACK ACK-ACK-
I tend to bring that out in people.
HEY.
CRACK ACK-ACK-ACK-ACK-

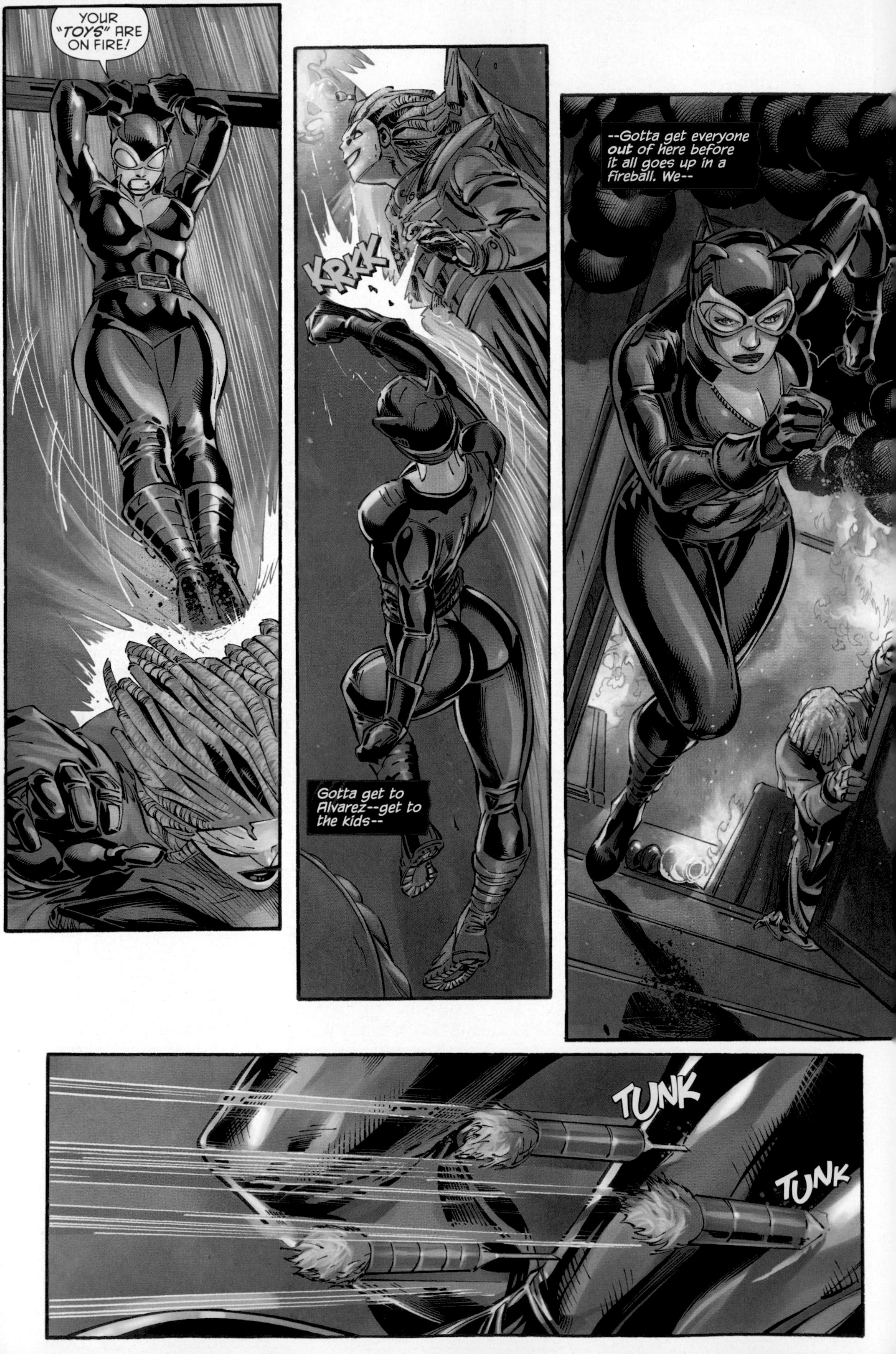
YOUR "TOYS" ARE ON FIRE!
KRKK
Gotta get to Alvarez--get to the kids--
--Gotta get everyone out of here before it all goes up in a fireball. We--
TUNK
TUNK

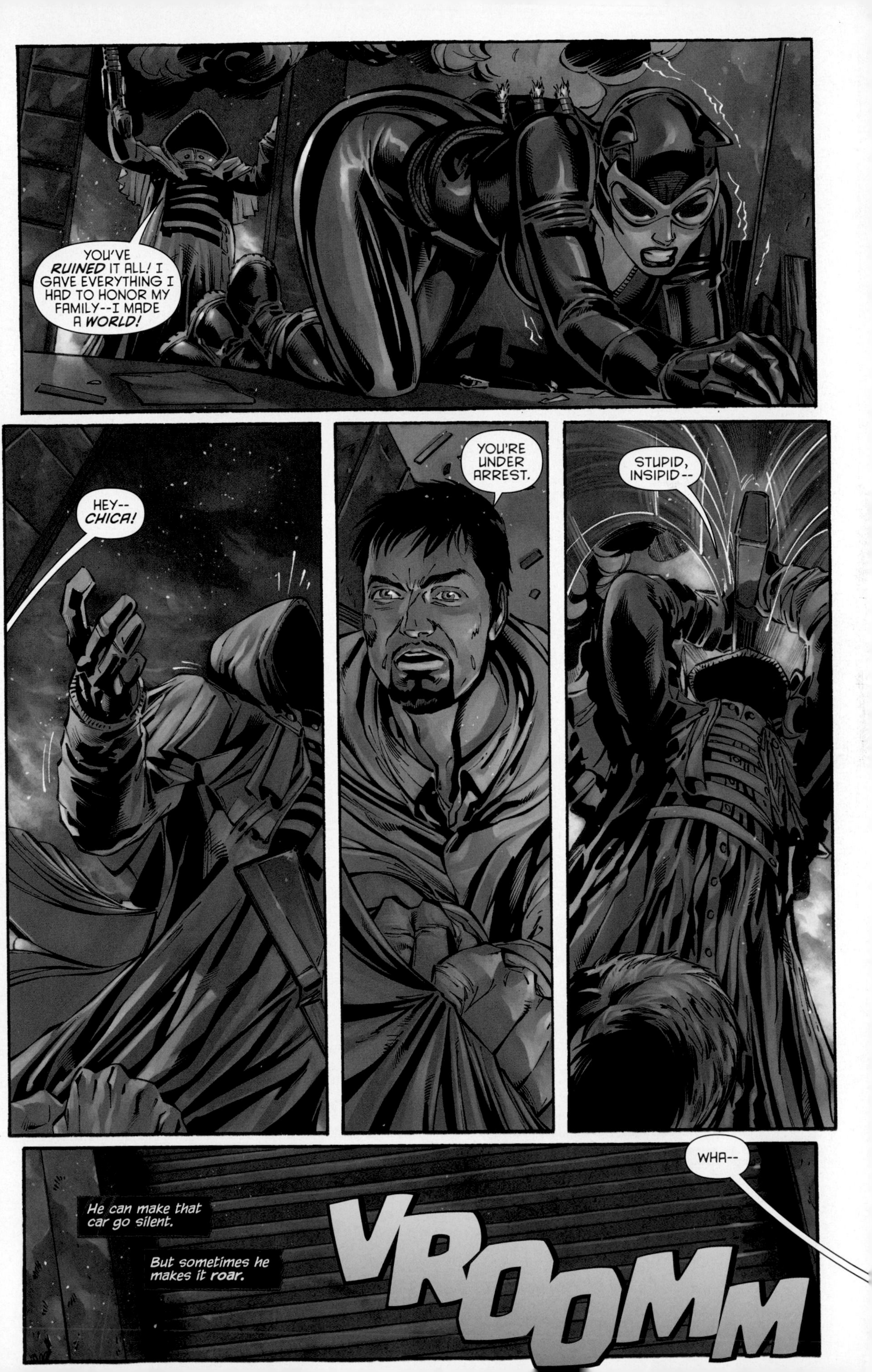
YOU'VE RUINED IT ALL! I GAVE EVERYTHING I HAD TO HONOR MY FAMILY--I MADE A WORLD!
HEY-- CHICA!
YOU'RE UNDER ARREST.
STUPID, INSIPID--
WHA--
He can make that car go silent.
But sometimes he makes it roar.
VROOMM

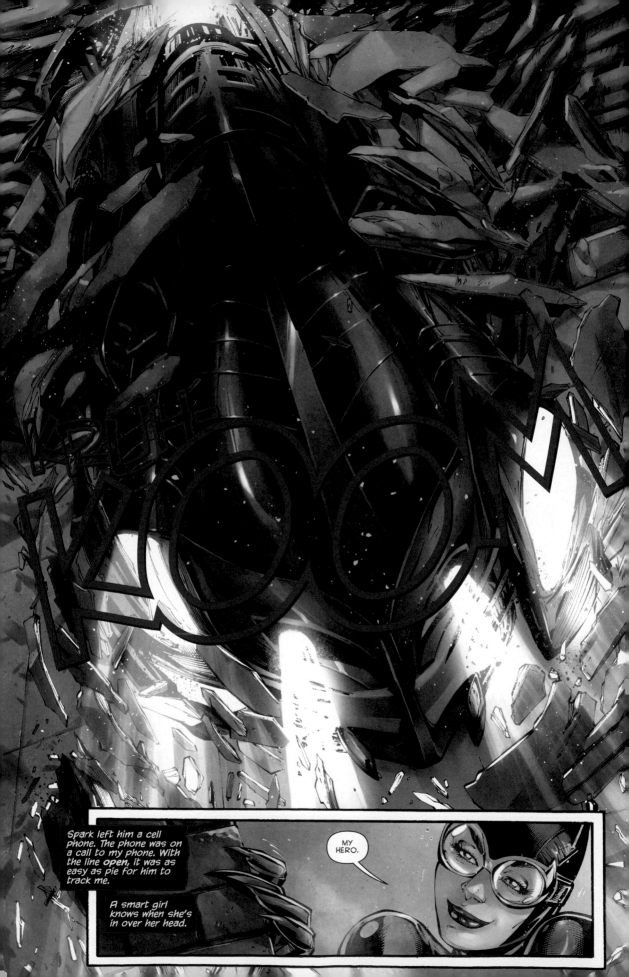

Spark left him a cell phone. The phone was on a call to my phone. With the line **open**, it was as easy as pie for him to track me.

A smart girl knows when she's in over her head.

MY HERO.

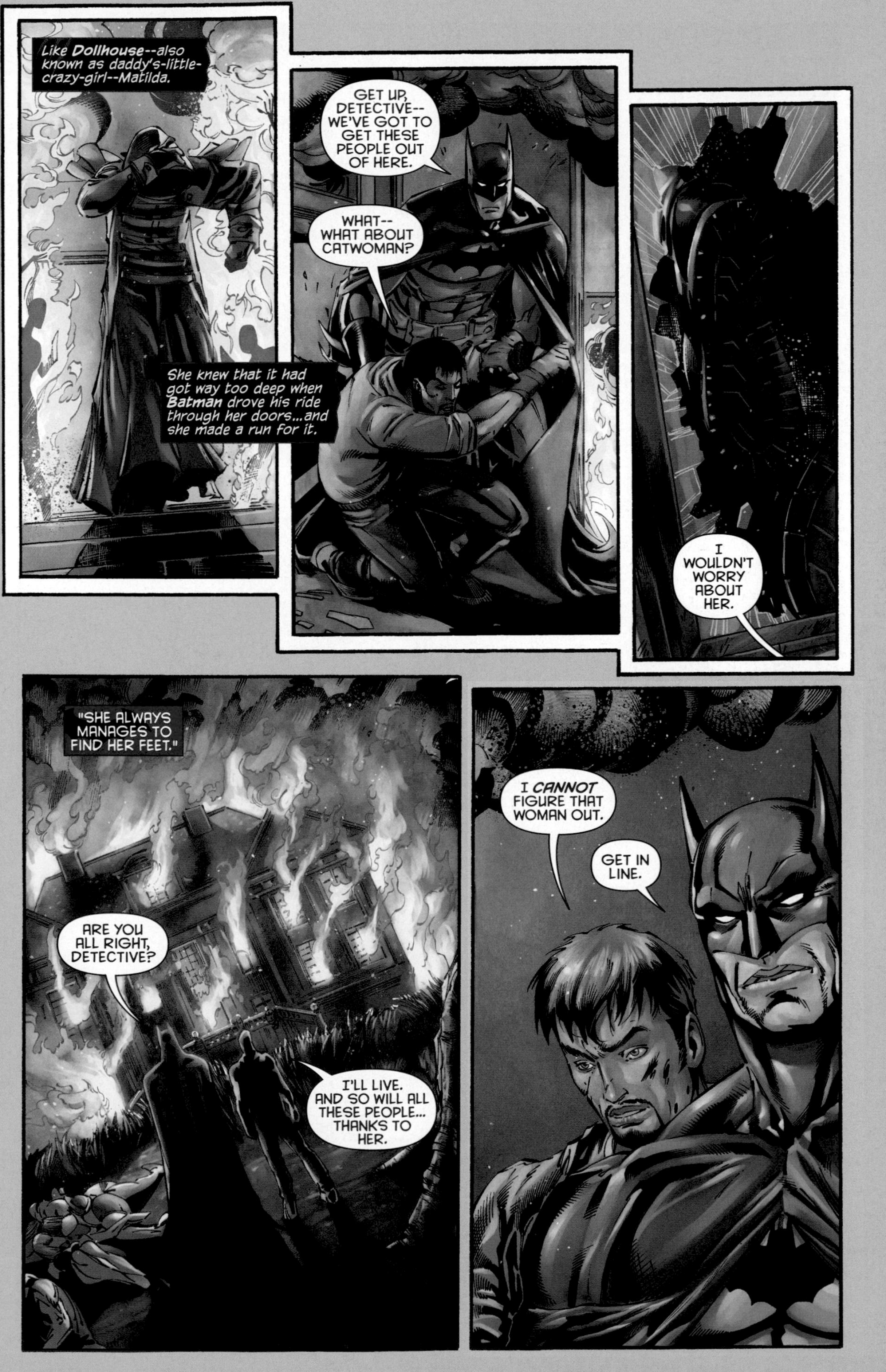
Like Dollhouse--also known as daddy's-little-crazy-girl--Matilda.
She knew that it had got way too deep when Batman drove his ride through her doors...and she made a run for it.
GET UP, DETECTIVE-- WE'VE GOT TO GET THESE PEOPLE OUT OF HERE.
WHAT-- WHAT ABOUT CATWOMAN?
I WOULDN'T WORRY ABOUT HER.
"SHE ALWAYS MANAGES TO FIND HER FEET."
ARE YOU ALL RIGHT, DETECTIVE?
I'LL LIVE. AND SO WILL ALL THESE PEOPLE... THANKS TO HER.
I CANNOT FIGURE THAT WOMAN OUT.
GET IN LINE.

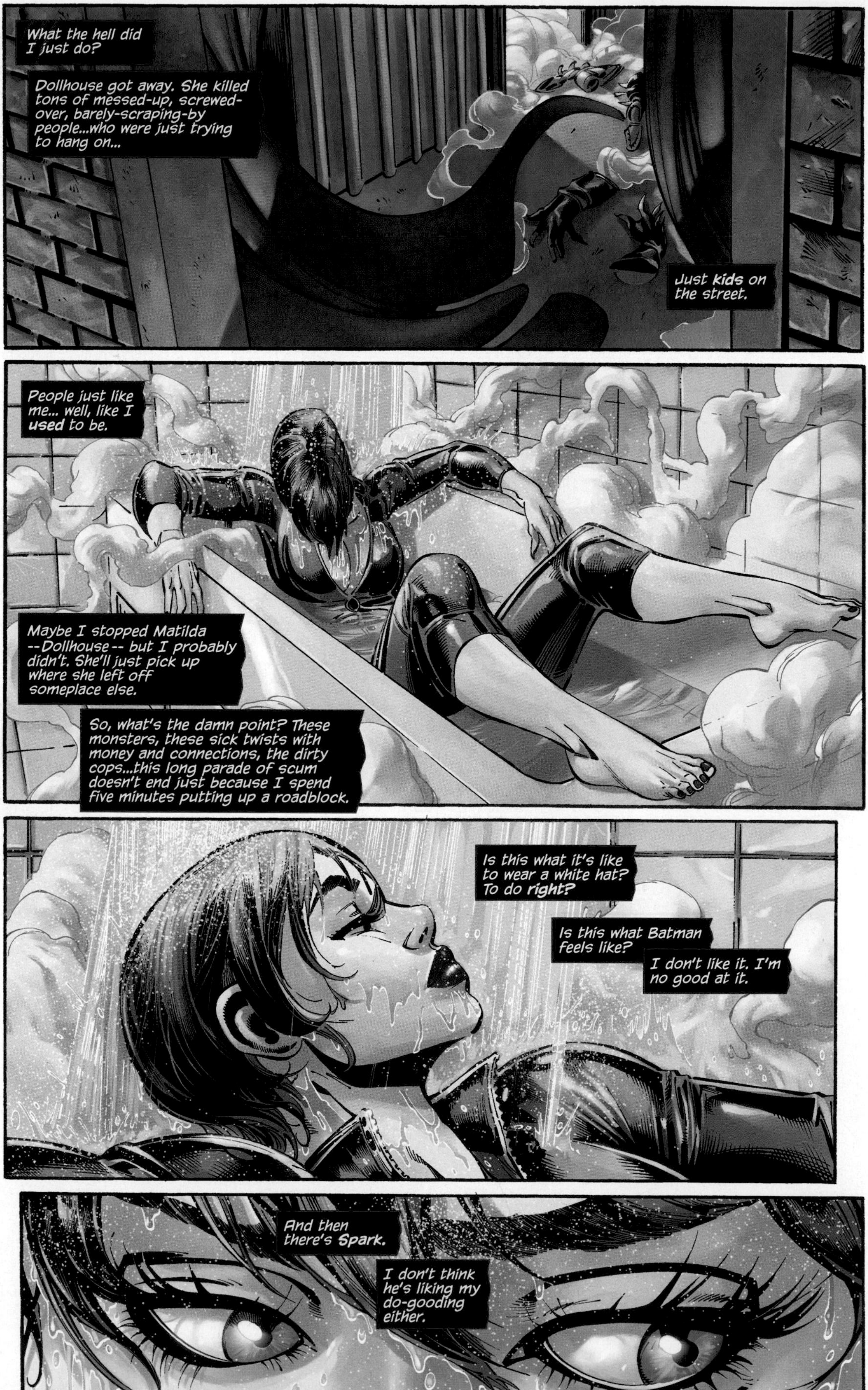
What the hell did I just do?
Dollhouse got away. She killed tons of messed-up, screwed-over, barely-scraping-by people...who were just trying to hang on...
Just **kids** on the street.
People just like me... well, like I **used** to be.
Maybe I stopped Matilda --Dollhouse-- but I probably didn't. She'll just pick up where she left off someplace else.
So, what's the damn point? These monsters, these sick twists with money and connections, the dirty cops...this long parade of scum doesn't end just because I spend five minutes putting up a roadblock.
Is this what it's like to wear a white hat? To do **right?**
Is this what Batman feels like?
I don't like it. I'm no good at it.
And then there's **Spark.**
I don't think he's liking my do-gooding either.

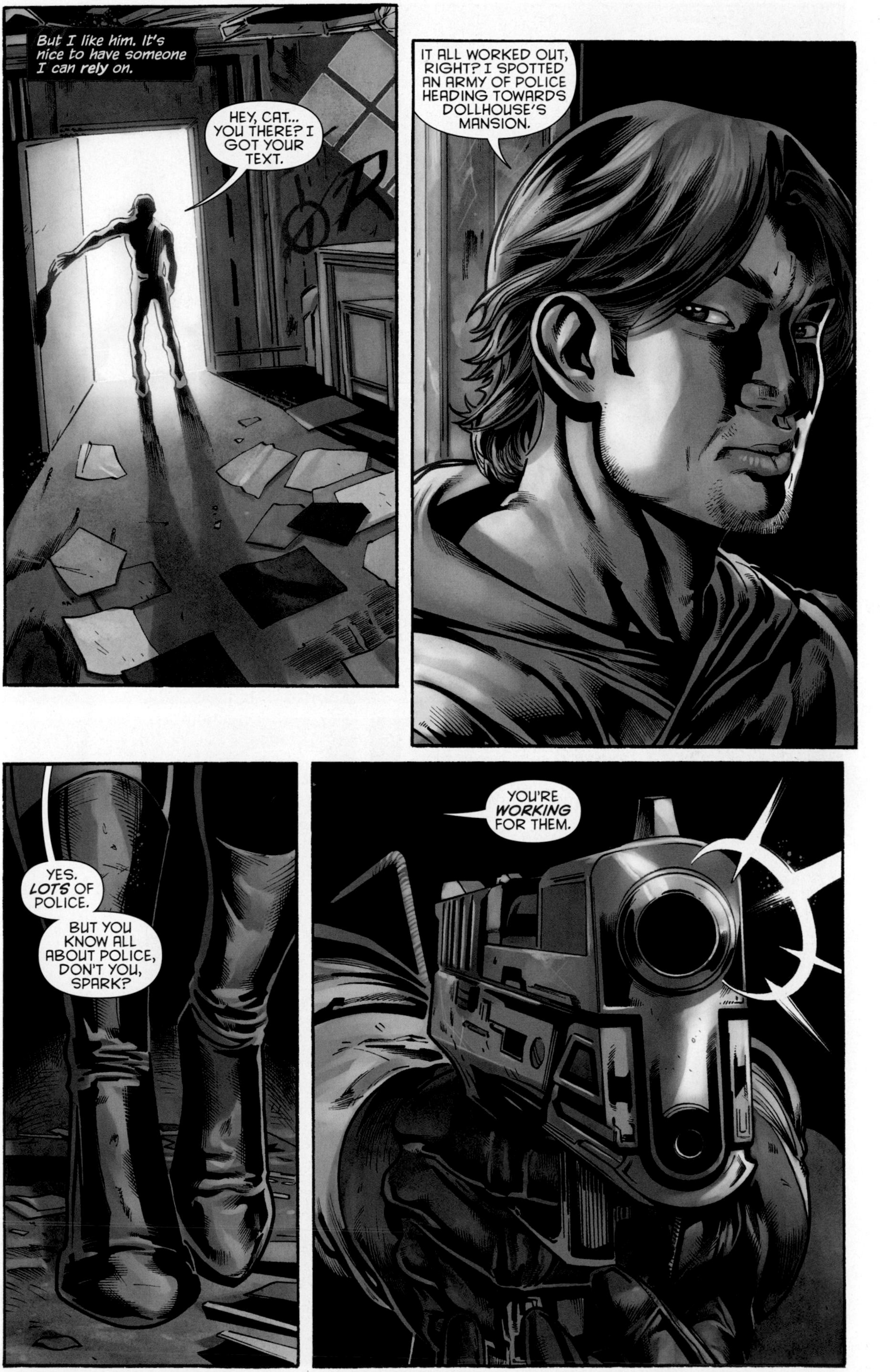

But I like him. It's nice to have someone I can *rely* on.
HEY, CAT... YOU THERE? I GOT YOUR TEXT.
IT ALL WORKED OUT, RIGHT? I SPOTTED AN ARMY OF POLICE HEADING TOWARDS DOLLHOUSE'S MANSION.
YES. ***LOTS*** OF POLICE.
BUT YOU KNOW ALL ABOUT POLICE, DON'T YOU, SPARK?
YOU'RE ***WORKING*** FOR THEM.

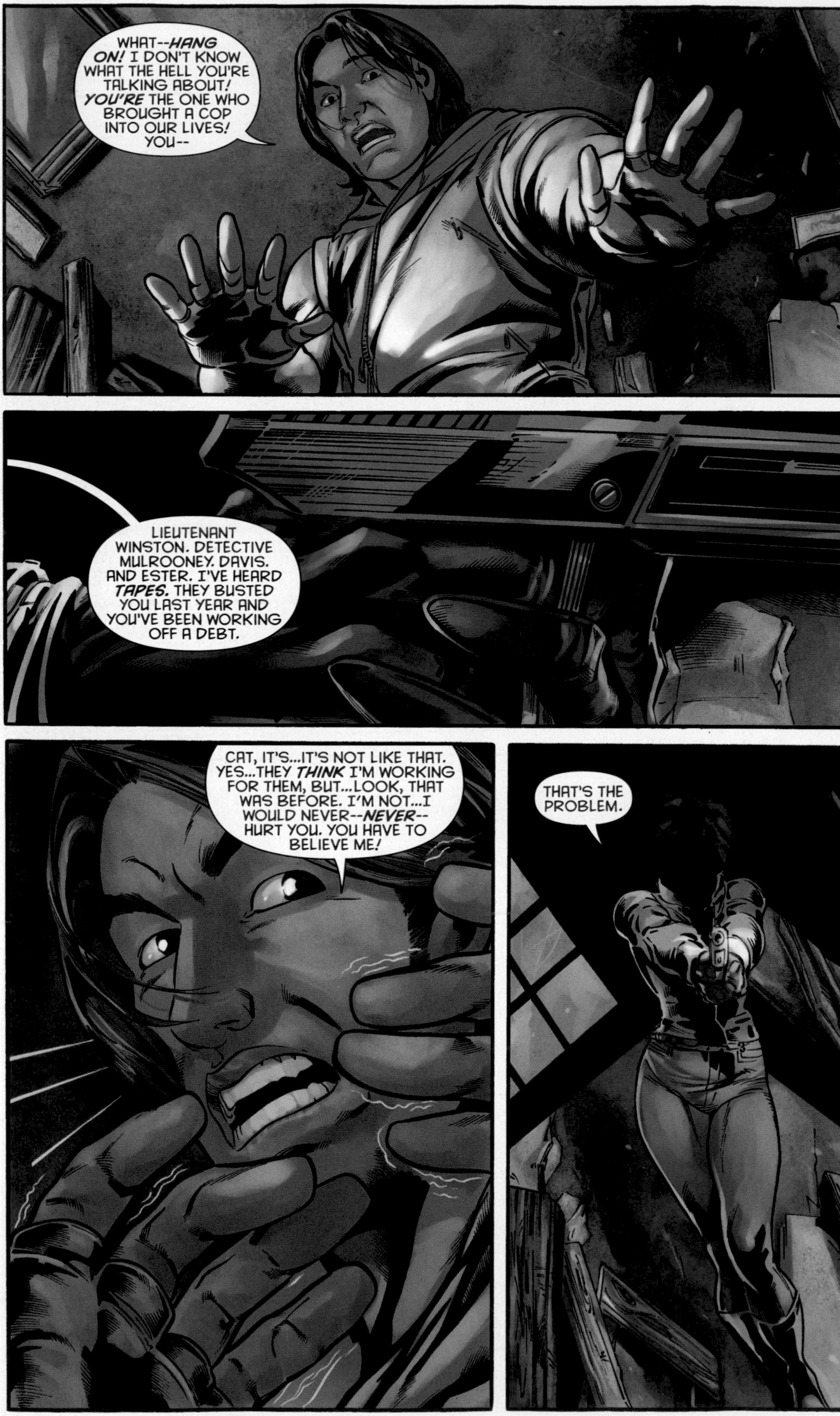
WHAT--HANG ON! I DON'T KNOW WHAT THE HELL YOU'RE TALKING ABOUT! YOU'RE THE ONE WHO BROUGHT A COP INTO OUR LIVES! YOU--
LIEUTENANT WINSTON. DETECTIVE MULROONEY. DAVIS. AND ESTER. I'VE HEARD TAPES. THEY BUSTED YOU LAST YEAR AND YOU'VE BEEN WORKING OFF A DEBT.
CAT, IT'S...IT'S NOT LIKE THAT. YES...THEY THINK I'M WORKING FOR THEM, BUT...LOOK, THAT WAS BEFORE. I'M NOT...I WOULD NEVER--NEVER--HURT YOU. YOU HAVE TO BELIEVE ME!
THAT'S THE PROBLEM.

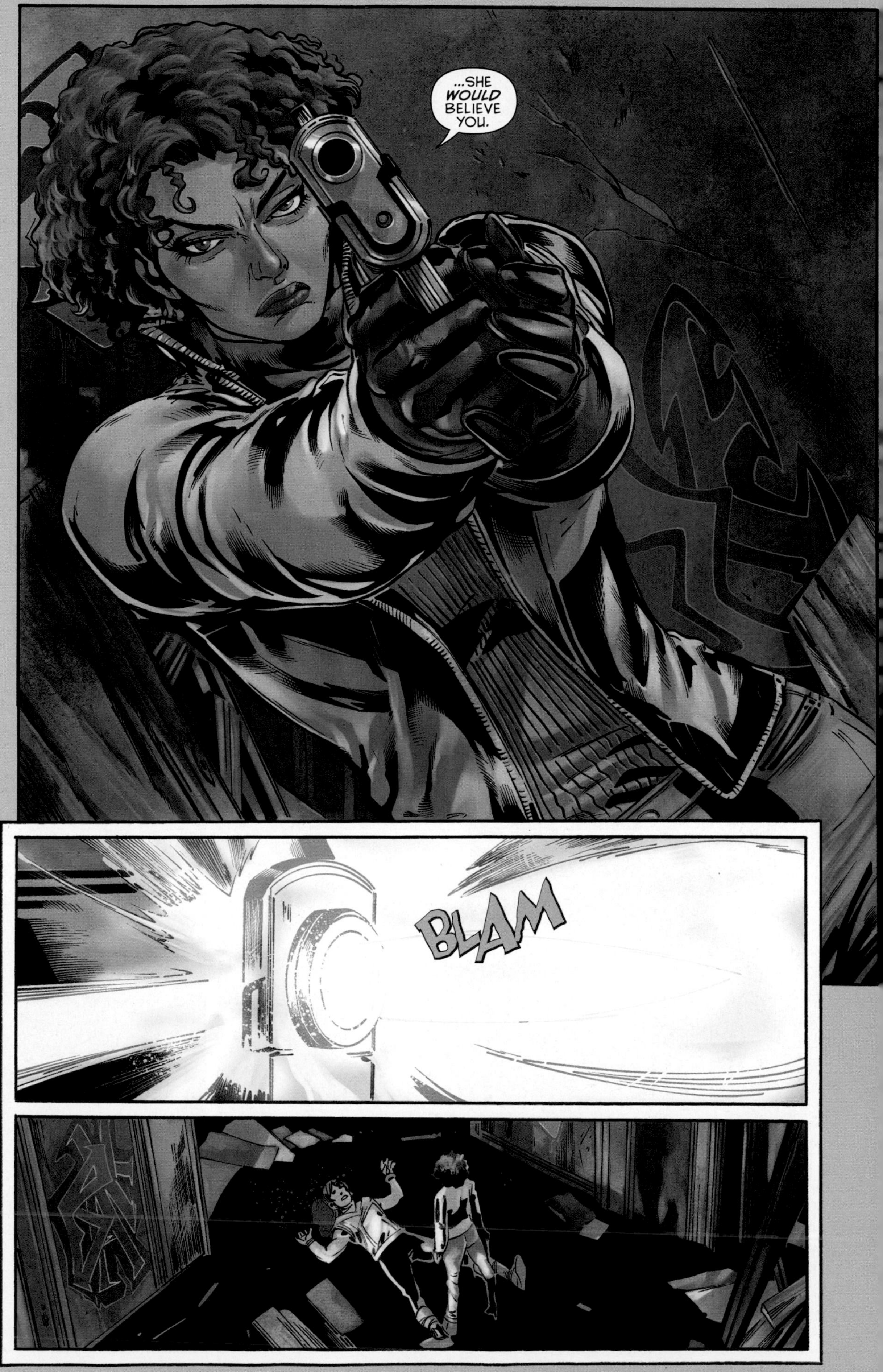
...SHE WOULD BELIEVE YOU.
BLAM

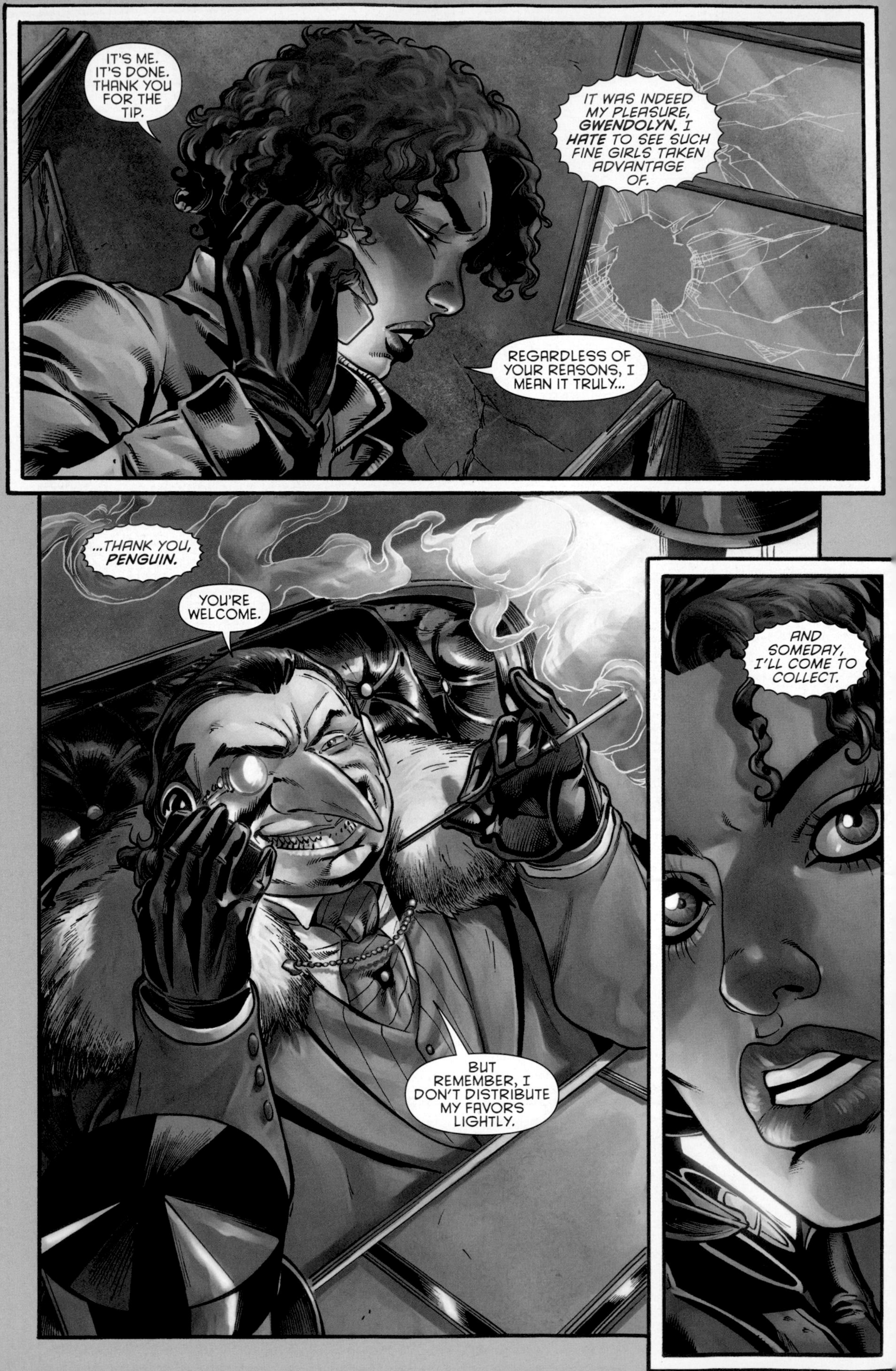
IT'S ME. IT'S DONE. THANK YOU FOR THE TIP.
IT WAS INDEED MY PLEASURE, **GWENDOLYN.** I **HATE** TO SEE SUCH FINE GIRLS TAKEN ADVANTAGE OF.
REGARDLESS OF YOUR REASONS, I MEAN IT TRULY...
...THANK YOU, **PENGUIN.**
YOU'RE WELCOME.
BUT REMEMBER, I DON'T DISTRIBUTE MY FAVORS LIGHTLY.
AND SOMEDAY, I'LL COME TO COLLECT.

CATWOMAN
COVER SKETCHES BY **GUILLEM MARCH**

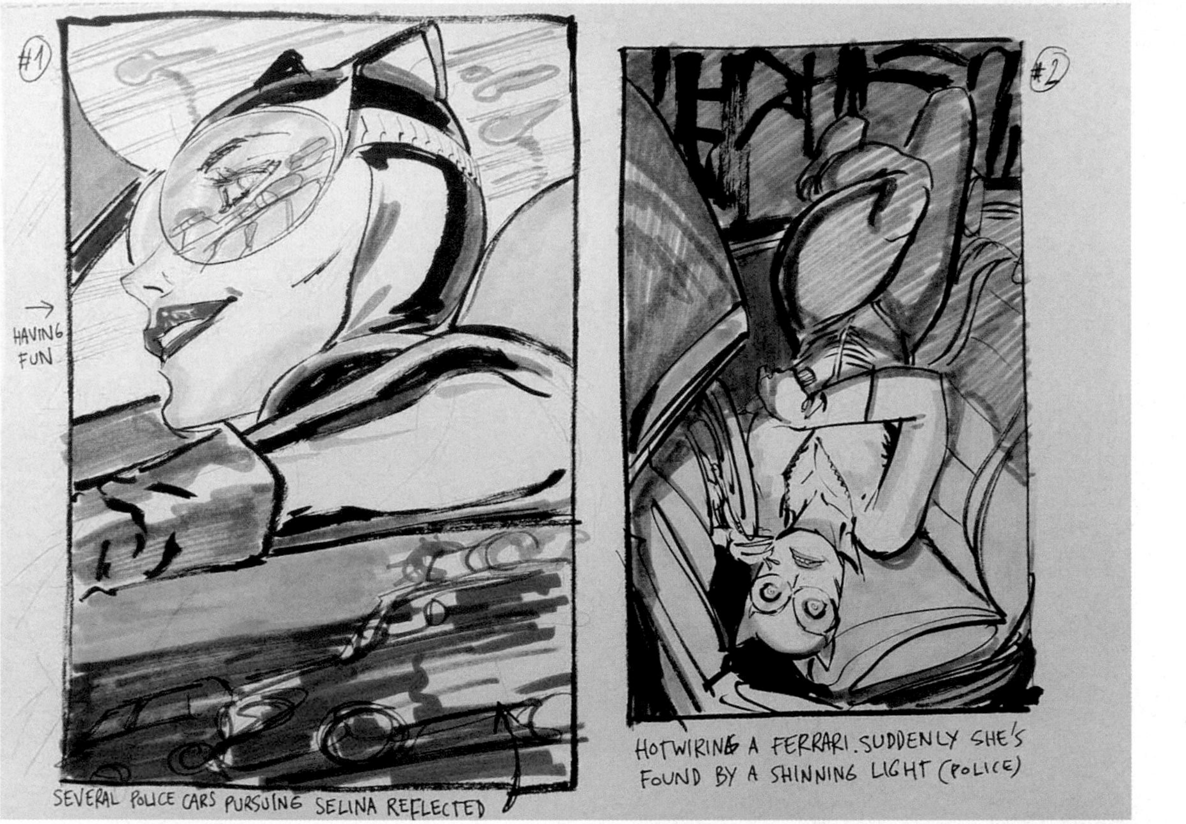
#1
HAVING FUN
SEVERAL POLICE CARS PURSUING SELINA REFLECTED
#2
HOTWIRING A FERRARI. SUDDENLY SHE'S FOUND BY A SHINNING LIGHT (POLICE)

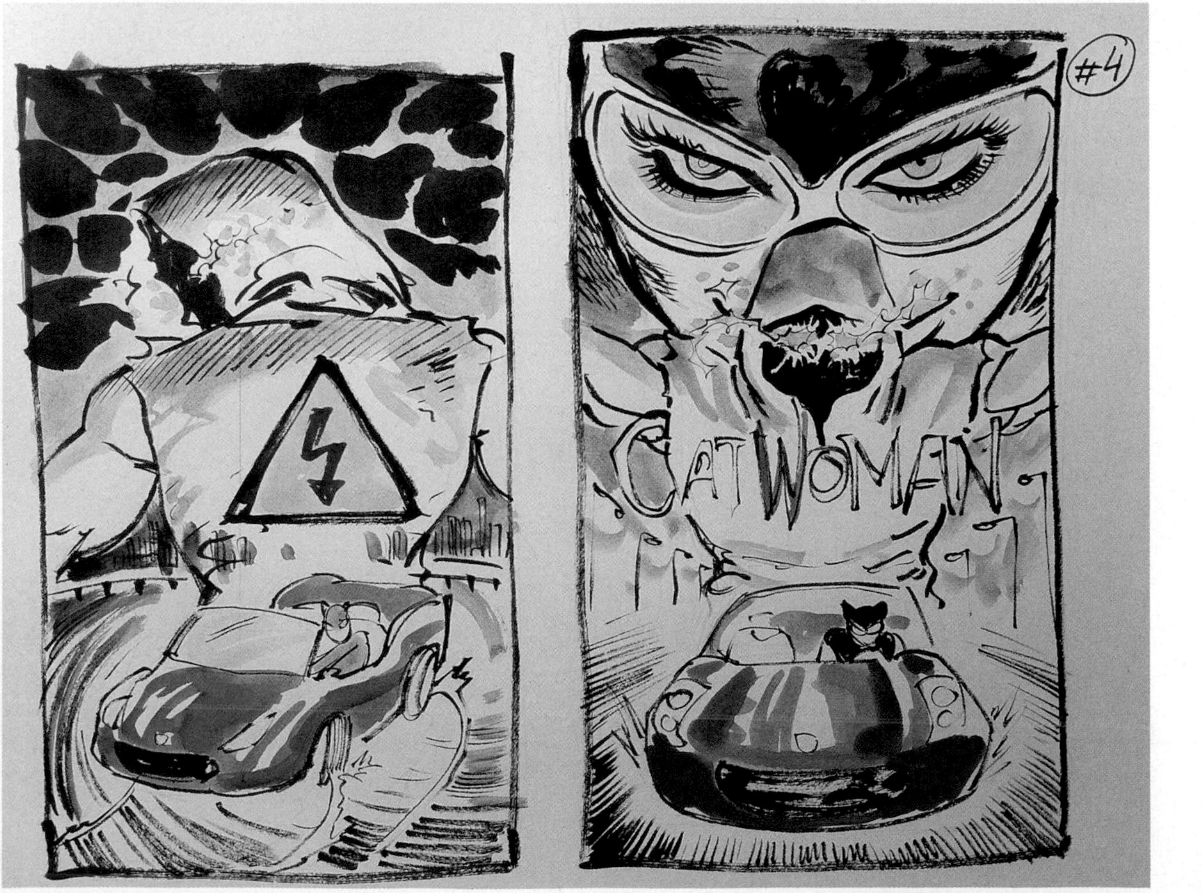
#4
CATWOMAN

CATWOMAN #7 cover sketches

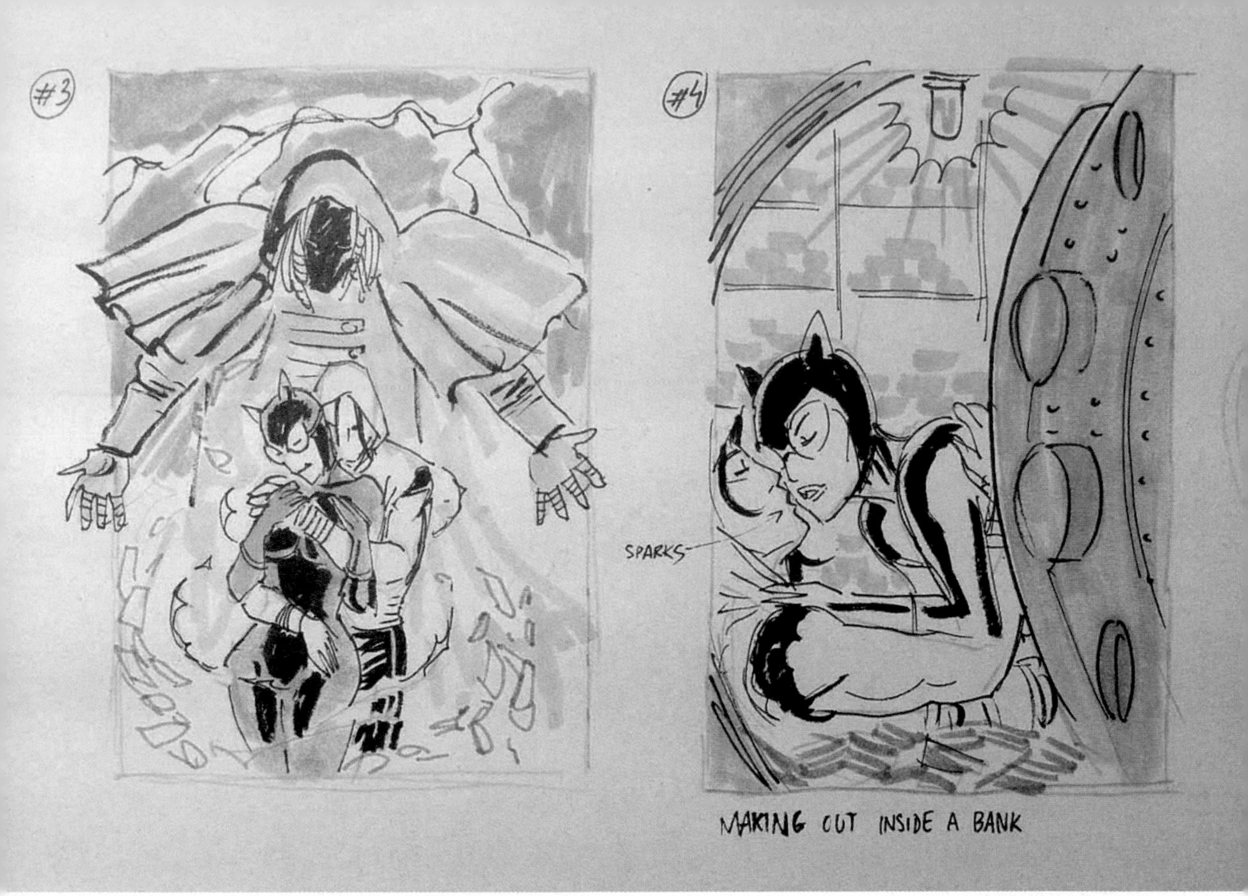
#3
#4
SPARKS
MAKING OUT INSIDE A BANK

CATWOMAN #8 cover sketches

CATWOMAN #9 cover sketches

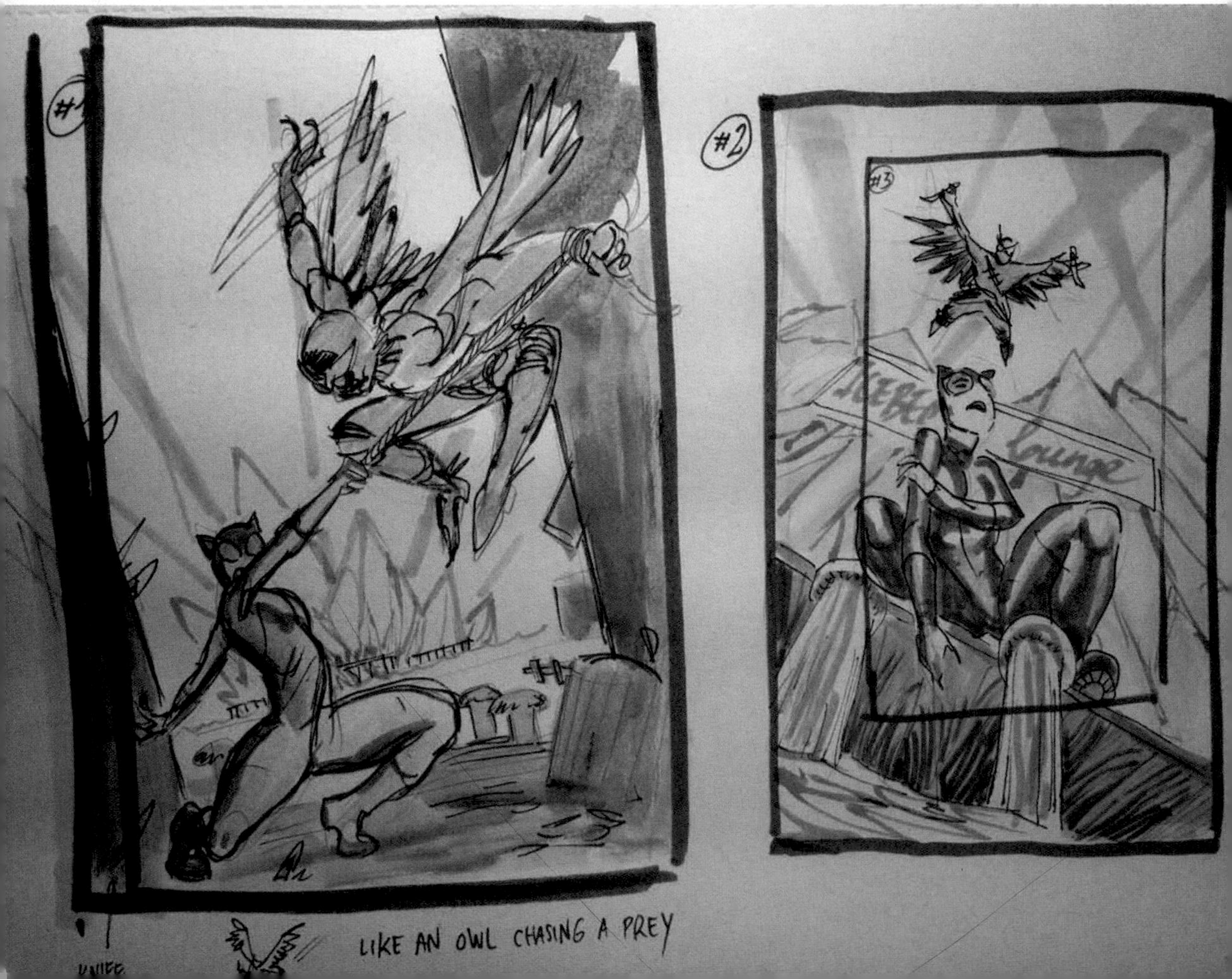
#2
#3
LIKE AN OWL CHASING A PREY

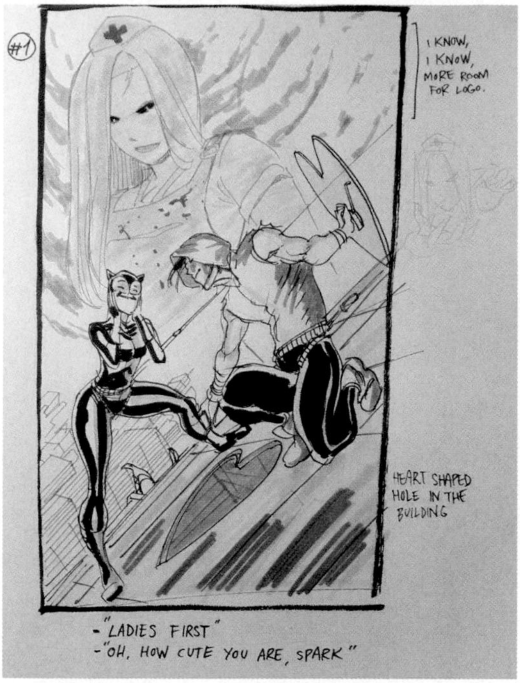
#1
I KNOW,
I KNOW,
MORE ROOM
FOR LOGO.
HEART SHAPED
HOLE IN THE
BUILDING
-"LADIES FIRST"
-"OH, HOW CUTE YOU ARE, SPARK"

CATWOMAN #8 cover sketch

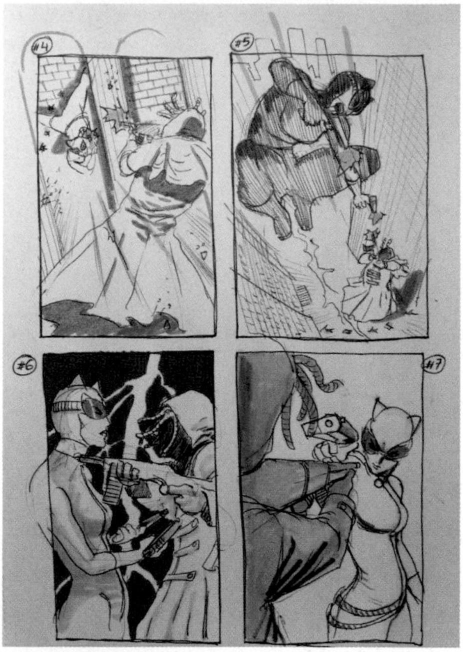
#4
#5
#6
#7

CATWOMAN #10 cover sketch

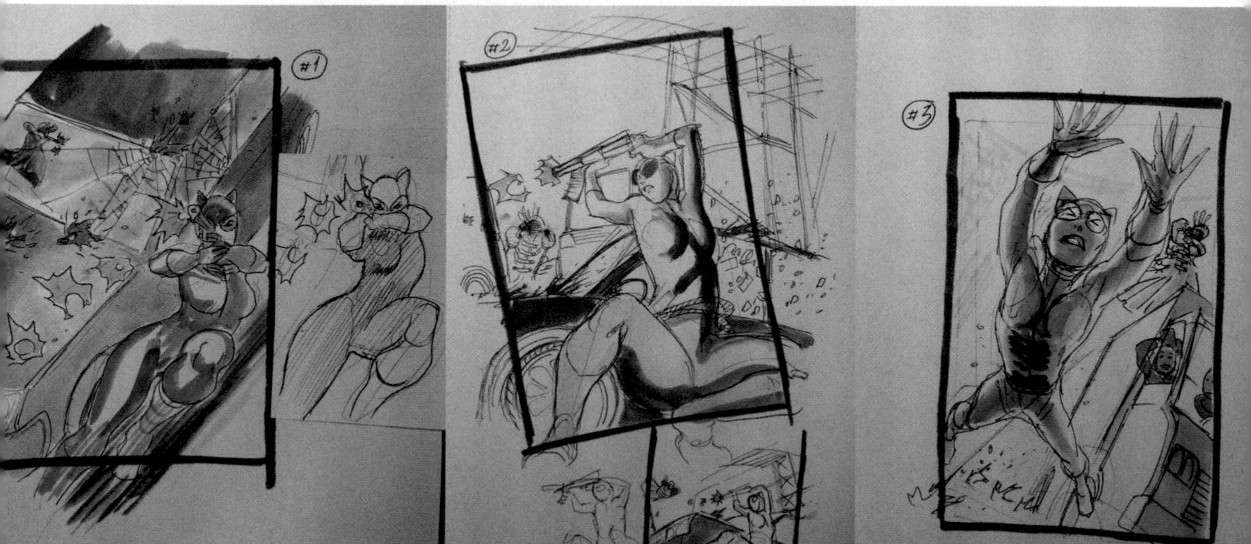
#1
#2
#3

CATWOMAN #10 cover sketches

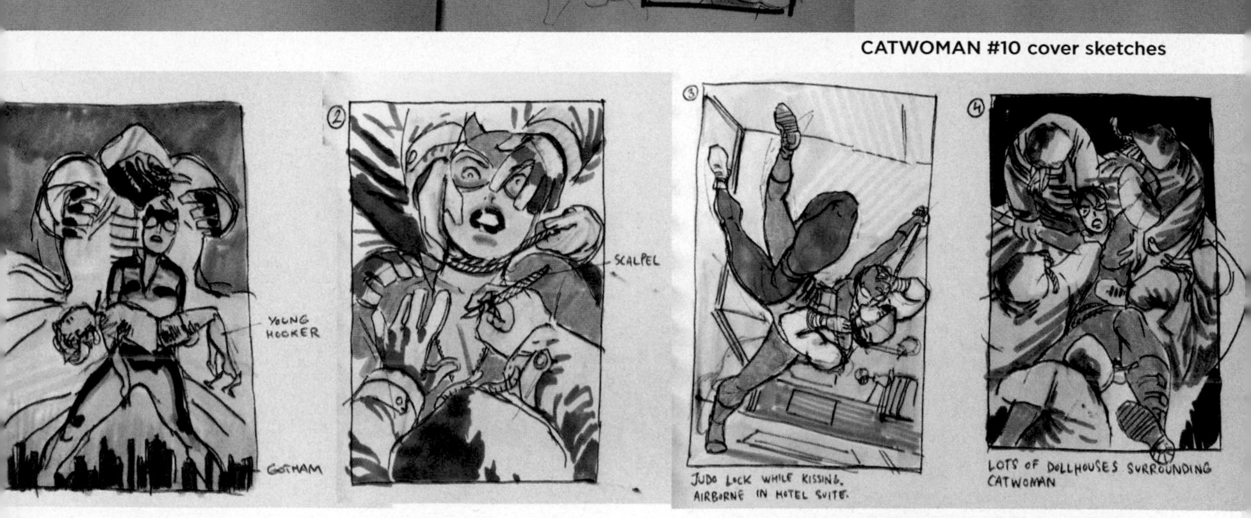
YOUNG
HOOKER
GOTHAM
2
SCALPEL
3
JUDO LOCK WHILE KISSING.
AIRBORNE IN HOTEL SUITE.
4
LOTS OF DOLLHOUSES SURROUNDING
CATWOMAN

CATWOMAN #11 cover sketches

CATWOMAN #10 cover sketch

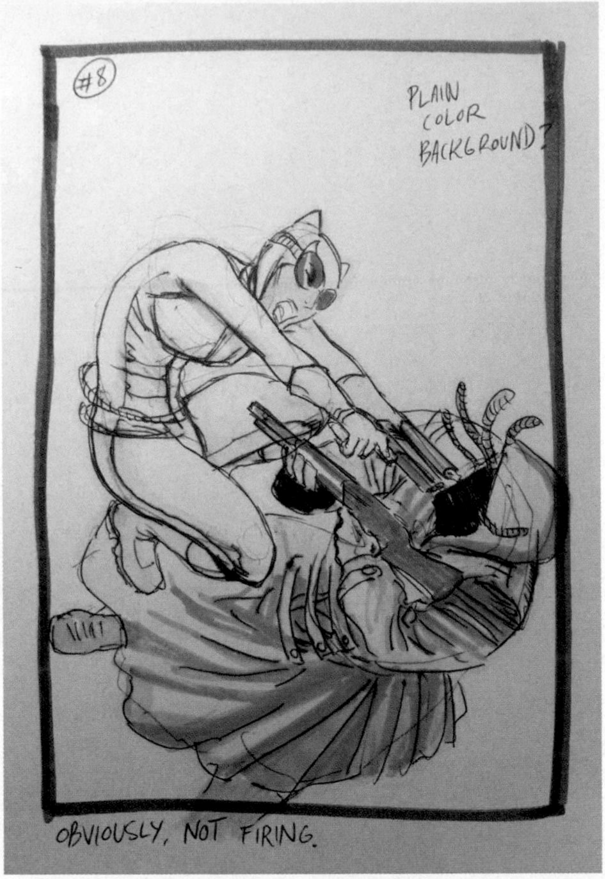
#8
PLAIN COLOR BACKGROUND?
OBVIOUSLY, NOT FIRING.

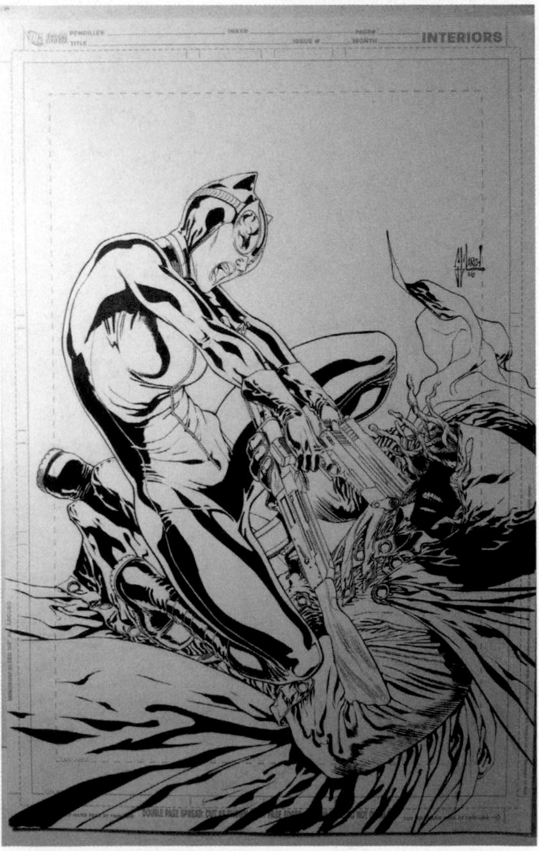
INTERIORS

CATWOMAN #10 inks

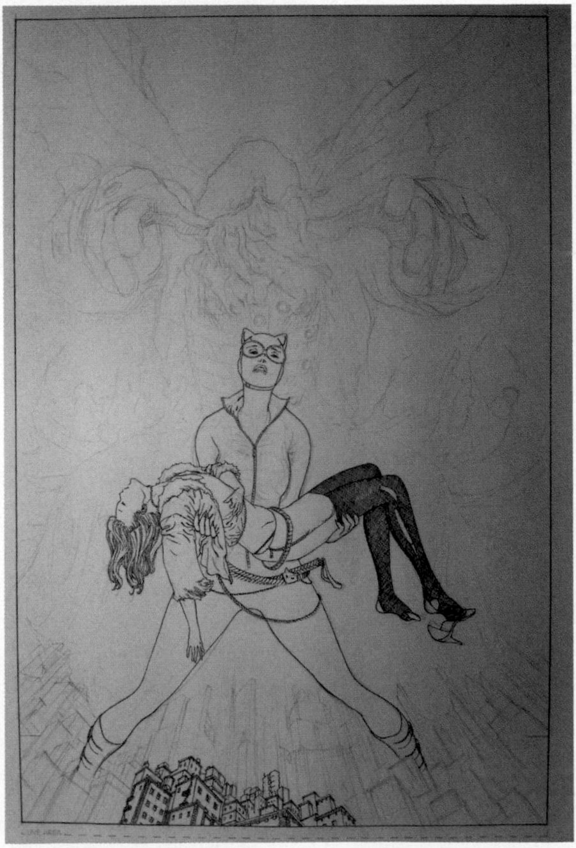

CATWOMAN #11 pencils

CATWOMAN #12 cover sketches

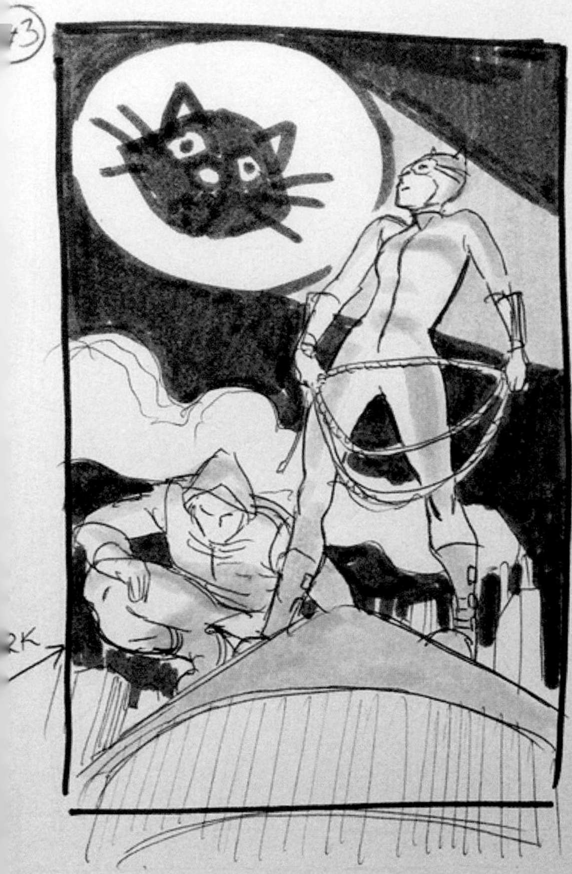
#3
2K

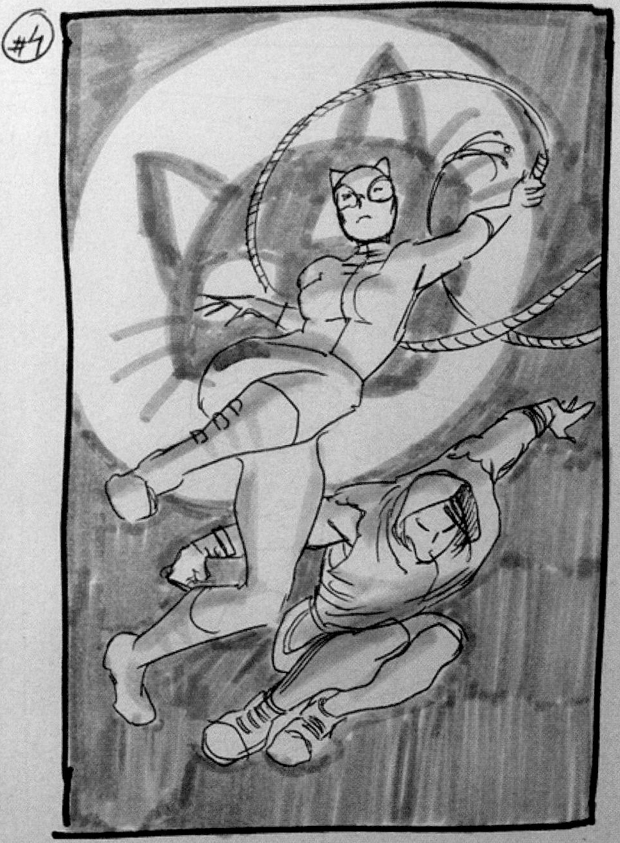
#4

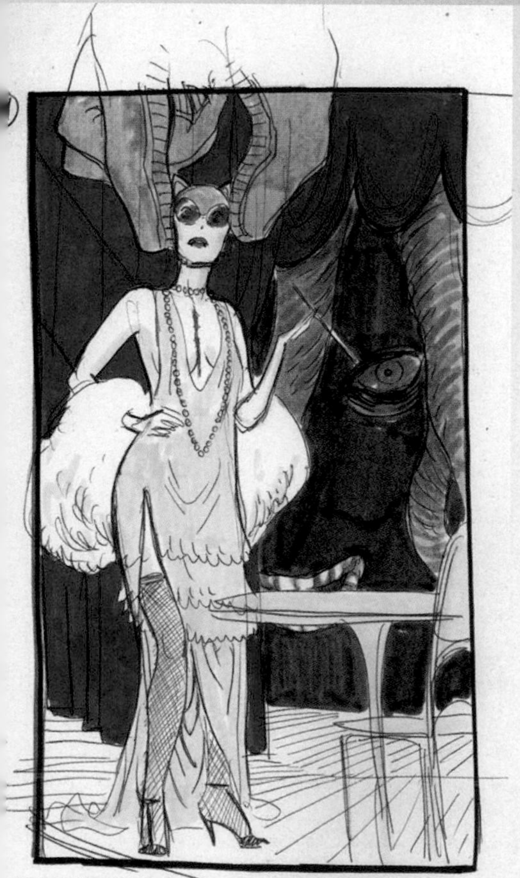

* CATWOMAN AS A DOLL IN THE DOLLHOUSE.
* TAXIDERMY SCAR IN CHEST.
* ROARING TWENTIES CLOTHES AND BACKGROUND.

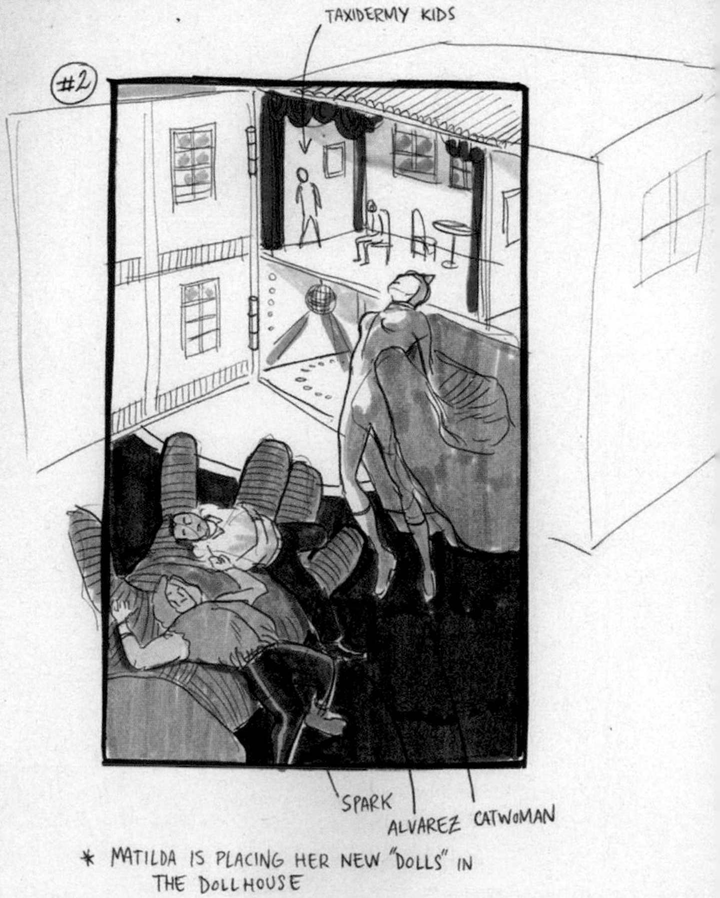
TAXIDERMY KIDS
#2
SPARK
ALVAREZ
CATWOMAN

* MATILDA IS PLACING HER NEW "DOLLS" IN THE DOLLHOUSE

CATWOMAN #12 cover sketch

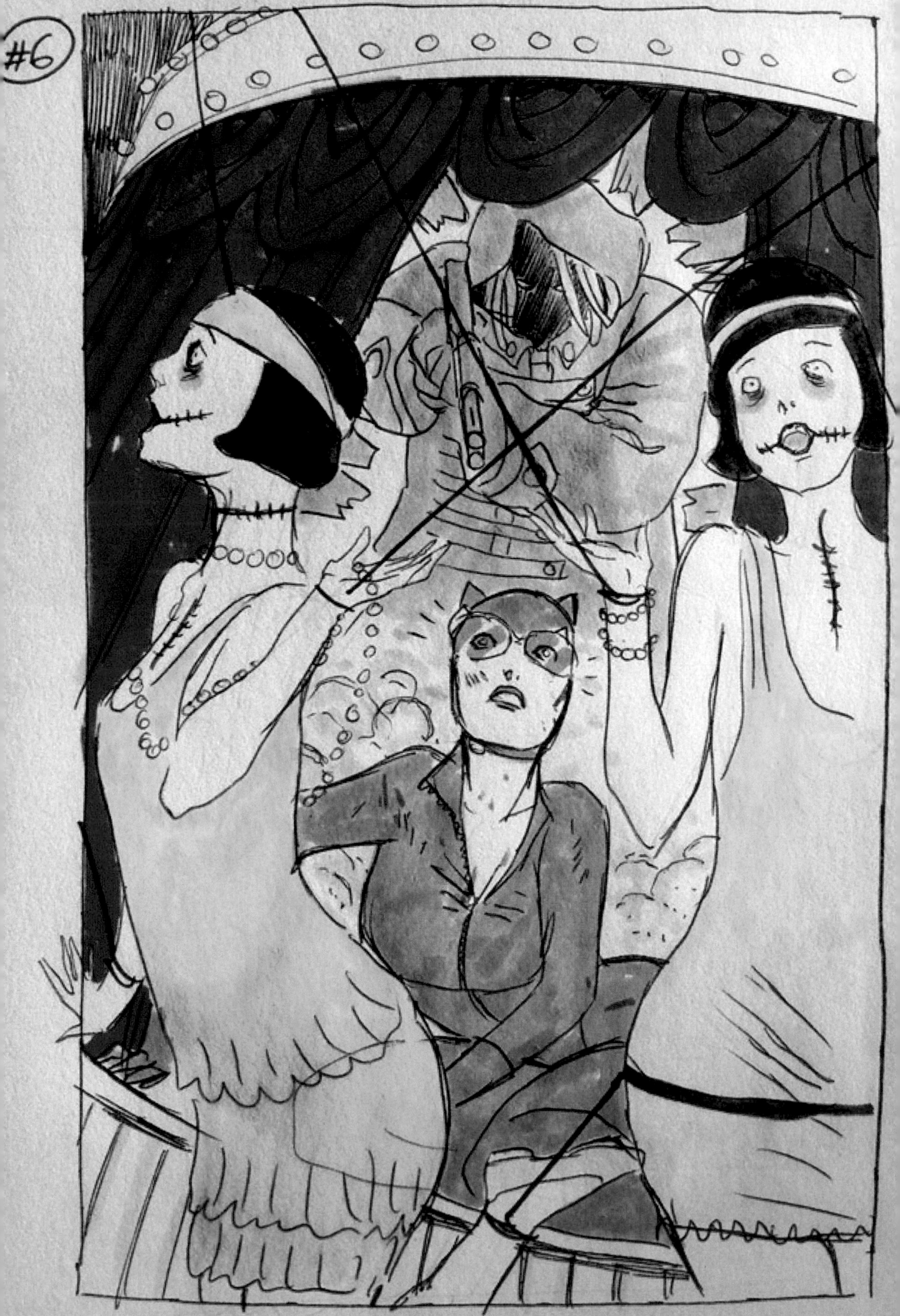
#6

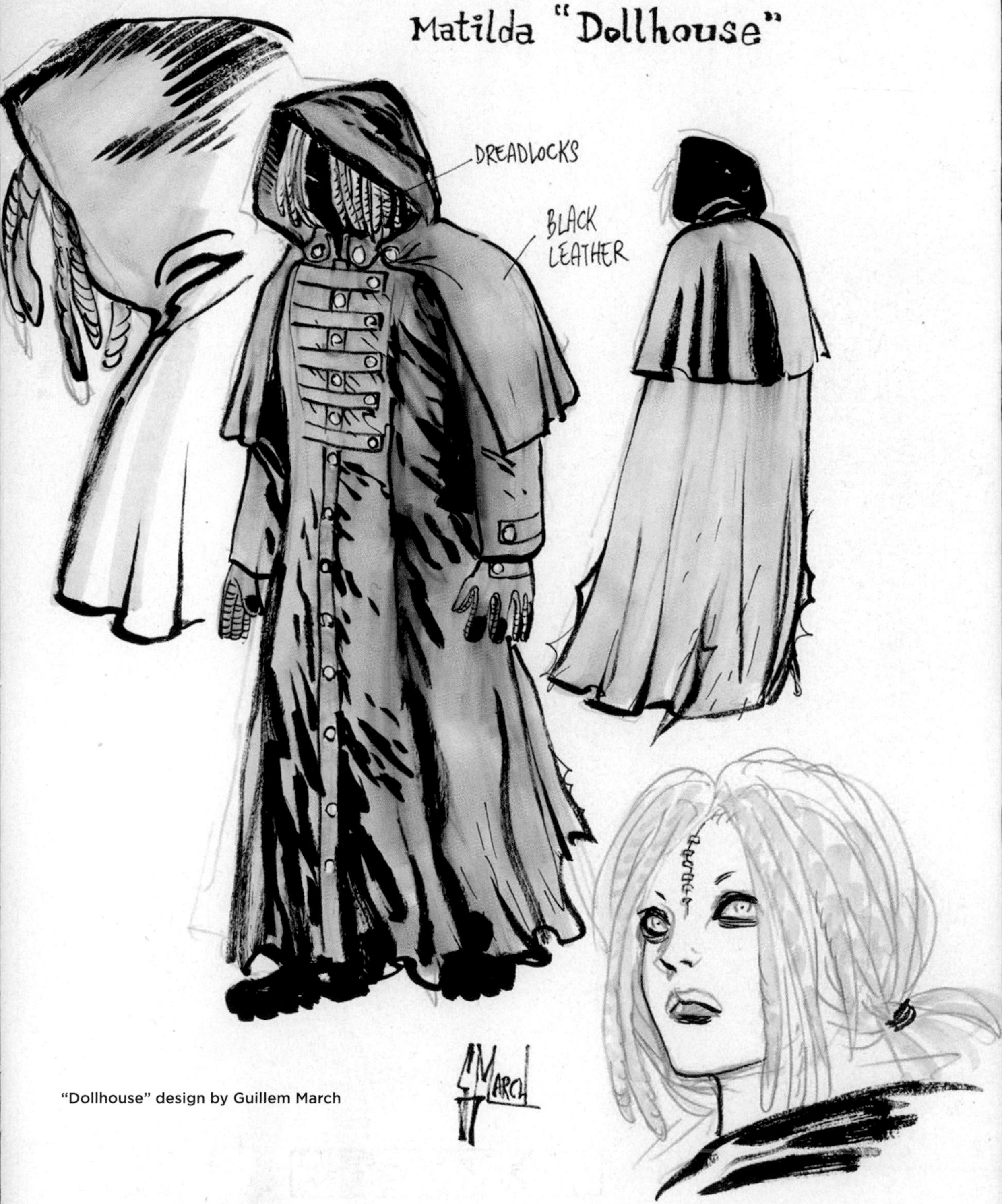
Matilda "Dollhouse"
DREADLOCKS
BLACK LEATHER
MARCH

"Dollhouse" design by Guillem March

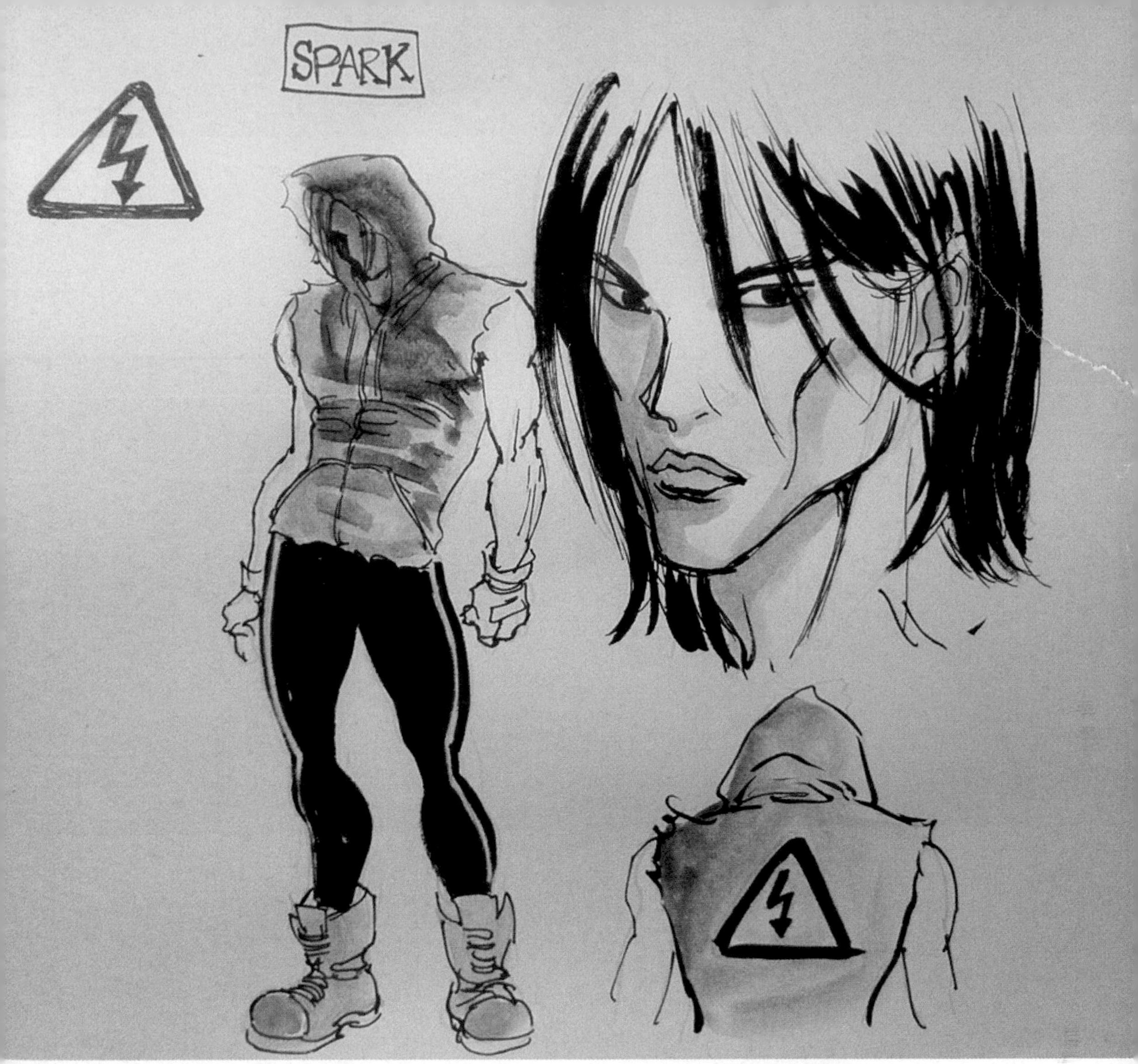
SPARK

Spark design by Guillem March

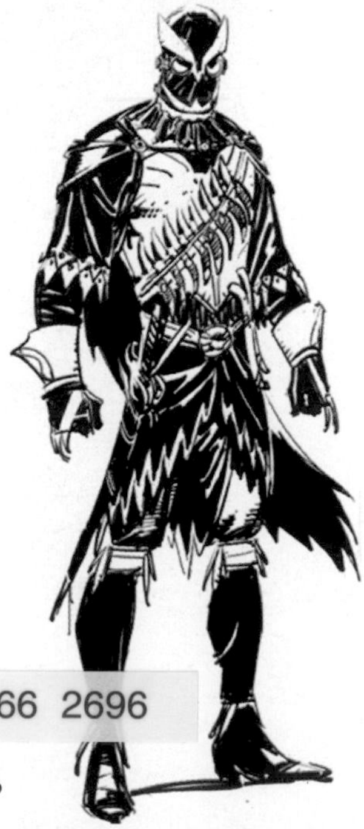

1660 Talon design by Greg Capullo